Walking in my Shadow

*a pilgrim walk to
Santiago de Compostela*

David Gibson

First published in November 2002 by
Cluain Mhuire
274 North Circular Road
Dublin 7

© David Gibson
All rights reserved
Photography courtesy of David Gibson

ISBN 0 9543894 0 9

Typeset and designed by Guildhall Press, Unit 4, Ráth Mór Centre, Bligh's Lane, Derry BT48 0LZ
info@ghpress.com www.ghpress.com
Printed in Republic of Ireland by ColourBooks Limited, Dublin

All rights reserved. No part of this publication may be reproduced or transmitted in any form or by any means, electronic or mechanical, including photocopy, recording, or any information storage or retrieval system, without permission in writing from the publisher. The book is sold subject to the condition that it shall not, by way of trade or otherwise, be lent, re-sold or otherwise circulated without the publisher's prior consent in any form of binding or cover other than that in which it is published and without a similar condition including this condition being imposed on the subsequent purchaser.

Acknowledgements

I wish to acknowledge the help of Brother John McCormack, who worked on the early drafts of the book, and Michael O'Hanlon, who continued the work of editing the manuscript. In addition, I would want to thank Paul Hippsley and Joe McAllister for their superb work in bringing the book to its final state. Paul, of Guildhall Press, was unstinting in ensuring that the book reached its present state and Joe displayed a real flair for the design and layout.

My thanks also to my community and family who were such a great support along the way. Without them all, this dream would have remained simply that. I take full responsibility for the rest of the project, hoping that it contributes somewhat to making the camino accessible to a greater number of people.

The Author

David Gibson, Dublin born and bred, has been a Christian Brother since 1965. Having trained as a Primary School teacher in Belfast, he taught in Belfast and Newry for a total of ten years and then was transferred to Rome to teach at secondary level. He is currently the Province Leader of the Christian Brothers in the Northern Province. Having walked the camino for the first time in 1998, David has returned each year to complete part of the pilgrim route. A keen amateur photographer, he has included some of his photographs in the book, most of which were taken on subsequent walks. This is his first book.

To Lori, a fellow pilgrim on the journey through life.

Contents

Camino di Santiago
de Compostela Maps — vi-vii

Beginnings — 1

Week One
St Jean-Pied-de-Port to Viana
Map — 6
Days One to Seven — 7-49

Week Two
Viana to Castrojeriz
Map — 50
Days Eight to Fourteen — 51-91

Week Three
Castrojeriz to Astorga
Map — 92
Days Fifteen to Twenty-One — 93-129

Week Four
Astorga to Palas de Rei
Map — 130
Days Twenty-Two to Twenty-Eight — 131-163

Week Five
Palas de Rei to Santiago
Map — 164
Days Twenty-Nine to Thirty-One — 165-178

Epilogue — 179

Bibliography — 180

Beginnings

The time had come for me to leave Cluain Mhuire, my home in Dublin, to catch the plane for Pamplona in northern Spain. All the months of planning and discussion were over and now, on 21 June 1998, I was about to embark on the pilgrim walk or, as it is better known in Spanish, the *camino*, to Santiago de Compostela, in the north-western part of the Iberian Peninsula.

A certain fear lurked in me that I would not be able for such a long walk. Maybe I had bitten off more than I could chew. And yet I knew that this decision to walk was something that had been with me since July 1997, when I had embarked on a 30-day retreat in northern Wales at St Beuno's Jesuit Retreat Centre. During the long retreat I was afforded the opportunity to reflect on my wayward journey through life and re-live the significant moments of my almost 50 years.

One day, walking the back roads of Wales, the idea of pilgrimage became a small seed that continued to germinate all along the route to Denbigh, six miles from Beuno's. Much travel literature deals with the urge to journey that lies at the heart of people's imagination and creates a restlessness that demands some response. It seems that the human quest for meaning is acted out in physical movement where the outer journey of walking allows the journey inward to begin. Travel literature had not attracted me up to then. But somehow, the idea of walking in the footsteps of the millions of pilgrims who in the past had travelled to Jerusalem or Rome or Santiago began to draw me in. And I had living exemplars to inspire me.

Two Italian friends of mine, Lori Bonetti and Davide Gandini, from Sovere and Pietra Ligure respectively, had completed the camino to Santiago. They talked about the experience in glowing terms, describing it as a significant highlight in their spiritual growth. Davide had subsequently written a book entitled *Il Portico della Gloria* (The Door of Glory) in which he charted his spiritual itinerary with honesty and imagination. I had just finished reading his book, and as I set out on the walk to Denbigh, its impact on me must have lain hidden in my psyche.

During the year that followed the 30-day retreat, what began as a remote possibility – a fanciful dream – gradually crystallised into a very definite project. There was a specific movement from thinking about Spain and Santiago in a vague and hypothetical way to actively setting about planning the journey.

The planning primarily involved getting myself fit to undertake the long 500-mile (800 kilometres) trek under very hot weather conditions. I had never really walked any great distances and indeed was more a couch potato than a regular hill-walker. However, Brother David Clarke, a Christian Brother like myself, and who lived in the inner city of Dublin's poorest environs, was a great help in encouraging me to move away from the office during the weekends to venture into the fresh air. Many a time he would cajole me out to the Wicklow hills on the occasional Sunday, or encourage me on the odd evening to join him in walks of two and three hours around the Clontarf area of Dublin. David himself had lost a considerable amount of weight due to walking, and he convinced me that I could do the same. Initially, the idea of walking for hours on end was something that I had no interest in, but as I began to take regular exercise, the breaks from the daily routine of work became most welcome. Walking, I soon discovered, creates a pool of deep silence in which all personal issues can float to the surface and become accessible to deeper scrutiny. I was beginning to catch the hiking bug and to feel healthier and more alive into the bargain.

The decision to take Tuesday afternoons off from work in order to give myself the opportunity to exercise in preparation for the challenge of the long pilgrimage proved to be very beneficial. I would walk from Phibsboro to Sutton Cross, turning right towards Howth Hill and around the cliff walk, into Howth village and back to Sutton Cross before making for home again. This was a circuit of about 44km; a walk that took up to nine hours and one that would have tested the strength of a horse. Walking long distances helped me face the struggle with tiredness and thirst. Frequently I was faced with the temptation to grab a bus or taxi, especially on the homeward route. But if I were going to walk 800km to Santiago, it was important to experience these moments of fatigue that would surely face me on the camino. As time progressed, I was beginning to feel more confident that it would be possible for me to stand the physical challenge of covering 24 to 32km a day. This Tuesday afternoon period became a time to treasure as I gradually grew to savour the privilege of being alone with my thoughts and with my God. The desire to arrive at Santiago was indeed growing and the anticipation of such an adventure brightened the dull months of the winter.

Walking 800km demands that the walker has proper equipment. In all the literature provided by the Confraternity of St James in London, the prospective pilgrim was constantly warned to procure the correct gear in order to face the journey with some hope of completing it. Many a pilgrim has had to abandon the enterprise because of faulty equipment.

Eventually I ended up with sturdy walking boots, a good waterproof yet breathable jacket and a medium-sized rucksack whose limited capacity would not permit me to carry a tonne of non-essentials. The comfortable boots and well-fitting rucksack would be tested at various moments along the way. There were also the special shirts that filtered out and controlled perspiration. These were to prove a real boon during the hot, sticky days of July when the perspiration would certainly flow. Included in the list of equipment were, as I thought at the time, some luxuries like the aluminium walking stick and special water bottles. These, however, would also turn out to be more than necessary during the 800km journey.

I came across a very handy invention for holding the guidebook open and dry as I would walk along the camino. Effectively, it was a waterproof bag with plastic folders inside (generally used for holding maps) that hung around the neck allowing me to consult the book without having to remove my rucksack. This talisman dangled about my neck as I made my way along the route, eager to know where I was going and where I had just come from.

My family insisted on sponsoring the equipment for the walk. Support could easily have come from my Christian Brother community but the family were keen to become involved. In many ways, it was an expression of their own desire to participate somehow in the journey and a token of their admiration for what I was about to undertake. Making my way along the Spanish roads, I would be ever grateful for the their generosity and financial support. I often uttered a prayer for them as I tightened the straps of the rucksack, unlaced my boots or washed the perspiration from the specially treated shirts, all of which they had bought for me. In fact, almost every day of the walk my sister and brothers became very close to me. I reflected on each of them: Darina, Peter, John, Michael and Richard. And the prayer uttered by me was related to the particular circumstances that confronted each of them at the time of the walk.

There are quite a few guidebooks for the camino. The best by far is *A Practical Guide for Pilgrims* by Lozano, which subdivides the walk into 31 manageable stages. It indicated the *refugios* or *albergues* (both words are used to describe basic Spanish hostels where pilgrims generally stay), where one could get a bed and a shower. It also recommends the places where one could get a good meal or indeed, more comfortable accommodation. The book proved to be an invaluable source of useful information all along the route. Not only did it provide very clear maps of the journey for each day but it also supplied a more than adequate commentary of the towns and villages through which I was to journey. Though many pilgrims simply followed the ubiquitous yellow arrows that dotted the countryside, enjoying whatever turned up around the corner, I was most interested to know exactly which village I was passing through and which church I could see on the horizon. I was never tempted to depart from Lozano's guide.

The origins of the pilgrim walk to Santiago are found in the very name of the city. *Sant Iago* is the Spanish for St James and refers to James, the brother of the apostle John, the beloved disciple of Jesus and the son of Zebedee and Mary Salome. After the death of Jesus, when the apostles went to preach the Good News, tradition has it that James went to Spain. Having preached there for some years, he returned to Jerusalem where he was arrested and executed for his beliefs. Some of his disciples took his body back by ship to Spain where they buried him in a place called Librédon. Two of the disciples, Theodore and Athanasius, devoted the remainder of their lives to watching over the tomb of their master, and on their death they were buried on either side of St James.

With the passage of time, the tomb of St James was lost in the memories of the people and though tradition always held it that he was buried in Galicia, the exact location was not known. Then in the ninth century, a hermit named Palagius, living in the area, began to witness during the night strange lights over a certain area nearby. On investigation, he found that the lights hovered over a small wood and, knowing of the legend that St James was buried in the area, he went to his bishop, Theodomir, and told of his experience. Theodomir visited the site and had it excavated. He discovered a small building that consisted of two levels: an upper level with a small altar and a lower level, which had three tombs. They immediately identified them as the bodies of St James and his faithful disciples, Theodore and Athanasius.

The king of the Asturias, Alfonso II, built a small basilica over the site of the tomb and also a Benedictine monastery nearby. From these small beginnings, the town of Compostela was born. The name derives from the Latin *Campus Stellae* (Field of the Star) which refers to the vision of Palagius so many years ago. It is to this place, Santiago of the Field of the Star, that pilgrims began to journey especially from the ninth century onwards.

The Pilgrim's Guide, contained in the twelfth-century Codex Calistinus, written in Latin by Aymeric Picaud, a priest from Poitou, describes the four routes originating in France that lead to Santiago. One begins in Le Puy, another in Vezelay, a third from Paris through Saintes and Bordeaux, while the fourth starts from Arles. It seems that the first three routes lead the pilgrim to journey through St Jean-Pied-de-Port, a small French town literally at the gateway to the Pyrenees; whereas to integrate the four routes together one would have to take Puente la Reina in Spain as the meeting place.

I liked the idea of beginning in France and walking into Spain across the Pyrenees in the tradition of Picaud, one of the first ever to write about the camino. This was a way to honour my Francophile tendencies. Ever since leaving school, I had had an interest in the French way of life, and it seemed very appropriate that I would acknowledge this abiding passion. As much as I would have loved to have undertaken the entire route from Le Puy to Santiago, a distance of almost 1600km, time would not permit it. A good compromise was to begin at St Jean-Pied-de-Port and traverse the northern territories of Spain.

I would be walking generally in a westerly direction, starting at St Jean-Pied-de-Port and heading for Santiago near the west coast of Spain. This meant that for the most part, I would be walking in my shadow with the sun at my back. The Jungian symbolism of the shadow (or anima) was caught beautifully in a photo of my shadow, which I managed (with difficulty) to take, holding the camera with one hand, while my companions and I walked along the path to St Juan de Ortega. All that was visible in the photograph was my elongated shadow stretching out in front of me along the earthen pathway. But the photograph became far more symbolic for me in that the entire journey became an exploration of the shadow side of my life. In true Jungian fashion, I began to explore during the walk those elements that are often hidden from consciousness amidst the business of everyday life. Shadow work can be frightening when fragility and brokenness, or in a word, humanity, all co-mingle in what could be termed a tapestry of layer upon layer of shadowy images. The warp and the woof of memory and imagination interlace to create a picture that reveals itself but gradually.

I put up a large map of Spain on our community noticeboard and stuck pins on the places along the camino where I would rest for the night. Beside the map were listed the places where the refugios were situated, together with the phone numbers for each one. It looked a bit obsessive and overly organised, and yet I felt it reassuring that I was not that far away from contact with the Christian Brothers. I hoped also that members of the community would occasionally contact me as I walked along the way. At the same time, part of me wanted to have the month away from contact with those with whom I live each day. I was certainly looking forward to the break from the daily business of administration that is my usual responsibility in the Christian Brothers of Ireland.

How strange it is that what appears far in the horizon of one's dreams can approach almost by stealth and overpower one suddenly. Before I knew it, the time had arrived to begin the pilgrimage. I had decided to leave Dublin on 21 June and to return by 27 July. This would give me time to complete the walk from St Jean-Pied-de-Port, to visit Santiago and even to contemplate walking to Finisterre, a further 80km beyond Santiago. However, this notion seemed almost presumptuous; I had not yet completed the 800km and was already adding another long stretch to the journey. Humility is a very valuable asset to any pilgrim! It is a lesson that I would have to learn along the route.

On the morning of Sunday, 21 June, the religious community I belong to gathered at nine o'clock in the community chapel to bestow a blessing on the lone pilgrim who was ready to depart. We had prepared a missioning ceremony based on a medieval rite of pilgrim blessing that is preserved in the Missal of Vich Cathedral in Barcelona and which dates back to AD 1078. The rucksack, walking stick and hat were placed before the altar and Tim, one of the senior members of the community, stood with his hands extended towards me and intoned the ancient blessing, "May the Lord always guide your steps and be your inseparable companion throughout your journey." I was presented with the rucksack and also with the 'pilgrim passport' that would be stamped at each of the refugios at which I stopped along the way. The ceremony was surprisingly moving, in that it provided me with a sense of support and encouragement from my community as I was about to commence what was essentially a solitary enterprise.

Brother James drove me to the airport and before leaving, he took a photograph of me standing beside the car in full pilgrim regalia. The intrepid traveller was somewhat overcome with feelings of privilege mingled with uncertainty as he made his way to the check-in for the flight to Pamplona via Barcelona. I uttered a prayer to the Lord to lead me along the right path in faith and trust.

Once, however, I entered the terminal and handed in my flight ticket, I began to allow the sense of excitement to take hold and just marvelled at how the dream of St Bueno's from

The author leaving his community house in Phibsboro in North Dublin.

the year before was about to unfold right before my eyes. The planning of the route was over and the real journey was about to begin. The practice walks would now be for real. I was stepping forward on the path to what is considered to be one of the more important places of Christian pilgrimage after Jerusalem and Rome – Santiago de Compostela, St James of the Field of the Star. The image of the apostle James was still a distant figure; but he was already beckoning me forward. The cry "*Ultreya*" (onward!), the ancient Spanish shout of encouragement to pilgrims, sounded in my ears and put a spring in my step.

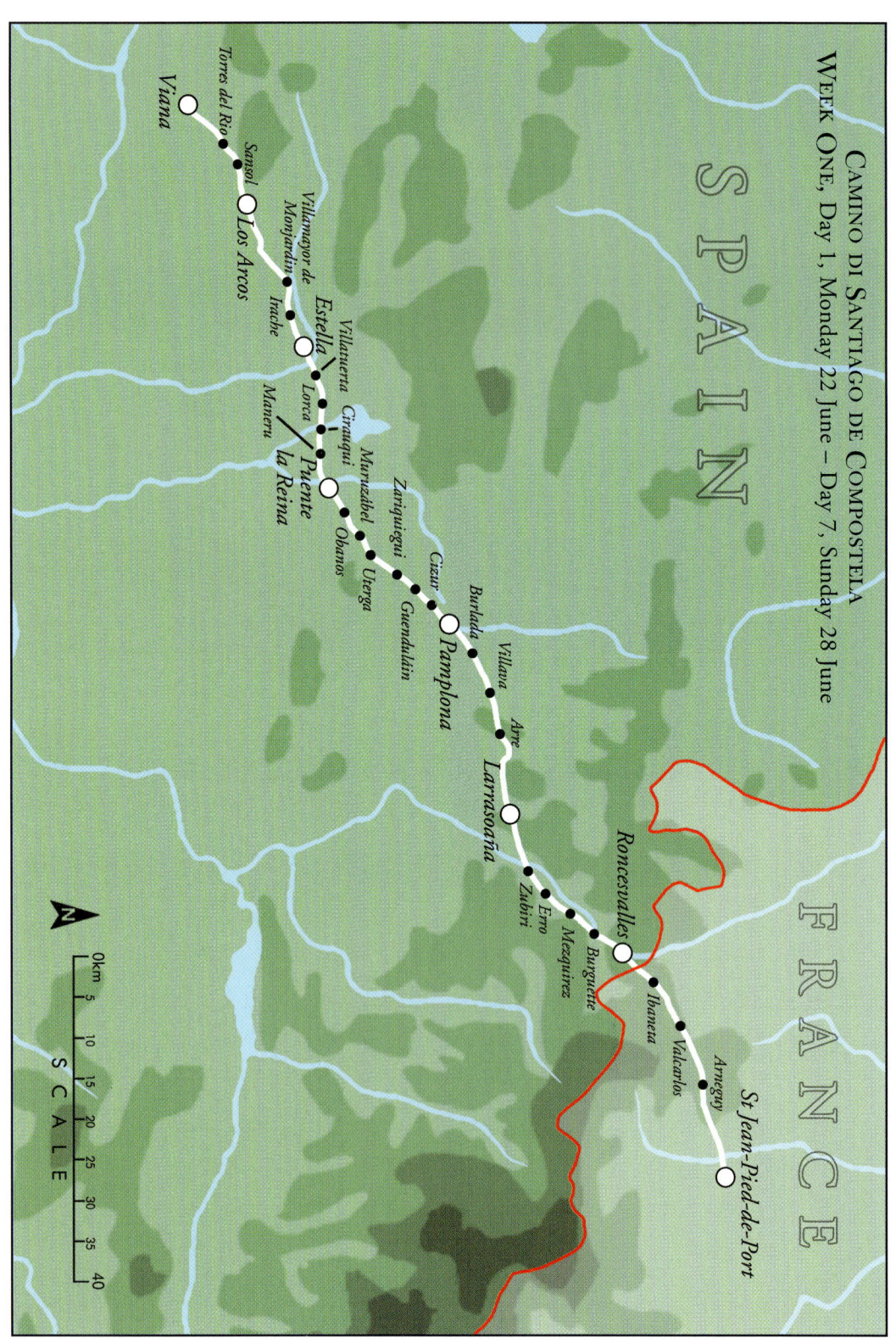

WEEK ONE

DAY ONE
St Jean-Pied-de-Port to Roncesvalles
Monday 22 June 1998

Flying from Dublin to Pamplona via Barcelona was somewhat inconvenient and time-consuming. I took off from Dublin at 12.30pm arriving in Barcelona at 4.30pm. After a few hours wait in Barcelona, the plane touched down in Pamplona around 8.00pm. In a sense, the trip was almost a blur, with most of my time spent studying Hugo's *Spanish in Three Months*. I was really in need of revising the rudimentary basics that I had managed to touch on since Christmas. I ignored, therefore, much of what was happening about me during both flights and during the stopover in Barcelona. Before I knew it, the plane had landed in Pamplona and the time had come to begin my long adventure.

A taxi took me to the *stacion autobus* (bus station), where I hoped to catch a coach to Roncesvalles. Roncesvalles in Spain is the closest town to the French town of St Jean-Pied-de-Port from where I hoped to begin the walk. I tried to inquire in my rudimentary Spanish where I could board the bus to Roncesvalles. A very kind nun took me literally by the hand and directed me to a plaza quite a distance from the station. I walked around in circles asking, "*¿Donde Roncesvalles?*" only to get further instructions and more walking. I was getting rapidly more fluent in the use of these two Spanish words as time progressed. However, it gradually dawned on me that I was probably being directed to a street in Pamplona called Roncesvalles, though certainly not to the bus that would take me to the town in the Pyrenees. I eventually returned to the bus station to find out that the next bus to Roncesvalles would be at 7.00am the following morning. The route to Santiago would not be as direct as I imagined.

Just opposite the station was a *pensión* (small hotel), which was simple and clean though by no means cheap. It cost 4000 pesetas (€25), really far too expensive for what I was getting, ie a small room with little more than a bed and a side table. Along the camino, the refugios cost about one tenth of the cost of the pensión. However, I was too tired to continue searching for a cheaper one, seeing the advantage of having a place near the station for the morning bus to Roncesvalles.

I dumped my gear, took a shower in a nearby bathroom to freshen up and left to find a place where I could get something to eat. Walking down a pedestrian area dotted with bars and disco night-clubs, I became aware of the sacred undertaking that was about to commence. I had not really prayed much during the day and wondered how this had happened. It was almost as if studying Spanish had become the focus of the day, blotting out the very motivation for the pilgrimage. So, strolling down the busy narrow streets, I asked the Lord to be my guide each day of the walk and to be a presence to me even in moments of spiritual amnesia.

In a lighter spirit, I entered a bar and ordered some *tapas* (mixed food) and beer. Sitting there in the bar brought a sense of relief that I had landed and was ready to begin a real adventure. It was a moment to relax with a beer and Spanish omelette and enjoy experiencing the loud and spirited conversation of the locals in the bar. After about an hour in the bar and with my stomach satisfied, I left and decided to have an early night so as to be ready for the next day.

Sleep came with great difficulty. Between the heat, which was considerable, and the noise from the traffic just outside my window, I tossed and turned fitfully for many an hour. Using earplugs seemed the obvious solution but they proved to be useless; it was almost impossible to extract them from my ears. With a certain amount of anger and frustration, I consigned them to the rubbish basket. I discarded the bedclothes but even with a single sheet over me, I still found the heat uncomfortable for sleeping. Resting fitfully, I woke every hour afraid that I would miss the early morning appointment. I had yet to find the alarm clock somewhere at the bottom of my rucksack.

The next morning I left for the station only to find that, contrary to what I believed, there was no 7.00am bus to Roncesvalles. It transpired that the only one going there that day was due to leave in the evening. The only solution, it seemed, was to begin the walk from Pamplona. It was not worth wasting an entire day waiting for the bus. So I made my way to the refugio in Pamplona to get my 'pilgrim passport' signed so as to officially begin the pilgrimage.

The Confraternity of St James issues this pilgrim passport to anyone who applies for it in his or her country of origin. It can also be purchased at some of the more important refugios in Spain. Then the passport is stamped at each refugio to guarantee that the pilgrim has indeed walked through the town in question. At the conclusion of the walk, the pilgrim is presented with a 'Compostela' (certificate) to show that they have walked at least 150km. Most pilgrims are not like David Lodge, the novelist, who in his book *Therapy* walked the route without bothering to get a passport. Access to refugios may require a passport and for most pilgrims, the Compostela is a prized possession.

When I went to the refugio, however, it was closed. Although it was 6.30 in the morning, I had presumed that some eager pilgrims would be on the verge of departure but there was no sign of life. I rang the bell and a voice responded in Spanish. Once they heard the foreign stutterings of an obvious pilgrim, the door automatically opened to allow me ascend the narrow almost spiral staircase that led into a small but welcoming lobby.

The first person I saw was a young American woman sitting beside her rucksack. She was a small lightly built girl with long hair and a friendly face. I explained how I had hoped to travel to Roncesvalles but was now resigned to starting from Pamplona. Kristen was in exactly the same position and suggested we share the cost of a taxi that would take us to Roncesvalles. This seemed an excellent idea. I first got my passport stamped so that I could begin walking from Pamplona should the taxi not work out; and together we went hunting for one in the deserted streets of sleeping Pamplona.

Eventually we found one outside the bus station and the driver agreed to take us to Roncesvalles for 6000 pesetas (€40). He took off at great speed and before long we were outside the city and travelling towards the mountains visible in the distance. There was a slight drizzle, which surprised me considering the heat of the previous day. We passed our first pilgrim walking towards us on the route as we continued to climb. Poor Kristen became quite queasy in the back of the car and was ready to be sick on a number of occasions. Her pale face underlined the discomfort she was suffering, so the conversation was kept to a minimum, while she comforted herself and generally calmed down.

Later on, she announced in panic that she had no paper money with her, having spent all her cash the previous day on presents for her friends in Madrid. Having assured her that I would pay for the taxi she promised to refund me when she got the opportunity. Already I was contemplating asking the taxi driver to continue beyond Roncesvalles to St Jean-Pied-de-Port in France, which would mean that Kristen would be a day ahead of me. She promised, however, to leave her share of the fare for me on the noticeboard at the Pamplona refugio.

We parted at Roncesvalles, and I reluctantly said goodbye to her. She seemed to be an exceptionally nice girl and it would have been interesting to have her company on the first stage of the pilgrimage. But my sights were on France! The taxi driver agreed to take me to St Jean-Pied-de-Port for an extra 3000 pesetas (€20); so we continued on towards the highest point in the gap through the Pyrenees and then descended sharply along a tree-lined motorway for what could not have been more than 20 minutes. The driver pulled up at the archway leading into the busy main street of St Jean-Pied-de-Port where I alighted. I was in France – the place of my dreams!

The rain continued to drizzle, covering the streets with a film of water and creating a freshness that banished the discomfort of a dusty road. Crossing the street, I met with a New Zealand couple who seemed weary after their walk along the final stages of the Le Puy route. We exchanged simple pleasantries but I was anxious to find out where to get the passport stamped and where to begin the first stage of the pilgrimage.

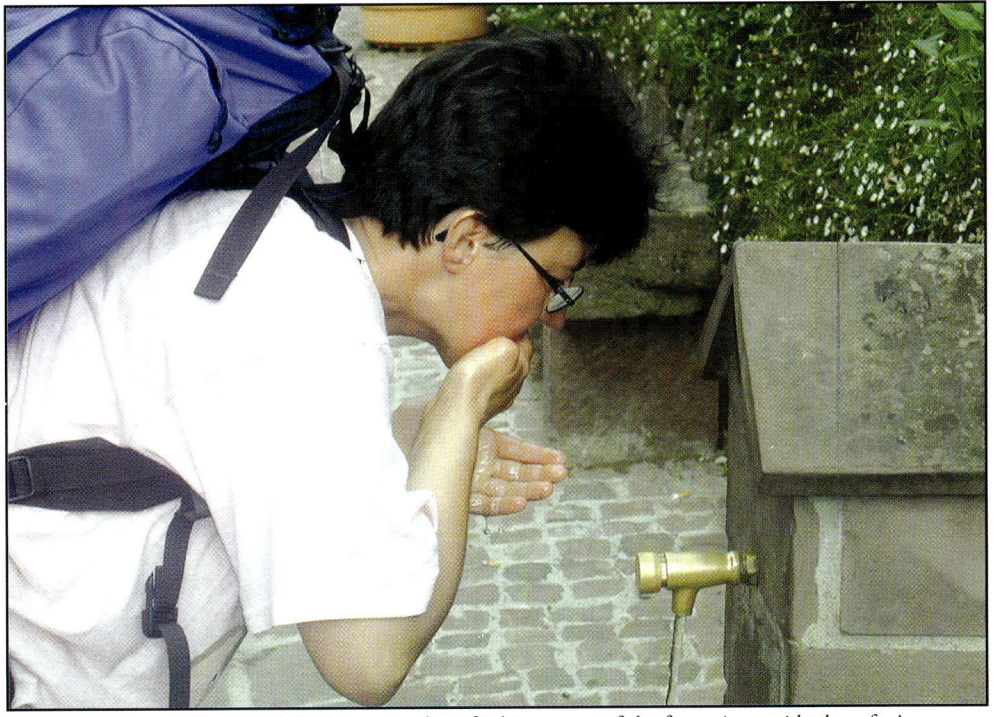

Pilgrim at St Jean-Pied-de-Port tastes the refreshing water of the fountain outside the refugio.

I came across L'Eglise du Sacre Coeur, a charming gothic edifice that exuded a sense of the sacred. This air of sanctity had developed over a long period of deep spiritual strivings and devotions by the people of St Jean-Pied-de-Port. The cleaning lady in the church explained that I would have to take the passport to the pastoral office of the *curé* (parish priest) some distance away in order to get the first pilgrim *sello* (stamp).

However, it was pleasant to remain for a while to absorb the atmosphere in the church before I took off in search of the curé. As I sat in the silence of this sacred place, I prayed to the Lord for his guidance during the pilgrim walk and expressed my joy at having the opportunity to travel in the footsteps of thousands of pilgrims who had gone before me.

Eventually I found the curé's house some distance away from the church. He came across as friendly but distant; this was reflected in the totally functional stamp that he inserted into the passport. The stamp only bore the name of St Jean-Pied-de-Port on it, but was bereft of any form of logo or design. However, it was the first sello of the camino, and it did indicate the start of the walk. So, for this simple reason it was for me a special stamp.

I bought a baguette and some ham and cheese at a local market to sustain me on the journey, setting off immediately along the rue d'Espagne. The rain persisted, so it was necessary to keep the raingear on for the time being. Stopping at the road signs that pointed to Roncevaux (French) or Roncesvalles (Spanish) and to the Route Napoleon, I came upon the place where the taxi had left me. I had decided that I was not going to follow the example of Bettina Selby, author of *The Pilgrim's Road,* who took her bicycle over the mountain pass despite rain and wintry conditions. Instead, I made for the more leisurely route to Valcarlos along the main road to Roncesvalles. The latter route seemed the wiser one considering my poor physical fitness and the fact that this was the first day of the camino.

None of the famous yellow arrows designed to guide the pilgrim on the camino were to be seen; any inquiry of the locals resulted in a shrug of the shoulders and a, *"J'en sais rien"* (I don't know). Having examined the map, I decided to follow the road until I could see a clearer sign. The only delay was stopping at the road signs to ask a woman carrying her child to take a photograph of me in front of the signpost to Roncevaux. The plan was to take a photograph at the signpost of each of the towns at which I would gain a passport stamp. This would prove to my friends that I had in fact done the walk!

The rain eventually stopped and the sun made its appearance soon afterwards creating a warmth and vibrancy that lifted my spirits. Still I could not find the correct route. The pathway across the River Nive was clear to see but every attempt to cross the river and join the path was thwarted either by high fences or wide ditches. Finally, I decided to keep to the

Don Elias Valina Sampedro, the parish priest of O Cebreiro, was the first to introduce yellow arrows as indicators of the camino.

main road for the duration of this stage. The guidebook indicated a place where one could leave the road after Valcarlos – the valley of Charlemagne – and head up into the Pyrenees, but it seemed more prudent to stay with the road and take things easy.

After Valcarlos, having crossed the border at Arneguy, it was time for a rest-break. Although quite tired by this time, I was in no humour for eating and after a nibble or two from the baguette, it was consigned to the nearby bin. I needed to drink plenty of water and restore the liquids that had already been lost in the heat of the climb. During the walk it would be necessary to carry two litres of water at all times, one of which was tied to my rucksack straps that could be easily reached and the other litre stored in the rucksack for emergency use.

The route was all uphill and things seemed to be getting tougher. However, the impressive sight of the spectacularly surrounding countryside with the rugged Pyrenees to my left and the wooded valleys to the right more than compensated for the struggle. At the same time, it became necessary to take rests at more frequent intervals. Towards two o'clock, four hours into the walk, I decided that a siesta was needed to revive my flagging energy. There was a good shady spot amidst a copse of coniferous trees, and using the rucksack for a pillow, I slept for about half an hour. When I awoke, I felt relaxed and ready to resume the walk.

By now, the route was in descent, and the going was much easier. Walking alone on the road, I began to enjoy the whole experience. After about an hour though I started to have a sinking feeling. Judging by the kilometre markers, it became obvious that I had retraced my steps and was walking back towards Valcarlos instead of on towards Roncesvalles. How could it have happened? What an idiot I was. I ranted at myself, and all spirituality went out the window at the stupidity of what I had done. The expletives that emerged involuntarily from my mouth could not be reconciled with the traditional perception of pilgrim behaviour. But at that stage I did not care – I just had to let my anger explode. What a mistake to make on the very first day! I could not believe what I had done.

It took some time before I cooled down and paused to review my options. I decided to hitchhike back to the point where I had slept, with the intention of continuing the rest of the walk on foot. There was no time to debate as to the morality of such an action but even as I stood there hitchhiking, I felt I was cheating. However, I need not have worried for the speeding cars simply whizzed by with no intention of stopping. Obviously, the drivers could see no point in giving lifts to pilgrims who were supposed to be on foot. The choice remained of either continuing the journey to Roncesvalles from where I now was or of walking back to Valcarlos and taking a room there for the night.

Then, amazingly, I noticed a sign indicating where I should originally have taken a path into the higher ground. I had missed it on the first time around and now I was being invited to observe the correct route. It was almost as if fate had brought me back to the spot I had decided to ignore on the first day of the pilgrimage. Was God reprimanding me for the decision to go my own way? I do not really think this is the way the divine operates; yet, in moments of crisis, all the more atavistic beliefs surface and demolish any degree of sophistication. I laughed at the very absurdity of walking back along the road already travelled. T S Eliot has something to say about this in his poem, *Little Gidding*:

> We shall not cease from exploration
> And the end of all our exploring
> Will be to arrive where we started
> And know the place for the first time.

I certainly was discovering that path for the first time.

The sign that had stopped me in my tracks was quite interesting. It showed a matchstick man with a stylised sun in the background whose rays pointed in the direction to be followed. These signs had been recently erected by the European Community Cultural Commission when the Santiago camino was given the status of a European cultural project and would become a regular feature all along the route to Santiago. However, thankfully they do not replace the traditional yellow arrows painted by volunteers from the Confraternity of St James on trees and walls all along the route. I always find these hand-made indicators much more natural and user-friendly.

The pathway led along a rushing stream and followed the electricity pylons that clung to the rocky crags. Nature was at its best, with the recent rain still discernible in the undergrowth and everything appearing fresh and lush. As time wore on, however, I began to feel increasingly tired and had to rest more and more. A mist was beginning to form in the upper reaches of the hillside and the temperature was dropping noticeably. I struggled onwards but found myself often having to take a pause at the side of the pathway in order to regain some of the flagging energy. I began to get concerned that I could be lost in the hillside as darkness approached. Already I noticed that the level of brightness had lessened appreciably and my supply of water was coming to an end. Before I began to panic completely, I saw the outline of a cottage at the brow of the hill.

On reaching this lone cottage, I was greeted with the sounds of growling, barking dogs that thankfully were behind wire netting. A yellow arrow indicated the general way forward but left me uncertain as to the proper pathway. I inquired about this from the occupants of the cottage, but they were most unhelpful and gruff, muttering something about the arrows. I suppose they were tortured by pilgrims like myself asking the same questions. The arrows, however, soon led to Ibaneta where a church stood shrouded in a deep fog. I mistakenly took the right turn and found myself on the N135 to Valcarlos once more. This time, however, I recognised the mistake after 100 metres, turning back up the hill, past the incongruous contemporary-styled church and down towards Roncesvalles.

At this stage, the fog was so enveloping that nothing could be seen beyond 20 metres. Still I continued on, mechanically placing one foot ahead of the other for I was exhausted at that stage. As if by magic, then, the cluster of monastic buildings that nestled in a depression to the left of the motorway made their appearance before my very eyes. A large crane dominated the dull grey buildings. Obviously, the ancient twelfth-century Augustinian monastery was being renovated in preparation for the influx of pilgrims that would surely arrive in 1999, when the feast of St James fell on a Sunday, thus creating a Holy Year. This occurs every six, five, six, then eleven years.

What a relief I felt at the end of this long first day. It was now almost nine o'clock and I had spent the best part of eleven hours on a walk that should have taken about six hours to complete.

At the entrance of the monastery, there was a couple who were waiting for a priest friend. There were no pilgrims within sight, so I left the foyer and eventually discovered where the dormitories were situated. However, the pilgrims there kept telling me that I would have to go back to the foyer in order to register. My frustration almost overwhelmed me and I was fit to be tied. All I wanted to do was to find my bed and then go for something to eat. So I stormed back to the main entrance and hammered on the bell demanding service, knowing full well that I was behaving in a very un-pilgrim like way.

Finally, a monk came out and he must have realised I was at the end of my tether. He could not have been more welcoming and gentle as he led me once more back to where the groups of pilgrims were gathered. We climbed innumerable steps until we reached the foyer for pilgrims. There we signed a form that indicated our motivation for going on pilgrimage. I ticked the religious box and signed my name. I was later told that the categories included religious, spiritual, health and cultural reasons for going on the camino. On reflection, I think I could have filled in all categories because, in a way, I was undertaking the pilgrimage for spiritual and religious motives but also for health reasons and certainly because of the interest I had in the culture of the Spanish people.

Although I needed a shower badly, the need for food was greater. I left my rucksack near the bunk bed where I would eventually sleep and exited back into the fog to a rather high-class hotel nearby. On entering the hotel, I became very aware of how dishevelled I must have looked. However, the waitress hardly batted an eyelid and led me to a table discretely at a distance from the rest of the guests. I was ready to eat a horse.

A rucksack rests against the wall of the refugio in Roncesvalles.

By the time I had finished my meal, I felt almost human again and most magnanimous to the waitress who had shown such consideration to a tramp-like pilgrim. All the efforts of the first day had been worth it and I felt elated at having finally achieved the first stage.

It was time for sleep. My eyes were beginning to close as the effects of the Rioja wine began to kick in. I considered taking the next day off in order to recover from the rigours of the first day, but I resolved to put off the decision until then, when a proper assessment could be made of my physical condition. In fact, although tired by then, I had no sensation of sore feet or blisters.

Before sleeping, I thanked the Lord for his guidance and protection, praying for all pilgrims on the way to Santiago. I wondered how Kristen had fared on her journey to Larrasoaña. I still regretted that we had not been able to walk together on the first day. And yet, in a sense, I felt united to all the pilgrims who were walking to Santiago. I was part of something bigger than myself, something greater than I could ever be. It was like the communion of saints and sinners, all joined by a common bond – the camino.

Day Two
Roncesvalles to Larrasoaña
Tuesday 23 June 1998

I was awoken by the muffled movements of pilgrims anxious to set off on the journey in the cool of the morning. Although I had thought of taking a day's rest after the exertions of the journey over the Pyrenees, I was now feeling in better shape and anxious to continue. I had slept quite soundly despite the claustrophobic arrangement of the bunk beds and the stentorian habits of my neighbours. Without too much difficulty, I found my torch and

Detail of St James at Roncesvalles in the thirteenth-century collegiate chapel.

managed to locate the various elements of equipment without turning on lights and disturbing the pilgrims who were still sleeping. It was six o'clock, and considering that the journey would take at least seven hours, I resigned myself to the fact that there would be no time to visit the grandiose abbey of Roncesvalles.

Roncesvalles, meaning 'the valley of the thorns', has a proud history that goes back to well before the twelfth century. It is considered to have one of the earliest hospices founded by the Augustinian canons regular to welcome the 'sick and well, not only Catholics but also pagans, Jews, heretics and vagabonds' (from a twelfth-century Latin poem). At the height of its power, the hospice catered for up to 40,000 pilgrims a year.

Of course, Roncesvalles is also famous for its connection with the 'Chanson de Roland', which immortalised the place where Charlemagne's army, 20,000 strong, was devastated by the Basque and Aragonese troops. It also marks the place where Roland was betrayed and perished in the fighting while the plaintive sound of Olifant's horn rang out in vain to summon assistance.

It would have been most interesting to have visited the thirteenth-century collegiate chapel that houses the famous fourteenth-century gothic image of Our Lady of Roncesvalles, made of cedar wood covered with silver and encrusted with jewels. The remains of Sancho 'the Strong', one of the great kings of Navarre and his wife Clemencia of Toulouse, are here in a magnificent thirteenth-century mausoleum.

However, on the second day of the camino, I did not consider delaying even for cultural reasons, as my focus was on continuing the walk and arriving safely at the second stage in the journey. There would always be the dilemma of whether to view the beauty of historical monuments or concentrate on arriving at the next stage. Resolving that was not always easy.

In the quietness of a fog-bound dawn, I set out along the road and came almost immediately upon a large roadside map of the area indicating the route of the camino. Other walkers appeared before and behind me, some taking the main road and others venturing into the pathway that bordered the road. I took the latter and before long, the welcome yellow arrows made their appearance, contributing in no small measure to a sense of security and confidence.

Ten minutes into the walk, I came across a local café crammed with pilgrims. Inside, one could pick out the sounds of at least four European languages: French, Spanish, German and

Norwegian. Each language group huddled together, chatting excitedly and with humour. The sound of English was noticeably absent. Obviously there would be many occasions on the walk when pilgrims have to contend with incomprehension but this too is part and parcel of the experience. I thanked the Lord that I had had the opportunity to study French and Italian and could also make a stab at understanding Spanish: this would prevent total isolation. Travelling abroad always strengthens one's resolution to add to one's repertoire of languages, though that determination weakens with the passage of time, as one settles back into the daily routine at home.

So, in my best Spanish accent, I asked for *café con leche* (coffee with milk) and for some *magdalenas* (fairy cakes), which are supposed to be nourishing for the weary pilgrims. They turned out to be sickly sweet buns, almost like sawdust in their consistency. I would not be ordering the same again, preferring to stick to the more humble but equally nourishing bread.

Somewhat overawed by the sheer volume of foreign chatter and sensing a feeling of isolation and confusion, I beat a hasty retreat only to be followed out by the waiter. He handed me the bread rolls that I had purchased for the lunch-time snack and had forgotten to take with me. A few *muchos gracias* (many thanks) could not express my admiration for this simple gesture of running out of the café to assist a lone pilgrim on his way.

I passed through the neat hamlet of Burguete and visited the modern church dedicated to St Bartholomew. Having finished saying a prayer in the silence of this empty but impressive contemporary-styled church, I continued along the way admiring the fertile verdant fields that surrounded the town and the purple distant hills of Alto de Erro. The camino led through the town and began to bear left, heading to the top of the hill covered with hazel and beech trees.

Just across the C135 at Mezquiriz, there was a fine stone stele with the image of the Virgin and Child, with beautifully carved script in French, Spanish and Basque, inviting the pilgrim to pray to Our Lady of Roncesvalles for protection on the journey. Standing before the statue, tears came to my eyes as I began to recite the Memorare.

Scenes from my childhood flooded back to me. I used to go daily with my father to the Jesuit church in Milltown Park, Dublin, to serve at the 6.30am Mass. After Mass, we would walk with our bicycles over to the grotto of Our Lady that had been erected by a Jesuit in exile in Ireland during World War II, and together we would recite the Memorare. I lovingly recalled my father and how I got in touch with his faith, which he never shied away from professing in very practical ways. I stayed with this image for quite some time, praying for both my deceased parents. The time I spent in prayer before the stele at Mezquiriz was one of those moments that would occur along the camino – a subtle epiphany-like sequence, when insights entered my consciousness with a new clarity and power.

Journeying onwards, the route passed through Viscarret intersecting the C135 twice until it came to a small village called Linzoain where I purchased some fruit to slake the thirst that had been growing in the morning sunshine. It was also necessary to rest a while before beginning to climb up the Alto de Erro. I sat outside the shop where I had bought some oranges and sampled one of them. Everything in the village was quiet; hardly a living thing moved. It was as if the village was having a communal siesta, though it was only ten in the morning.

On the way up through the pines, beeches and holm oaks, three young walkers passed by, two women and a bearded youth who all seemed to be on a day's outing judging by the speed they were walking. Each wore light sports shoes and carried small rucksacks on their backs, too big for a single day's outing and almost too small for the long trek. I let them pass with an *hola!* (hello) and they responded likewise. I was tempted to quicken my pace to prove to myself that I was indeed fit and healthy, but I resisted the temptation to delude myself. The experience of the walk from St Jean-Pied-de-Port was still fresh in my memory. And I still had almost 800km to go.

There was no sign on the route of the two-metre-high stone block that is supposed to represent the footsteps of the great Roland whose story I had just recalled in Roncesvalles. I was probably too concerned with negotiating the deeply rutted pathway down Alto de Erro to pay attention to historical sights and decided to let it go unexplored.

The camino continued on this treacherous pathway, crossing the C135 once again until I arrived in Zubiri, a Basque word meaning 'village of the bridge'. As I was in need of some refreshment, I decided to go into Zubiri to buy some water. As I crossed the bridge, I entered into what looked like a village in the process of urban renewal. The houses had the appearance of being recently constructed with reinforced concrete, creating sharp rectangular outlines that were inclined to portray more functionality than style. There was little to attract me there.

As I took off my rucksack outside the local supermarket, I realised that the precious shirt I had hanging from my rucksack to dry was missing. I contemplated for a moment or two the option of retracing my steps to find it but I simply hadn't the energy to seriously think of doing so. I had no idea where I might have lost it; indeed, it could have happened quite early on in the day. Maybe I had left it in the church at Burguete. Returning there would have taken some hours. I decided I would simply have to do with the other two shirts I had, the one I was currently wearing and the other packed away in the rucksack. For a moment, I became very aware of being alone on this walk; of the need to be very careful of my belongings and of my very person. Carelessness could result in having to abandon the walk.

Just as I was undoing the rucksack to pack away the water, I let the bottle drop, its contents splashing all over the pavement outside the shop. The shopkeeper saw it happen, and when I returned to buy another bottle, I half expected him to offer the second one gratis. My faith in humanity, however, took a dent. There was neither any expression of sympathy nor an offer to replace the broken bottle. I handed over 30 cents with a certain sense of regret and maybe with a more realistic assessment of how the locals view these strange creatures travelling their roads in all sorts of peculiar gear.

I crossed back over the ivy-covered bridge that spanned the River Arga. This gothic bridge with two arches is called 'the bridge of the rabies' where, in former times, animals were cured of this dreaded disease by being driven three times over the bridge in an ancient ritual ceremony of cleansing. I continued along the path until I came to what appeared to be a cement factory in all its hideousness alongside the beautiful Arga river. How companies manage to obtain planning permission for such eyesores continues to amaze me, though given the sleazy revelations about such matters uncovered in Ireland recently, nothing would really come as a surprise.

By this time, I was beginning to feel the heat of the day more intensely. The track passed through Osteriz near the fountain and ancient church at Llarraz. It then bordered the Arga and a town could be seen in the distance on the far side of the river. I imagined it to be Larrasoaña, but on checking the map realised that it was Urdaniz, the village adjacent to Larrasoaña. Then came Esquiroz, with its quaint and ancient farm dwellings, and a path going alongside a field that led to a clump of trees and some undergrowth. Suddenly, through the branches, I could see the famous Bandits' Bridge, a fourteenth-century gothic bridge infamous for being the place where pilgrims of the period were relieved of their precious possessions by the local outlaws. Larrasoaña lay before me.

Just across the bridge was the parish church of San Nicolas of Bari. The camino continued along the narrow main street with the family coat of arms emblazoned on some of the terraced houses. The refugio came into view before long; what a welcome sight it was to see the doors open and pilgrims moving easily in and out.

What was immediately obvious was the friendly atmosphere created in no small part by the *hospitalero* (guest master), a certain Subiri who, I learned later on, was also the Mayor of the town. He was a small man, obviously very fit and strong, with an inner energy that belied his age. But above all, he was full of enthusiasm for his job and for the refugio, which he kept with loving care. He seemed to thrive on meeting people and kept up an unremitting chatter with everyone despite the fact that most could not understand a word of Spanish. This did not seem to faze him one whit.

He proudly displayed his visitors' books, which were real works of art. There were messages of acknowledgement in all languages from grateful pilgrims who had passed through; and many had drawn pictures or cartoons to accompany their amusing or touching comments. In his office nearby where he took pilgrims to get their passports stamped, the walls were covered with postcards from every corner of the world and again these witnessed the gratitude of pilgrims for his gracious welcome to them.

It was about 2.30pm, and I had been walking for about seven and a half hours in the heat of the day. What a relief to get a shower and wash my clothes in preparation for the next day's stage. I was beginning to see that the daily rhythm would be to shower, wash the sweat-stained clothes and hang them out to dry, rest for a while and then find food for the evening.

Rather than take a bunk bed that appeared very short for my almost two metre frame and would have necessitated me adopting the foetal position all night long, I inquired if there was the possibility of sleeping on the floor. The hospitalero led the way to a room upstairs where I could roll out the sleeping bag on the floor without any restrictions. I was the first occupant.

Later on, I made my way down the main street to the only shop cum restaurant where I met Liam, a fellow Irish man from Carlow who was just finishing his meal. He kept me company as I ordered my *tortilla espagnol* (Spanish omelette) and a much-needed beer. I took an instant liking to Liam. He seemed open and ready to engage in conversation. How pleasant it was to be for a while in the company of someone who spoke English. The Spanish chatter of the Mayor was still ringing in my ears; I was exhausted by the effort to understand even a scintilla of what he was saying.

We were joined by Bernard and Rolf, a French and German duo that had met Liam in Roncesvalles and had struck up a partnership almost immediately. Bernard seemed totally engrossed in the camino and it became apparent that he had studied by way of a project the historical development of the Santiago camino down through the centuries. He had recently been given early retirement as an engineer with Air France and was undertaking the walk to reflect on the unexpected termination of his employment. His companion, Rolf, spoke equally fluent English and was a teacher of religion and philosophy in a secondary school in Germany.

As each one of us attempted to explain why we had decided to undertake the journey, we revealed aspects of ourselves that many of our day-to-day acquaintances would not have been privy to. This initial sharing with pilgrims inspired me no end and augured well for the rest of the journey where stories would reveal the inner lives of the pilgrims.

Evening approached and darkness crept towards us, so we decided to call it a day and return to the refugio to rest ourselves for the next stage of the journey. As we entered the refugio, the television was blaring and many a pilgrim was glued to the World Cup. Never one to get excited by the world of sport, I went to the bedroom to sleep after such a varied and challenging day. Stretching out on the floor in the silence of the evening became a moment of prayerful thanks to the Lord for his protection over me during the walk.

However, the silence was rudely shattered about midnight when the three young Spanish people who had passed me at Alto de Erro, noisily entered the room and began to prepare to bed down. I found it difficult to have to listen to their chatter, which seemed endless. Part of me wanted to object to their lack of consideration; yet I realised that a pilgrim was invited to practise tolerance and accept any daily inconveniences along the route. This was a first test!

What a change after such a marvellous day when I felt enthused and inspired by the people I met and the various moments along the way. Even as I reflected on this, I calmed down somewhat and gradually slipped into the realms of sleep with a prayer of thanksgiving for the blessings of the day.

DAY THREE
Larrasoaña to Pamplona
Wednesday 24 June 1998

The walk to Pamplona was only 19.7km. Generally a most engaging and pleasant route, it offered the pilgrim the enticement of a richly historical place where myth and legend meet.

Having had an early breakfast in the crowded café in Larrasoaña where we had dined the previous night, I set off on my own, passing the church of San Nicholas and crossing the Bandits' Bridge over the Arga. The route rose gently towards a copse of beech trees and then descended once more to continue along the river. What a feeling of *joie de vivre* I experienced in the early morning air! Light was just beginning to appear and the moon was still visible in the brightening sky. The beaten earth pathway alongside the river was bordered by wild yellow and purple flowers, which I would love to have been able to identify. It is a long time since terms like *umbreliferae* and *leguminosae* were part of my learning repertoire; now all I can do is to classify them all with the generic term of flowers. Someday, I will once again become acquainted with world of plants and trees. It seems such a pity to be among a profusion of plant life and not he able to identify what one is looking at, or indeed to appreciate the uniqueness of each species. It is at moments like this that the concept of lifelong learning offers an invitation and a challenge!

The morning walk reminded me of when I used to go with scouts to the Dargle River in Enniskerry where we would camp and hike during the weekends. The beauty and vibrancy of the Arga River cascading over the rocks and meandering through the Esteribar valley likewise filled me with intense joy. I began reciting the Morning Prayer I had composed during my 30-day retreat at St Bueno's the year prior to the walk:

> Loving Father, thank you for the gift of this new day.
> May I spend each moment of it loving you
> With all my heart and all my soul and all my strength,
> And may Jesus and Mary be my constant companions
> As I journey towards you, O Father, source of every good.

As I continued to admire the rich vegetation alongside the river and between the trees, I wanted to repeat over and over again, "Thank you, Father, for the gift of trees, of hills, of streams, and of all creation." I was filled with an extraordinary sense of gratitude for the chance to travel this journey as a pilgrim, gratitude for the very gift of life. This sense of thanksgiving welled up inside me and engulfed my spirit with indescribable happiness. What a day to be alive amidst the abundance of rich vegetation!

I crossed the Arga over an ancient Romanesque bridge and met the *carreterra* (motorway). By this time, Rolf and Bernard had joined me, and it was most pleasant to be in their company as we made our way towards Monte Narval, a hill on the side of the road. Liam, their other companion, had not yet appeared on the scene, intending to join us later.

Rolf's manner of carrying his gear was rather amateurish in that he had his rucksack strapped at a rakish angle to his back, and the outside of the rucksack was cluttered with various objects hanging from it: shoes, plastic bags, a cup, among other things. He also carried a hand-held bag with other bits and pieces in it, giving the impression of someone on a shopping spree. I wondered how he could continue the pilgrimage in this fashion, but it did not seem to bother him.

In contrast, Bernard had everything neatly and tidily stored in his compact rucksack with not a sign of any extraneous objects dangling from it. In fact, he told us how he had weighed each item in the rucksack so that the overall weight would not exceed 12 kilogrammes. There was not a single unnecessary item in his bag. Bernard was methodical to a fault.

He walked with the assistance of his magnificent staff or, as the Spanish call it, a *bordón*, that a friend of his had carved especially for the walk. The bordón was of a hard wood weighing almost five kilos and measuring about five feet in height. On top of the bordón the scallop shell, symbol of the Jacobean pilgrim, was beautifully carved, and around the upper part of the staff were various hieroglyphics with astrological and religious significance. It was the envy of many a pilgrim.

We found ourselves walking high up on the hillside when we were hailed by a rough-looking Spaniard who indicated that we had taken the wrong route. Scrambling down the hill, we exchanged a few words of thanks with this local farmer who explained that the signage had not been restored after the recent repairs to the pathways.

On we went away from the Esteribar valley and crossed the River Ulzama over an impressive Romanesque bridge with six arches. Right before us stood the basilica of Trinidad de Arre; it used to house a pilgrim hostel in the sixteenth century. Unfortunately, the basilica was closed when we arrived, so we decided to continue on our way through the suburbs of Villava and Burlada on our way into Pamplona. Just before entering the city, we crossed over the Magdalena bridge, which spans the Arga, and stopped at the stone cross bearing the image of St James dressed as a pilgrim. We took photographs of each other sitting on the bridge and walking towards the city fortifications. This was a moment to relax before reaching the city walls that towered over us.

We were entering into the ancient city of the Roman general Pompey the Great from whose name in Latin (Pompaelo) Pamplona derived its name. The city apparently dates back as an Episcopal See to the sixth century, although it was not until the eleventh century that it began to flourish under the influence of Sancho III who was a great promoter of the Santiago pilgrimage. He established groups of foreign artisans and merchants to provide a service of support to pilgrims on the way. Many of these artisans had themselves been pilgrims and had been enticed to remain in Pamplona to create a centre of hospitality.

Our way took us past the city walls and we arrived through the narrow streets of Valle Curia at the refugio, which was closed until midday according to a sign on the door. It was eleven o'clock and the sun was beaming down unmercifully on the city streets. We parked ourselves just outside on the benches of the Plaza de los Burgos where we decided to relax and wait for the hostel to open. Before long, one of the hospitaleros approached us and explained that they had seen us outside and were prepared to open early to accommodate us. Gratefully we gathered our gear and followed them into the refugio, the same one I had visited three days previously on my way to St Jean-Pied-de-Port.

The refugio was very compact, if not cramped, with a narrow corridor leading to a long narrow dormitory where lines of bunk beds were closely stacked to accommodate the maximum number of pilgrims.

The place exuded a spirit of hospitality with smiling faces and ready advice. A very enthusiastic young hospitalero explained that the staffing of the refugio was on a voluntary basis and that quite a coterie of the friends of St James existed in the city who took it on themselves to provide a ministry of welcome to the weary travellers.

I got my passport stamped with their sello for the second time. I had already got it stamped on the first day of the walk when I had almost given up hope of making the journey to France. However, I wanted to have the impressive Pamplona stamp in proper sequence in the passport, that is, between Larrasoaña and Puente la Reina. Some pilgrims take this practice most seriously and indeed collect as many stamps as they can along the way. It becomes almost a competition to see who has the greatest number and the most unusual stamps. I did not have much choice as to whether I would enter the competition or not since my Irish pilgrim's passport had only 36 spaces where I could obtain a stamp. Anyway, I had decided that I would only seek the stamps from the places where I would rest for the night.

Then I remembered about Kristen's promise; I searched for her message on the noticeboard, on which pages of every shape and colour were pinned in a higgledy-piggledy fashion. Sure enough I found an A4-size page folded over with my name, David Gibson, written large on one side. On opening the sealed pages, there was her share of the taxi money that I had lent her. What amazed and disappointed me was that there was no accompanying note. The pages that had been used as an envelope were part of a bulletin on women's issues written in Spanish. I could not understand how she could simply have returned the money without any expression of gratitude or acknowledgement. It was not that I would have demanded such a message, but it seemed the least she could have done under the circumstances. I wondered if I had judged her incorrectly. She had come across as someone trustworthy; someone indeed that I would have wanted to walk with for some of the journey. This, however, indicated a definite lack of graciousness never mind appreciation.

Having showered and done my laundry, I went in search of somewhere to eat. I found a typical Spanish eating-house along a side-street adjacent to the refugio. The place was packed with locals, all from a very working-class section of society. Bare tables and noisy music mingled with the smell of strong Spanish cigarettes and the loud chatter of friendly arguments. I found a corner well away from the smoke and picked up the menu, only to be faced with words that meant little to me. All I could do was take pot-luck and order what I could pronounce! I soon discovered I had ordered a large ball of white rice covered in red sauce, which tasted like heated ketchup. To the weary pilgrim it was most welcome, especially as it was being washed down with cheap Spanish wine.

A breaded piece of meat, probably beef, followed, but it was so greasy that I simply nibbled at it. Dessert came in the form of a decent ice-cream cone; strong black coffee followed to complete the repast. When I took the time to digest all that I had eaten, I realised that I was really tired. All I was fit for was to return to the hostel and sleep off the effects. I was in good company for it appeared that all the pilgrims had decided to take their siesta as a matter of principle. The snores were almost deafening, but nothing would have prevented me from dozing off.

A visit to the cathedral situated in the heart of the Navarreria district was next on the agenda. The Navarreria district is like the Liberties in Dublin, where the original inhabitants of the city resided. To reach this area, I had to walk the traditional Calle Curia with all the small specialist shops selling anything from the proverbial needle to an anchor. Obviously, Pamplona enjoys the economic benefits of a tourist town where luxury items and antiques of all sorts entice the acquisitive appetites of the well-heeled passers-by.

The cathedral was originally built by the famous Maestro Esteban (Stephen), one of the best known of the master builders along the Santiago way. Many of the significant churches along the camino are the work of pilgrim builders who, in lieu of completing the pilgrimage themselves, or even on completion of the pilgrimage, contributed to the pilgrimage by constructing churches or hospitals for the service of the fellow pilgrims.

A fire destroyed the cathedral in the late fourteenth century, and it was rebuilt in the Gothic style of the spectacular cloisters that had been completed 50 years before the fire. The present cathedral is built in the form of a Latin cross and has three naves, a polygonal apse and a wide ambulatory. The richly gilded reredos to be found at many of the altars contrasts with the bare stone floor of the cathedral. I was grateful that I had read something about the architectural features of churches over the years so as to appreciate the marvellous skill of the stonemasons.

As I walked around the cathedral and listened to the background organ music, I found tears coming to my eyes. This weeping was becoming a habit! I reflected on the faith of so many people who had motivated the construction of such a magnificent edifice. The vibrant faith would have filled the cathedral to bursting, and here I was almost alone in an empty cavernous reliquary. And yet, this surely could not explain the flow of tears! There was something lurking below the surface, and for the life of me, I could not get in touch with it. As I sat there, the thoughts that came to me were of the young men who had left the congregation of the Christian Brothers over the last eight years.

I began to recall them to mind and name them. I had known them well and had admired their enthusiasm and creativity. But they did not stay. In a sense, their leaving mirrored the wide-scale exodus from the Church in Europe over the last 50 years. Somehow, religious life is witnessing the same sort of departures, leaving congregations somewhat like deserted cathedrals, impressive but empty. These depressing thoughts welled up creating a sense of sorrow that things had reached such a low point. And yet, to place the blame on the institutions would be rather simplistic. Often the cause for the mismatch is far more complex than many sociologists would posit. The historical evolution of institutions and their impact on individual lives frequently create a cultural incomprehensibility on both sides and make for gradual estrangement.

As I sat in this glorious edifice listening to the strains of grandiose organ music, I prayed for those young men who had left the congregation. I hoped that their ideals would grow and develop and that the congregation would continue to seek ways of communicating the Gospel message in ever more articulate ways. Even as I prayed, I reflected that people also left religious life because they found the challenge of living the life too uncompromising, too radical. Analysis is always multi-layered.

Weary almost from such ponderous thoughts, I emerged into the unrelenting sunshine and walked along the almost deserted streets. It was siesta time, and only the proverbial mad dogs and pilgrims ventured onto the streets. I was looking for a fruit shop to augment my diminishing supplies and eventually found a beautifully organised fruit and cheese emporium. I was no sooner within the confines of the shop when a smiling shop assistant came to my help. However, I was still very shaky with Spanish, and so beat a hasty retreat. I would return later when there were more customers and less time to receive this overpowering attention!

After exploring the shopping area of the Piazza Consistorial, I returned to the fruit shop and managed to purchase the fruit and cheese without the somewhat embarrassingly close attention of the friendly shop assistant. What impressed me particularly about the food shops in Spain is their obsession with cleanliness. Everything is simply spotless and impeccably arranged for the maximum effectiveness. People seem to take pride in how food shops are arranged, and this creates in the customer a sense that he or she is important.

By this time I was bushed. There was only one thing for it; I would return to the refugio and get some sleep. Others had the same idea for the dormitory was quite well populated with sleeping pilgrims recovering from the effects of many hours walking in the heat of the day. I lay on my bed with my Spanish grammar and eventually dozed.

That evening I met with Rolf and Bernard in a local hostelry to sample the tapas. We exchanged stories and shared how the day had been for each of us. Before long, however, the three of us were giving signals that it was time to sleep. Since we had decided to rise early each morning in order to avail of the cool walking weather, it was becoming necessary to discipline ourselves to retire before 10.00pm each evening.

On our return to the refugio, I was lucky to find the nearby church of San Fermin open. I had tried earlier to visit the famous 'Virgen del Camino' (the Virgin of the Way), only to find the place locked and barred. Entering now the darkened thirteenth-century church, I was

San Fermín's gold-encased statue in the Basilica of San Fermin in Pamplona.

just about able to make out the statue of the 'Virgen' and as I stood before it, I prayed to Mary that she would accompany me on my journey to Santiago as she did Jesus during the flight into Egypt.

Lying on my bed that night I reflected on the events of the day. It had indeed been a truly enriching time. Though the memory of the departed Brothers and the slight disappointment over Kristen's 'ingratitude' lingered with me, I thanked the Lord and the Virgen del Camino for their protection of me along the way. At this stage, I was truly on my way and more and more like a pilgrim. Pamplona had certainly improved on the second visit; I was no longer lost or floundering.

Day Four
Pamplona to Puente la Reina
Thursday 25 June 1998

In the midst of packing the rucksack in the darkness of the early morning hours, I came across the paper in which Kristen had wrapped the money she owed me. I don't know how I had missed it but there, towards the bottom of the page, was a message from her, thanking me for lending her the money and wishing me the best for the pilgrimage. The note was a real gift, especially after the initial feelings of disappointment I had experienced. Amidst the feelings of gratitude, however, there was also a sense that I had misjudged her in the first place. How easy it is to jump to conclusions, even when on a spiritual journey! I blessed her for her kind wishes and prayed the Lord's blessing on her. The fact that Kristen was a day ahead and was only intending to walk for ten days would mean that I would never be able to express my thanks for her prompt repayment nor indeed would I learn of how she had experienced the camino. I resigned myself to the fact that there might be many people like Kristen whom I would only meet for a day or two.

Leaving Pamplona along the narrow Calle Major, I saw Bernard in the distance as he walked through the Parque de la Traconera. On reaching him, I became aware of his need to be alone with his thoughts and pulled back, wishing him well and arranging to meet in Puente la Reina. It is vital to allow people on the camino to have space for themselves to reflect and to pray. There is always the danger that the need for companionship will prevent the pilgrim from developing their own spirituality. In solitude, the pilgrim faces into the inner journey of self-knowledge alone; each person finds themselves longing for these moments along the camino. It would be crucial to judge when to engage with pilgrims and when to leave them alone.

I was somewhat anxious when I saw the Sierra del Perdón mountain rising up in the distance. Not having done much hill-walking up to then, it seemed that my day would be quite strenuous, and I had some misgivings about how I would fare. By now, dawn had given way to the light of the day, with a cool breeze stirring around the base of the mountain, making it cool enough to put on my windproof jacket.

The first village on the route was the small hamlet of Guenduláin, where there had once been a pilgrim's hospital run by the Confraternity of St James. All that now remains are the ruined church of San Andres and the Palace of the counts of Guenduláin. The path led on to the small village with the almost unpronounceable name of Zariquiegui, and there I met Rolf. We were both dying for a coffee but not a bar was to be seen. An elderly local woman kindly filled Rolf's flask with the cool water from the local well, and off we went towards the summit of the Sierra.

Our conversation was rudely interrupted when I discovered that I had lost my walking stick. My old faithful companion had vanished somewhere between the village and where I was now standing in bewilderment. Unwilling to go on without my bordón, I encouraged Rolf to continue on his way while I retraced my steps in search of the missing ally. Fortunately, I came across it lying on the ground just outside the village. It seems that I had simply let it fall to the ground inadvertently. Although losing the bordón would not have been the greatest tragedy, I certainly would have missed my 'companion'. So it was with a sense of relief that I set off once more with my stick to head for Alto de Santa Maria de Erreniega, 789 metres above sea level, the highest part of the Sierra del Perdón.

The climb up the side of the Sierra was made all the more enjoyable by the Van-Gogh-like mixture of colours made up from the patchwork of tilled and untilled fields that spread like a quilt in the valley below. The shades of golden wheat, with what appeared to be some fields of green unripe wheat, the browns of fallow fields, the sun-scorched hedges that defined the margins between the fields, all formed a kaleidoscope of nature's hues in a scene of breathtaking beauty. All this contrasted with the azure skies, where wisps of clouds broke the intensity of the almost lapis lazuli sky. And on the top of the mountain, majestic against the skyline, was a phalanx of windmills rhythmically revolving in unison.

The monument at the top of Sierra del Perdón commemorating the 'Fuente de Reniega'.

The beaten path wended its way along the side of the mountain and thus, with each step, I approached the windmills in an oblique fashion. Shortly before reaching the Alto del Perdón, there was a modern sculpture of cutout bronze figures silhouetted against the skyline. Apparently, the monument commemorates the ancient legend of the 'Fuente de Reniega', the Fountain of Denial, according to which an exhausted and parched pilgrim was tempted by the Devil who offered to show him a spring of water from which to quench his thirst on condition that he would deny his faith. The pilgrim resisted the temptation and, for his steadfastness, was rewarded by the apparition of St James dressed as a pilgrim who uncovered a mountain spring and gave him water from his scallop shell. Strangely, I could not find the modern fountain, although there is supposed to be one. Nevertheless, it seemed a good moment to delve into the rucksack to retrieve the backup water bottle and quench my thirst.

Standing on the top of the mountain was like being on the edge of two worlds: the world of rich pasturage and intensive cultivation contrasting unbelievably with that on the other side of the mountain. Stretching down into the distance was an immense expanse of almost desert barrenness interrupted by the three villages of Uterga, Muruzábel and Obanos. It seemed impossible that two totally contrasting views could co-exist within such close proximity and under the one sky. And yet, there it was before me! I was almost reluctant to leave the fertile half of the mountain to face into the rugged and harsh terrain on the other side.

Descending Santa Maria de Erreniega was difficult because it was uneven underfoot and unyielding in its severity. The rains had worn away much of the earth, leaving rocky surfaces and deep irregular ridges as scars across the paths. This made walking downhill quite challenging and very tiring. By the time I reached Uterga, the first of the villages, my feet ached, and I generally felt quite exhausted from the unrelenting heat of the morning sun. Rather than continuing regardless, it seemed wiser to pay attention to the body before continuing on towards Muruzábel.

In the middle of the plaza in the centre of Uterga, just in front of a Gothic church dedicated to the Assumption of the Virgin, there is a fine fountain. Water gushed from a tap into a large trough, creating quite a din in the otherwise silent village. It was a relief to take off the heavy boots that had protected my feet against the rocky path of the mountain and liberate my feet from the oppressive woollen socks. There I lay against the side of the trough allowing the spray from the gushing fountain to sprinkle my hair and sweatshirt. And bathing my feet in the cool water was simply heavenly. What a relief and a sense of achievement after climbing almost 800 metres! For someone whose idea of climbing was often limited to climbing the modest slopes of Howth Head on the fringe of Dublin Bay on a Sunday afternoon, that was a major achievement – and there was more to come.

Just as I was about to depart Uterga, three women arrived in the plaza, speaking what sounded like Norwegian. They seemed equally exhausted after the mountain climb, but they were apparently more interested in food than in water. They made straight for what appeared to be a grocery shop and tried to make their needs understood to a local passer-by. What happened next I never found out for it was time for me to take off for the next stage of the walk. Were these three women the same Norwegians that I had heard in the small coffee bar outside Roncesvalles? They may have been, but for that day, I was not to find out.

The road to Muruzábel seemed straightforward. Yet the further I went along the path my misgivings increased, as there were no signs of the yellow arrows that had been so much in evidence up to that point. I was beginning to marvel that I could simply point myself in the direction of the next town and rely on the arrows that had been painted at strategic points along the way. But now they had let me down and I was unsure of where to go.

When I was about to retrace my steps for fear of having taken the wrong path, I came across a crudely written sign, simply saying 'Bar'. Looking in the direction indicated by the sign, I saw Liam standing outside the bar eating an ice cream as he made ready to continue his walk. He told me that the bar was more like the shebeen or unlicensed drinking den that one would find in Connemara in the early fifties than a bar in Spain. It was not clear what he meant until I entered the darkness of the unlit room whose cool air sheltered the clients from the merciless sun. I was met with the silent stares of ancient men who appeared to show no recognition that I had arrived. My friendly, *"Buenos Dias"* was greeted with a grudging murmur.

Towards the back of the bar sat a number of even older-looking men, each hunched over what appeared to be coffee, but staring suspiciously at the unwelcome foreigner. Their conversation had dried up abruptly on my arrival, and it seemed that my departure alone would enable them to take up where they had suddenly left off. The whole experience was both disappointing and depressing. What could have been a friendly refuge for the weary pilgrim – welcoming the stranger and offering some refreshment – was instead a dark and drab drinking hole. Feeling the need to knock the dust from my boots and walk immediately to the next village, that's exactly what I did, after I had extracted from the timid shopkeeper my longed-for ice cream. I could not get out of there quickly enough to feel the warmth of the sun and to meet some more human faces along the road. I would not be recommending anyone to stop by at Muruzábel!

Obanos was where I saw for the first time the word *ultreya* (onwards!) painted in yellow on the gable wall of an old house outside the village. It gave me great pleasure to see the word before my very eyes. I had seen it written in books, but there it was written where the pilgrim could see it as he or she entered the town. So here was Obanos and its people welcoming the pilgrim into their town and offering encouragement to continue along the route. What a contrast from Muruzábel just down the road where there seemed to be both mistrust and suspicion instead of warmth and openness.

Three pilgrims travelling along the camino. Dogs, horses and donkeys can almost be considered as pilgrims!

Liam was sitting outside the neo-Gothic early twentieth-century church of St John the Baptist, looking rather glum. He explained that he had hoped to visit the church to see the silver-coloured skull of St William, his namesake, but, as is often the case in Spain, the church was closed. It probably only opened at Mass times. He told me the story of St William, contained in *The Mystery of Obanos* written between 1965 and 1978 by the local canon Don Santos Beguiristain. It tells of Saint Felicia and her brother, William, Duke of Aquitaine. On returning from a pilgrimage to Santiago, Felicia decided to live the life of a hermit. William was furious about this and insisted that she return to court. When she refused, he killed her. On coming to his senses, he was grief-stricken, and in repentance, he decided to make a pilgrimage to Santiago. Then, on his return, he took the decision to spend the rest of his life in prayer and penance.

We left Obanos and headed for Puente la Reina where we intended to stay for the rest of the day. Just outside the town, a modern sculpture of St James greets the pilgrim, and we took turns to pose for photographs before the statue. Puente la Reina (Bridge of the Queen) is the place where the four main pilgrim routes converge. So, from Le Puy, Vezelay, Paris and Arles, pilgrims arrive at this town to walk together to Santiago.

We headed for the refugio, which was in the charge of the Padres Reparadores housed nearby. Having got the passport signed by a friendly priest who was keen to chat with the pilgrims from different nations, we entered the refugio.

An orderly chaos reigned, with over 50 pilgrims all trying at the same time to wash themselves and their smelly clothes. In vain, I tried to erect my clothesline, which had suction pads at each extremity. Every time I hung an item of clothing, the pads came away from the tiled surface and the sodden sweatshirt splattered on the floor and splashed anyone and anything that moved in the vicinity. So much for the useless gadget, which I had purchased

Puente la Reina bridge spans the River Arga.

in Dublin in the months preceding the departure. In the end, I simply tied the string from window to window and hung the recently washed clothes on the makeshift line. While I was busy hanging up the clothes, an unknown villain (or villains) 'borrowed' my liquid soap, so that when I eventually found the wretched tube, it was almost empty. Obviously, the spirit of 'share and share alike' had reached Puente la Reina! I would need to guard my personal possessions more carefully.

The town lies half-way between Pamplona and Estella and is built on the edge of the River Arga. My guidebook pointed out that 'Puente' refers to the bridge, 'Puente de Arga', a Romanesque construction consisting of six semi-circular arches and five pillars with spillways that span the river. 'Reina' refers to either Dona Mayor, wife of Sancho III, or to Dona Estefania, wife of Don Garcia de Nájera, of the eleventh and twelfth centuries respectively, who would have sponsored the construction of the mighty bridge.

From the twelfth century until their suppression in the fourteenth century, the Knights Templars had the responsibility of protecting pilgrims. Then the Hospitallers undertook the task. The Knights Templars were the first of the military orders founded to protect the pilgrims travelling to Jerusalem on pilgrimage. With the deliverance of Jerusalem by the Crusaders in the early part of the twelfth century, that precarious conquest needed to be consolidated by some group. The Templars adopted the Rule of St Benedict and eventually wore the Cistercian white habit, adding a red cross on the back. They became very wealthy and powerful, so much so that they had to be suppressed in the early part of the fourteenth century. The Hospitallers are said to have existed before the Crusades; their original function was to provide shelter for pilgrims going to Jerusalem. They were the infirmarians of their day, gradually becoming a military order. The Knights of Malta are descendants of the Hospitallers.

Liam and I sought out a place to have a bite of lunch. It was now almost two o'clock, and it seemed that the whole town had gone to sleep. However, just beyond the refugio, we espied 'Bar Very', a modern disco-like bar, in the midst of medieval Spain. On entering the bar, we were met with neon lights everywhere and music blaring with a beat that almost made the building shake. When we approached the bar, the proprietor explained that they were closed, but his wife intervened and offered to make us tortillas. This gesture of generosity expressed again the spirit of the camino where the ancient welcome of the pilgrim seems rooted in the traditions of the local population. And so we sat out in the sun, away from the decibels, sipping a beer and just recovering from the fatigue of the 23km walk from Pamplona.

When the tortillas arrived, again it was obvious that they had been prepared with loving care: beautifully cooked and presented tastefully on good-quality plates, with a side helping of salad. We continued talking, eating, and drinking beer, and by the time we had cleaned our plates and discussed our plans for the walk, I was beginning to feel quite drunk. Sitting in the sun imbibing ice cold beer was a formula for disaster. In fact, beer and sun do not really mix. We expressed our thanks to the kind hosts and made for the cool shadows of the Calle Major, one of the characteristically medieval streets along which pilgrims for hundreds of years have wended their way to the famous bridge at the end of the town.

We passed the Church of Santiago with its impressive multi-lobed portal and Romanesque façade and since it was closed, we continued until we reached the Puente de Arga, the bridge that spanned the eponymous river. As we looked over the bridge, one could almost imagine the ancient pilgrims stopping at the same juncture and admiring the higgledy-piggledy conglomeration of houses that pressed against the bridge for support. Looking beyond the bridge, we could make out the road that would lead us the following morning towards Estella.

Liam and I separated after agreeing to meet back at the refugio around seven o'clock so that we could dine together. Meanwhile, I began exploring the old parts of the town. By this time, the church of St James was open. I entered the cool and dark interior by the artistically beautiful west door. The eighteenth-century altarpiece in magnificent gold leaf dominated the apse and created an atmosphere of solemnity in contrast with the rather bare stone walls. There was a fourteenth-century statue of St Bartholomew and a famous Gothic statue of St James 'the Black' – the first statue of St James that I had come across. No doubt, there would be many more of his images along the camino.

The iconography of St James either portrays him as a pilgrim, an apostle, or a 'Moor-slayer'. The image of St James mounted on a mighty stallion, brandishing a wicked-looking sword and chopping off the heads of the wretched infidels, does little for creating a sense of spiritual contemplation. And yet often in the churches, I am told, the image of the pilgrim and the Moor-slayer exist side by side in unhappy proximity. Strangely, it was the image of the Moor-slayer that gave the impetus for devotion to St James in Spain in the first place. The battle of Clavijo (AD 834) signalled the beginning of the reconquest of Spain when Ramiro I of Leon defeated the army of Abdurrahman II. The story of the appearance of St James in a vision, where he was seen astride a mighty white stallion and liberating the hundred virgins demanded by the Moors as a tribute, has become one of the dominant legends in Spanish folklore. It was from this image that devotion to St James developed and, following the phenomenal growth in popularity of the camino to Santiago de Compostela, the image of St James as a pilgrim himself offered the ordinary pilgrim a model and a protection on the way.

Leaving the church, I went in search of postcards to send to some friends. I wanted particularly to remember Lori who had set out the previous year on the camino starting at Puente la Reina on her way to Santiago. Her taking such a step was, to a large extent, the reason why I myself was also on the pilgrim way. I wished to remember her, and indeed the various families in Sovere, a small village in the Bergamo region in northern Italy, feeling ever grateful for their friendship and fine example as people who have succeeded in making religion part and parcel of their lives. In the many trips I have made to their homes they have become a precious influence in my life and in writing to Lori, I wished to thank the Lord for the gift of friendship that has contributed enormously to my personal growth over the years.

Bernard appeared on the scene, and we agreed to dine together that night, together with Rolf and Liam. He even had researched the restaurant that gave the best value, and in his typical French manner made all the gastronomic sounds to indicate that what we would eat that night would more than satisfy four ravenous pilgrims.

Returning to the refugio, I entered the church of the Padres Reparadores attached to the seminary. It is called the Iglesia del Crucifijo because, suspended in the apse, is an imposing German wooden crucifix in the shape of a 'Y'. The cool and silence of the chapel afforded me the opportunity to meditate on the day's experiences. St Ignatius, the Founder of the Jesuits, emphasised the importance of taking time to look over the events of the day in order to discover how much the consciousness of the transcendent had been present in their lives. He particularly stressed the need to concentrate on feelings and to examine how they were linked to the various daily happenings. So this is what I did, beginning with the discovery of Kristen's letter and concluding with the meeting with Bernard. I simply let the events come into my mind and tried to get in touch once more with the feelings associated with each occurrence. The function of such an overview of the day is to create a contemplative stance in one's life, thus avoid living at a superficial and unreflective level.

When I joined Bernard, Rolf and Liam at Yony's Restaurant, I was pleasantly surprised to see that the three Norwegian women, whom I had first seen in Uterga, had tagged along. The three women had truly Nordic names; Ingrittberg, Littian, and Olga. They were on the camino for ten days and had decided to take in some of the more interesting parts of the route, avoiding the monotonous and less noteworthy parts. So they were going to leave Puente la Reina the next day by bus and head towards Estella.

The meal turned out to be most pleasant because of the sharing of stories and biographical details by each pilgrim. What we talked about that night, I simply cannot remember clearly, but the lasting impression was of three most vibrant, interesting and friendly women who knew how to live life to the full. They were a real tonic for us foursome who were inclined to be of the more serious type. They did not talk explicitly of their faith or indeed of their motivation for walking, but they obviously had chosen to take ten days of their holidays to undertake an experience that in itself is faith-provoking. At the end of the meal, our parting was tinged with regret that we would not see each other again; but there was also a sense of gratitude that for a short while we had been blessed with the presence of feminine graciousness. And there was always the possibility that we would meet again in Estella if they decided to explore that town.

Returning to the refugio, I was ready for sleep, as indeed were most of the pilgrims. The refugio was packed, and even in the foyer, there was an elf-like figure asleep on a table. He had arrived when all the bunks had been occupied. With a sense of real gratitude, I slipped into my sleeping bag, almost immediately falling into a deep slumber, despite the noise of snoring all around me.

Day Five
Puente la Reina to Estella
Friday 26 June 1998

Leaving Puente la Reina along the Calle Mayor and over the beautiful Romanesque bridge that spans the Arga, I was feeling elated in the early morning. Having walked for four days without a blister and without any real sense of tired or stiff limbs was very encouraging. Already 95km had been covered since St Jean. Almost an eighth of the journey completed without any real mishap. What probably also prompted the feelings of joy and gratitude was the sight that greeted me that morning in the refugio prior to departure.

A young pilgrim was sitting on a stool in the common room of the refugio, cautiously treating four or five blisters that apparently he had accumulated over the previous few days. His foot looked a real mess. Large areas of red inflammation surrounded smaller circles of deeper red where obviously the blister had burst. Carefully, he was removing old plaster, disinfecting the wounds and bandaging up the blisters. Feelings of sympathy flooded my mind alongside feelings of relief that the same fate had not befallen me. No doubt it would happen sometime, but there was no desire to hasten the fateful day. It is generally accepted that septic blisters, tendonitis or dehydration are the main physical disabilities that prevent pilgrims from completing the camino. So far, I had avoided all three.

It was 6.15am, and already I could see Bernard and Liam just ahead of me. They had said the previous day that their guidebook indicated a café just outside the town but none was to be seen. Liam was particularly embarrassed, as it was he who had insisted on the location of the café. Now it meant that we would have to wait a while for the daily caffeine fix. So the nuts and raisins I purchased the previous day would have to do me for the moment until we reached the first town that boasted a café.

Ahead of us were some Spanish pilgrims who were taking the motorway instead of following the arrows that pointed to a track skirting the road. It seemed a foolish thing to do; the hard tar road can be very trying on one's feet, whereas the track provides some protection as well as offering more interesting views, not to mention avoiding the roar of the juggernauts congesting the motorways. My own experience of walking from St Jean to Roncesvalles along the main road was enough to convince me that the paths and tracks are infinitely preferable, not only from the health point of view but also from the opportunities to be closer to nature and in the company of other pilgrims.

The path led through what is known as the 'Nuns' District', which alludes to a convent founded in the thirteenth century that used to care for the pilgrims. Not a sign of the convent remains although just past Eunea there were ruins of the Hospital de Bargota, which had been run by the Hospitallers whose influence can be seen in many parts of Spain, but especially along the camino.

I met Liam who was having a cigarette on the steps of the imposing ruined church at Mañueru; but rather than stop I continued on past the local cemetery. What surprised me about the cemetery was that the bodies were buried underground as is the custom in Ireland. I had expected to see burial vaults above ground, as is the custom in Italy where only the poorest of the poor are forced to bury their dead in the earth.

Already Cirauqui could be seen some three kilometres away standing on a hill. Cirauqui is a Basque word meaning 'vipers' nest', which refers to the rocky hill on which it is constructed. One of the most impressive monuments in this town is the Church of San Roman at the top

'Cirauqui' is Basque for 'vipers' nest'. The village is so named because it is built on a rocky hill.

of the village. Just like the Church of Santiago in Puente la Reina, this church has the multi-lobed main portal characteristic of Romanesque architecture. Both doors reminded me of the old portal in Christ Church Cathedral in Dublin, which may even pre-date these beautiful Spanish churches.

However, even though I reached the top of the village there was no sign of the church. Of two minds whether to spend time looking for it in the knowledge that it would surely be closed in the early morning or alternatively to continue walking, I decided to keep going and was soon descending towards the old Roman path. No sooner had I reached the stony path than a cyclist on a mountain bike and dressed in professional cycling gear overtook me as he bounced over the rocky surface. He must have been made of iron for the terrain was both uneven and steep. Indeed, the climb up to Cirauqui would test the skills of a Tour de France rider. The path led across the single arched ancient Roman bridge and rose up to meet the N111, where I paused for a drink from my water flask.

Carrying water is most important for the walker along the pilgrim route. With the merciless heat of the sun, a pilgrim without water is a pilgrim in danger. With one litre in the flask and another litre in the rucksack, there was little possibility that I could be caught short; but I was always conscious of the danger of this happening. Water is by no means lightweight, and many a pilgrim has been tempted to travel light by carrying the minimum water supply – not a good idea.

Liam caught up with me as I was energetically making my way along the path.

"Do you ever look back as you walk?" he asked.

"What do you mean?" I enquired.

"My mother told me that you should always keep looking back as you walk, because she believed that what is behind is as important as what is ahead."

"I never really thought of that," I said, "but it does make sense."

As I looked back I could see the old Roman path that had led me from the 'vipers' nest' to the motorway; there behind me was the village of Cirauqui perched precariously on the top of the hill. And in the distance, I could see the old path that had led me out of Puente la Reina, an ancient path along which pilgrims had, for hundreds of years, made their way to the point where I now stood. The rugged terrain had a beauty of its own, something I would have missed if it were not for Liam's mother's advice.

Liam was holding his plastic water bottle awkwardly, trying to open it while taking off his rucksack. The inevitable happened. The bottle flew out of his grasp falling onto the pathway and splitting at the side. Though the bottle still held the water once it was kept upright, this would be awkward for him along the journey. I immediately thought of my spare bottle in my backpack, yet fear and maybe selfishness halted my initial urge to loan it to him. What would happen if I did not come across another watering hole before Estella? Would I last with the supply I had with me? As I left Liam, I felt rather tacky and wondered how I could square my selfish decision with the whole spirit of the pilgrim way. The further I walked the more I realised that my self pre-occupation was, in fact, contrary to all that the camino stood for. I also knew that regret was a useless emotion; it would not change anything. I had simply put my own needs before another's and unless feelings of regret cause a real change in the future, they simply lead to further self-condemnation and depression. Actions do indeed speak louder than words.

Crossing the N111, I continued with such feelings of self-reproach, walking along the beaten path that was under major repair. Probably because of all the road works I missed the yellow arrow indicating a left turn, so only when I heard a distant call of what sounded like my name did I turn around and see in the distance Bernard pointing frantically towards the left. Retracing my steps, I saw where the arrow had almost disappeared behind the dust of freshly flattened earth. I followed along the widened path only to meet Liam who also had taken the wrong path. We made a detour to reach the road that led to the small double arched gothic bridge that spans the River Salado.

Aymeric Picaud's *Pilgrim's Guide* tells the following story about the Salado:

Take care not to drink the water here, neither yourself nor your horse, for it is a deadly river! On the way to Santiago we came across two Navarrese sitting by the bank, sharpening the knives they used to flay pilgrims' horses which had drunk the water and died. We asked them if the water was fit to drink, and they lyingly replied that it was, whereupon we gave it to our horses to drink. Two of them dropped dead at once and the Navarrese flayed them there and then.

So, I certainly was not going to refill my flask from this water. Before I left Ireland I had bought water-purifying tablets to drop into doubtful water sources, but I did not feel confident that these would really work and preferred not to use them unless absolutely forced to do so.

No sooner had Liam and I met than we came across Bernard sitting on the fateful bridge over the Salado. When Bernard saw Liam's leaky bottle he immediately offered him his spare flask. And here was me guarding my own personal supply in my rucksack. What a heel I felt. And I am supposed to be a religious who dedicates his life to service of others. Will I ever learn, I said to myself? The answer that whispered in my ear was none too reassuring.

Up the dirt track we continued to Lorca, a typical wayside village but with a fine fountain and washing area right in the centre of the village. It is amazing how even now in the villages, the locals often wash their clothes in the free-flowing ice-cold water from the wells. Usually there are large stone troughs with ridged flat appendices attached where the clothes can be pummelled and rinsed. It is not unusual to see a number of the women bent over the troughs and laying into a pile of washing. Whether they continue to follow this tradition out of necessity or because they feel this method is more effective, I never discovered. It seemed unusual, however, for people not to have the services of a laundrette in this day and age!

Bernard continued walking ahead while Liam and I rested at the fountain. The heat was intense, sapping our energies. As we sat there, along came a smiling young Spanish woman carrying a small rucksack. She greeted us enthusiastically and began speaking to us in broken English. Teresa was her name. She came across as someone who was sympathetic, compassionate and genuinely interested in people. It was as if she wanted to understand the viewpoint of others instead of imposing her own views. She declined an offer of water, saying that she tried to avoid drinking too much. She talked about her pilgrimage and of her enthusiasm in seeing all the places of historical interest. And with that, she took off with a sprightly step on the heels of Bernard who had just left us.

Liam and myself left Lorca after a good rest at the fountain and soon afterwards stopped along the motorway at a local café for a coffee. We had hardly sat down when three noisy Spaniards burst into the café and almost took over the proceedings. My friends from Larrasoaña were on to me again. Their energy and vivacity was too much for us in the early morning, and whereas both of us wanted to escape this invasion, Liam was too tired to move. He encouraged me to proceed at my own pace, an offer I was only too glad to accept.

Walking within sight of the N111, I marvelled at the amount of wheat that was growing in the surrounding fields. Acres and acres of golden flowing wheat created an impression of cloth shimmering in the wind. Obviously, this region of Spain must be the breadbasket for the entire country, supplying the more barren areas with wheat and other crops.

As I walked in the very strong sun, I prayed in thanksgiving for this chance to be a pilgrim. An enormous sense of thankfulness came over me for the opportunity to have this time to reflect on life and to get away from the many tasks that I had left behind in Ireland. Feelings of gratitude gave way to a growing sense of repentance. I found myself with tears in my eyes as I began to reflect on how easy it would be to waste my life without making any real contribution to this world. How easy it would be to glide through life without really attempting something worthwhile! I prayed that I would have the courage to do something practical with my life in the service of others. The water bottle incident came to mind again; this sobered me and forced me to refuse to wallow in self-pity and unrealistic dreams. True, I am called to make a real contribution to life but the reality is that this will be achieved in the day-to-day living-out of my vocation as a Christian Brother in the nuts and bolts of daily tasks. Self-pity was soon exorcised by a good self-inflicted kick in the pants, especially when I thought of my unwillingness to share my water!

Arriving at Villatuerta across a double-arched bridge over the River Iranzu, I saw Bernard's and Teresa's rucksacks outside the fourteenth-century Church of the Assumption. This was almost the first church that I had found open. Bernard and Teresa were with an old woman who had opened the church to give them a guided visit.

The interior was immaculately kept; it was clearly the pride and joy of this simple and kindly woman. Of particular note was the gleaming pavement that had seen many a waxing over the years. She explained in so far as my Spanish would allow me to understand that many of the ecclesiastical treasures that had formerly graced the church had recently been transferred to some museum. She said this with a tone of regret mixed with resignation. I could not really understand too much of what she said, though it was most enjoyable simply to savour the language and catch her enthusiasm.

I wrote a note in the visitors' book wishing God's blessing on this woman and on her family and before leaving she insisted on stamping our passports. Teresa was delighted with the stamp, whereas I would have preferred to stick to the original plan of only obtaining a stamp at the place where I would sleep each night.

The last four kilometres to Estella consisted of a narrow path that wended its way through olive groves, gradually descending towards a fine French Renaissance style building in the distance. The guidebook was no help in enlightening me as to the history or use of the building; but impressive it was and the path led inexorably towards the road that passed close to it.

The pilgrim route goes through the San Miguel district as it enters Estella and passes the Romanesque Church of San Miguel with its magnificent carvings on the portal that looks onto the pathway along which the pilgrim walks. I then came along a narrow street and saw Bernard and Teresa in a queue outside the refugio. Apparently it was not opening for another hour. It seemed that this refugio was run by the local council, unlike most of the others I had already experienced, which were organised on voluntary lines. It looked as if it had been recently constructed and the guidebook confirmed this. It had all the signs of a modern hostel with the latest facilities but personally, I preferred the more rustic refugios.

Liam arrived, as did Rolf. Together with Bernard and Teresa, we decided to look for somewhere to get a bite to eat. Having had a breakfast of raisins and nuts, it was time to find something more substantial.

A 71-year-old Spaniard walking with his 16-year-old grandson, and a third who was the grandson's school-friend, kindly offered to look after our gear as we went to search for a local café. I had noticed this threesome in Puente la Reina. In fact, they had taken the bunk beside me and I had exchanged some preliminary niceties prior to exploring the town. The grandfather seemed to be one of those men who, though of a certain age, belie their age by dint of physical activity and intense interest in all around them. We gladly accepted his offer to guard our valuables, leaving to explore Estella. Teresa, however, soon left us in order to look for the municipal offices to obtain another pilgrim seal. She was childlike in her enthusiasm to obtain as many stamps as possible. Obviously, we were more interested in filling our bellies than filling our books!

After lunch, we returned to the refugio. Although the facilities were very modern, I somehow felt that the place lacked soul; that efficiency seemed more important than the personal touch. It was very different from the friendly atmosphere I had experienced in the volunteer-run hostels I had stayed in until then. They had been so much more welcoming.

Having showered and done the laundry, it was time for the usual siesta. However, not wanting to waste too much time asleep, I set my alarm to give myself an hour to rest. I found, in fact, that I awoke feeling rested and refreshed before the alarm sounded and took off to explore Estella. Teresa met me at the entrance to the refugio and offered to show me the archaeological dig taking place in San Sepulcro, the church I had passed immediately prior to arriving in the refugio.

Unabashed, she approached the archaeologist on-site, who was very willing to explain the objective of the dig – examining the cemetery alongside the church. It seemed that they had come across some buried remains of pilgrims from medieval times. Teresa patiently explained to me in her broken English the various aspects of the dig, most of which I no longer recall. What I do remember, however, was her kindness and her willingness to share her enthusiasm with her companions on the journey.

The visit to the north portal of the church of San Miguel was certainly worth it, even though it was disappointing that it was limited to the covered walkway under the portal. The church itself was locked, again further emphasising the museum-like quality of many of the ecclesiastical monuments along the camino. The imposing church of San Juan Bautista was another case in point. From the vast Plaza de los Fueros the church looks gigantically impressive but once again the giant doors were firmly barred to the tourist.

Resigned to examining the exteriors of churches, I sauntered through the streets of Estella. Aymeric Picaud, in the twelfth century, said of Estella: 'the bread is good, the wine excellent, the meat and the fish are abundant'. This was still true in the last decade of the twentieth century. Shops proudly displayed their wares in all sorts of imaginative ways, enticing the chance passers-by to sample their produce. The fruit especially was magnificent and eventually I succumbed to some red, ripe strawberries.

Alongside the River Ega is the single-span and very steep bridge called the 'Puente de los Peregrinos', the Pilgrims' Bridge. Certainly the steepness of the arch would challenge many a pilgrim, not to mention the locals that would daily cross the bridge. I never did go on it that day for I had no occasion to cross to the other side of the river.

The next place on the itinerary became the highlight of the short stay in Estella – the Church of San Pedro del Rua. Liam had met me in the town and told me that the curate had indicated that the church would be open around 7.30pm. Walking up the steep steps towards the most impressive poly-lobed arches provided one with a panoramic view of the town and especially offered a better view of the Palace of the Kings of Navarre, just opposite the church. It was in this church that the kings of Navarre took an oath when passing new laws.

It is difficult to describe adequately the extravagant interior of the church. It would take a student of architecture to point out the significant features and express the uniqueness of this jewel of a building. What immediately struck me was the multi-levelled harmony between the crypt, the apse and the choir gallery. It was as if each connected with the other under a ribbed and vaulted ceiling. Many a time have I been tempted to buy one of those manuals that explain the various architectural features of ecclesiastical monuments. Indeed, I remember buying a small book on church architecture a few years previously when I was in France on holidays. Would that I had it with me as I admired the sheer genius of the stonemasons' work.

The curé also invited us to visit the cloister situated behind the church. As we entered, what met us were the significant remains of what must have been a truly imposing monastic enclosure in the twelfth century. Pilgrims who died on the camino would have been buried here. Liam was spellbound. He could not take in the sheer beauty of the capitals, especially the scene of the annunciation graphically executed on one of the cloister pillars. He talked about his interest in monastic life and of his experiences of visiting monasteries while living in England, telling me also about going on a Buddhist retreat immediately prior to undertaking the walk to Santiago.

What struck me as I listened to him was the seeming incongruity of a young man with an earring on his left ear having a deep spiritual interest in religious life. How many people would find earrings and religion an incongruous mix! And yet, why wouldn't young people with all their original ways of dressing have the same spiritual hunger that I had? It is really frightening how prejudiced we can become in the face of externals and blinded to the reality behind such superficial differences! Liam was obviously a deeply spiritual person; an honest inquirer into the meaning of life and the place of the spiritual in the midst of daily living.

The three Norwegian women, Ingritberg, Littian and Olga, together with Teresa, the sello seeker, arrived into the cloister soon after us, and the beauty of the place equally stunned them in the dying moments of a beautiful evening. They took their time to admire the details of the

The Church of San Pedro del Rua in Estella boasts a magnificent cloister with beautiful capitals.

capitals as we already had done and when we all had feasted enough on the beauty of the place, we decided to have dinner together.

Just as in Puente la Reina, the experience of sharing pilgrim stories over a meal was most enriching. The Norwegians explained how they had bussed it to Estella and were going to do the same on the next day, skipping Los Arcos and stopping probably at Nájera before moving on to Alicante, where they would continue their holiday at the beach.

It would have been interesting to learn more of these three valiant women but it was not to be. Our leaving them at the end of the evening was heart-warming. They embraced us and we wished each other good fortune for the journey; as they went to their hotel while Liam, Teresa and myself repaired to our rustic hostel.

Lying on my bed that night, I remembered these gracious women and prayed for them that the Lord would keep them safe as they continued on their camino through life. Tomorrow would be another day and new people would cross my path along the road to Santiago.

Day Six
Estella to Los Arcos
Saturday 27 June 1998

Just outside Estella and beside the Monasterio de Irache, is a fountain that pours forth red wine instead of water. The Bodegas Irache, a local commercial winery, installed the fountain a number of years ago. It was most tastefully constructed. Above the taps of wine and water was a statue of a pilgrim; then below on either side of the statue was the crest of St James of Compostela in brass. To the left of the taps was this quaint message in bronze relief: *'Peregrino! Si quieres llegar a Santiago con fuerza y vitalidad, de este gran vino echa un trago y brinda por la Felicidad.'* From my limited knowledge of Spanish I translated it to read: 'Pilgrim, if you wish to arrive at Santiago with strength and vitality, take a drink from this fine wine and toast to happiness!'

I took the wineglass, washing it in the water from the tap and half filled the glass with red wine. Sipping as I stood – there was no bench available – a young pilgrim arrived. He appeared almost like the image above the fountain. His hat had the characteristic scallop shell pinning the front rim to the crown. He had two walking sticks instead of the usual bordón and around his neck was wrapped a purple scarf. His rucksack was by no means new, and again the scallop shell image was prominently displayed. Having greeted each other, I finished the wine, handed him the only glass available and chatted for a while with him as he sipped a few mouthfuls. He was taking things easy and wanted to rest there for a while. So, after each of us took a photograph of the other, I bade him farewell. He seemed a fine young man and I looked forward to meeting him in Los Arcos, our ultimate destination that night.

It was a most pleasant day in the early morning walking through the gardens of the Monaster of Nuestra Senora la Real de Irache. As I continued through the gardens and made my way through a residential area, feelings of gratitude welled up in me once more for the privilege of having the time and opportunity to be a pilgrim. My feet were still holding out after walking 126km, something that really pleased me.

Passing the houses in the small hamlet of Azqueta, I wondered what the locals thought of all the thousands of pilgrims who passed through their village, especially during the summer

The 'Wine Fountain', established in 1991, offers pilgrims free wine on tap.

months. Did any of them ever feel the desire to take off on the camino themselves? Or did they simply classify the pilgrims as strange beings on a strange journey?

Just before reaching Villamayor de Monjardin, I came across the Fountain of the Moors, described as exotic in the guidebooks. For me it was not that impressive; it looked more like a disused shelter than a fountain. So I continued on and came upon a few pilgrims who had stopped to chat with their backup driver. Some people seem to look down on those pilgrims who rely on a backup service to carry their rucksacks or on those who take a bus ride from time to time. They consider that such behaviour somehow detracts from the integrity of the pilgrim code. Personally, I had no such thoughts and, though I would hate having to take a bus or a lift myself, I considered that anyone who followed the camino should feel free to do so by whatever means they wish.

I saw Bernard in Villamayor de Monjardin searching for water. We continued on together through the fields of wheat that reached as far as the eye could see. Undulating hills merged with each other and all were covered with the golden hue of ripening corn.

Occasionally, the monotony of the golden colour was broken by olive groves and vineyards in which the local farmers would be working by hand. I marvelled at the sheer volume of crops – the fields reached the horizon – in their golden covering of shimmering ears of wheat. The gold contrasted beautifully with the deep blue cloudless skies uninterrupted by even a trace of cloud.

We walked unhurriedly in the scorching hot sun. Bernard told me again about how he had been recently retired as an aeronautics engineer with Air France and was obviously coming to terms with this unexpected termination of his employment. In his late fifties, he was beginning to plan the second part of his life. The walk to Santiago was the fruit of many years of dreaming about making the journey. He was undertaking the camino for spiritual reasons that would provide him with the space and opportunity to reflect on what the future held for him. I felt privileged to be part of his musings as we walked together on the way. He had spent the last year studying everything he could get his hands on about the camino and it was obvious that he was indeed a good student. He was a mine of information on the historical background to the towns and villages through which he passed.

However, our time together was interrupted when I felt a slight discomfiture in my left foot and decided to stop to investigate. Up to that point, I had had no problems with my feet, but now it seemed as if something was causing soreness in one of my toes. Prior to setting out, I had been warned to listen to the body and act immediately if messages were being sent to the brain! At my peril was I warned not to keep going when the body cried out. So our conversation had to be interrupted and we agreed to meet in Los Arcos that evening. When I undid the shoe, there was no visible sign of irritation but for safety sake, I simply pared the nails. This seemed to do the job, for the irritation disappeared.

Approaching Los Arcos, I came across the young man who had taken my photograph at the wine fountain outside Estella. We stopped to exchange some introductions. He was with two Germans who had taken the route through Somport. They plied me with so many questions that I felt under interrogation! Emmanuel was much quieter and seemed amused by the insistent questions of the older Helmut. One question led to another. From where had I had come? What was I using for clothing? How long it would take me to complete the camino. On and on the questions flew until I was desperate to run from their barrage and escape into the solitude of my own company.

It was fortunate that the pair was ready for a break, which allowed me to escape, but they promised to meet me in Los Arcos, something that I did not really look forward to. And yet, the walk was gradually challenging me to be more open and accepting of differences. Certainly many people had been so accepting and welcoming of me that now the challenge was to imitate this attitude of hospitality and welcome, especially towards those who were not immediately compatible with me.

On arrival at Los Arcos, I found the refugio, which turned out to be a former school. The hospitaleros were Belgian if my memory serves me right. They were very welcoming and most attentive to our needs. Some of the pilgrims had written somewhat critical comments about the guest masters, but much of the criticism was due mainly to the hospitaleros' over-zealous concern to assist the pilgrims. For my part, I was very grateful for their attentiveness and willingness to help when needed. To me it was obvious that they had embraced the ethos of the camino – welcoming pilgrims in a spirit of loving attentiveness.

A walk around the town was in order once all necessary personal matters had been attended to. Already I had seen some monuments on my way into the town that merited closer inspection.

Los Arcos is a medieval town that was built on the site of a Roman settlement.

By far the dominant feature in this small town of 1500 people is the Church of Santa Maria, where the first noticeable feature on the spire was a stork's nest with the mother sitting graciously in their home. I never did come to learn the significance of this feature, which would remain a frequent sight for the following days. No doubt the bird had its own religious and secular meaning for the people of Navarre; its presence dominating the church was taken for granted.

Inside the church, I was met with an enormously rich and varied selection of altarpieces. that highlighted aspects of medieval theology as well as portraying the lives of local saints. What were particularly noticeable were the scenes of the final judgement and of heaven and hell. Gruesome carvings of the lost being engulfed in wicked-looking flames added a sense of the spirituality of the Middle Ages, where the four last elements of death, judgement, hell and heaven were never far from the lives of people and would have featured regularly in the sermons delivered by fanatical preachers. Having brought binoculars, it was possible to examine at close quarters the facial expressions of the damned as they became enveloped by the flames of punishment. The artistry in the wood was breathtaking.

In the apse, there was the most exquisite seated Madonna and Child in a little niche over the tabernacle. This work of art was simply wonderful in its delicacy and refinement. I could not take the binoculars away from the image as I examined each detail. And as the evening Mass was about to begin, the statue was illuminated, revealing a richly deep red backdrop, which served to further bring out the gold ornamentation in the dress of the Madonna. The artist had captured the restrained nobility of the Virgin and Child.

Before then, it had not always been possible to attend a Eucharist along the route; so it was very satisfying to take the occasion to thank the Lord for his protection during the journey so far. Although I could not make out much of the ceremony with my elementary grasp of Spanish, the Gospel seemed to be about the servant who put his hand to the plough and then turned back – a really good medieval theme, which would have reeked havoc in the small community of Los Arcos, reducing to blubber the most hardened of sinners!

After Communion, the priest invited all the pilgrims to assemble before the main altar where he imparted a special blessing on them and distributed a leaflet containing a prayer for the journey. The ceremony was very simple but rather moving. To stand there, united with fellow pilgrims and before the Christian community, created a sense of communion with the wider church and offered a promise of solidarity along the lonely roads to Santiago. I was particularly taken with the prayer, with its quaint English style that approximated the original Spanish version:

> Lord, you who recalled your servant Abraham out of Ur of the Chaldea and who watched over him during all his wanderings; you who guided the Jewish people thro' the desert; we also query to watch your present servants, who for love for your name, make a pilgrimage to Santiago de Compostela.

Be for us:
A companion on the journey
The guide on the intersections
The strengthening during fatigue
The fortress in danger
The resource on their itinerary
The shadow in the heat

The light in the darkness
The consolation during dejection

And the power of our intention so that we under your guidance, safely and unhurt, may reach the end of our journey and strengthened with gratitude and power, secure and filled with happiness, may join our home. For Jesus Christ, Our Lord. Amen.

That evening Liam, Bernard, Rolf and myself met near the town plaza at a small bar cum café named 'La Gruanja'. We decided to order a pizza and were somewhat taken aback when we saw the barman taking pre-packed and frozen pizza from the deep freeze. It was the last thing we expected to find in the heart of rural Spain where one is accustomed to finding everything home-made and genuine. However, we succumbed to the Americanisation of the

The statue of Santa María de los Arcos is enthroned over the high altar of Los Arcos' church.

takeaway and sat in the plaza in the warmth of the declining sun and sipped our *cerveza* (beer). The pizzas were passable though obviously not fresh. Our meal was ruined when we examined the bill that had been placed under one of the plates. Almost 6000 pesetas (€40) for four pizzas and beers was extremely expensive by Spanish standards, when one considers that the standard pilgrim four-course menu can often be had for around €7. We were furious at being exploited as tourists, never mind pilgrims, and found each mouthful of the pizza rather bitter in our mouths as a result. We complained to the barman who expressed little sympathy for us. We felt like putting a curse on the café on behalf of all future pilgrims.

We promised ourselves that we would forward our findings to the Confraternity of St James in London. The Confraternity brings out a pilgrim guide to the camino on a regular basis, updating the information in the light of comments of pilgrims who go each year. We felt a certain sense of justice as we thought of how future pilgrims would be warned about the over-pricing at the bar 'La Gruanja' in the plaza of Los Arcos.

Day Seven
Los Arcos to Viana
Sunday 28 June 1998

Setting out for Viana at 6.15am was a beautiful and invigorating experience. The cool breeze and overcast sky augured well for the journey, and I was hoping to make the 18.5km to Viana before the sky cleared and the sun began its merciless onslaught on the exposed pilgrims along the route. I took out the pilgrim prayer that we had received at the Mass of the previous day and began reciting it as I walked. It was amusing to note the literal translation from the Spanish 'may join our home' to express the wish that pilgrims would reach the final destination in safety, but the sentiments were ones I sincerely expressed as I passed the cemetery on the outskirts of the town.

Over the entrance of the cemetery was a sign with the phrase: '*Yo que fui lo que tu eres, tu seras lo que yo soy*' which translates as: 'I was once what you are, and you will be what I am ', a rather sobering thought on this bracing morning as I headed for the town of Sansol just off the N111. Still, death was once a grim reality for many a pilgrim who may have drunk from the poisoned river that Picaud alluded to in his *Pilgrim's Guide.* In fact, the guidebook mentioned that opposite the cemetery once stood the hospital for patients struck down by poisoned water or by the plagues that ravaged the lands.

Passing through Sansol, I came to Torres del Rio, where there was the Templars' Church of San Sepulcro. This small church shows the influence of Byzantine and Hispano-Arabic styles and is often considered one of the real architectural gems of the camino. It is extremely small, more like a baptistery than a church. Its octagonal shape and clear lines created a unity and a perfection that immediately drew me to visit it. The gate was locked, however, with a badly-written message on it referring to pilgrims being able to get the key of the church from a neighbouring house on Wednesdays. It was far too early in the morning to be ringing at any doorbell. Anyway, it seemed strange to me that a mid-week opening policy would be in force in this sleepy hamlet. Surely the inhabitants of Torres del Rio would have all the time in the world to welcome the pilgrim to see its twelfth-century church. All I could do was read the description of the church in my faithful guidebook and hope that some day I would return. I

The sun catches the earthen colour of the farm buildings outside the village of Sansol.

journeyed onwards up the steep hill beside the church; at a junction, there was a sign indicating refreshments for weary pilgrims.

Not having eaten anything that morning, it was time to sample the local coffee and baked bread, the aromas of which could be detected from where I stood. Following the sign, I came across a recently converted garage that had been made into a simple snackery where pilgrims could get tea and coffee with bread and bocadilos. Bernard and Liam were already busily engaged with breakfast and invited me to join them while my coffee was being prepared.

To all intents and purposes, the bar was still a garage with a few tables and chairs scattered around the centre of the enclosure. The bright green door created a homely atmosphere; books lined a number of shelves that clung to the unplastered walls. Curiosity got the better of me and I went along the shelves examining the titles of the volumes on display. My heart leapt with excitement when I came across Davide Gandini's book, *Il Portico della Gloria*.

This was the first book I had read about the camino, and the fact that it had been written by Davide, a friend of mine, made seeing it before my eyes something incredible. Originally, I had met Davide and Tina in Dublin on their honeymoon and had spent a day showing them around the sights. And from that first meeting, we had kept in touch over the years, especially when on the number of occasions I had visited Italy. Synchronicity could only explain the likelihood of seeing such a book in this isolated village. I took the book off the shelf and inquired of the young woman who was bringing my steaming coffee to the table how she had come upon the Italian book.

She broke into a heart-warming smile as she exclaimed, "O, Davide and Tina, what a lovely couple! And they are expecting a baby before long." Apparently, she had met Davide in

Milan while she was studying Italian in the university and had kept in touch with the couple over the years. She introduced herself as Carmen Pugliese and she gave me her business card so that I would remember to tell Davide that I had met her. The network of human connections was being expanded, as I stood there holding a book that had inspired me to undertake the walk to Santiago in the first place. I promised myself that I would send a postcard to Davide and Tina from Torres del Rio to mark the chance meeting with their friend, Carmen.

By this time, more pilgrims had arrived; and among them were the two Spanish girls and their young male companion who had kept me awake in Larrasoaña. It turned out that they were from Burgos and were taking 12 days of their annual holidays to walk some of the camino, intending to complete the walk the following year. They were most friendly and keenly interested to hear our story. Bernard, Liam and myself shared something of our lives; it was obvious that the three newcomers were fascinated that us three very different characters had been brought together along the road to Santiago and bound together by the one desire to arrive at the sanctuary of St James. I was glad, too, that I was meeting the three young people under very different circumstances where I could come to know them better.

Part of the fascination of the camino is the telling of one's story. Each pilgrim or walker undertakes the journey for diverse reasons. However, motivations change or are modified as the journey continues. One who perhaps began at Roncesvalles for cultural or health reasons may find, with the passage of time, that a spiritual dimension seeps into their consciousness until they may find themselves reflecting on the very raison d'être of their lives. And often it is in the listening to others' stories that our own story is challenged and deepened. To listen to a pilgrim sharing their search for meaning in their life or reflecting on significant moments of their history creates the space for the listener to pause and meditate on their own life journey. No two stories are the same. The personal nature of each narration underlines the uniqueness of the person and demonstrates the varied nature of human experience.

I became aware, however, that the morning was passing and that it was time to move on. Having taken my leave of the small group of pilgrims, I began to reflect that I have a tendency to withdraw from social groupings and seek the solitude of my own company. It must be the introvert in me that prefers to be alone after a certain exposure to human contact. And yet, I can see that the challenge of pilgrimage is to allow oneself to be affected by the stories of those on the same path and in turn to reveal some of the more intimate aspects of one's own story.

The walk towards Viana was very pleasant, with the warm sun at my back and a cool gentle breeze protecting me from the direct heat. Liam joined me soon after I had left Torres del Rio and began telling me of his early life in London. He had joined the Simon Community when he was nineteen, and this experience of working with the poor became for him one of the formative periods in his life. He continues to work with the marginalised of society; I could see that his care and compassion were the direct result of his own inner journey towards holistic freedom.

He revealed how fear was the one factor that, for him, prevented growth and freedom. He talked about the place of fear in his life and how reading Susan Jeffers' book, *Feel the Fear and Do it Anyway,* had helped him enormously to confront situations of fear with greater courage. It had taken him many years of personal work to overcome such fear; but as he shared, I could see that he was braver by far than I was in revealing his weaknesses and mistakes. I, too, had read Jeffers' book and had devised workshops based on it, which I had given to various groups over the previous three or four years. And yet I can still see that fear often prevents me from expressing what is within when it would be more than appropriate to do so. The guarded nature of many of my interactions with others prevents me from getting hurt but also stops me from experiencing the gift of real friendships.

Liam was a faster walker than I was, and so he moved on towards Viana skirting the N111 along the flat wheat fields that led to the town. However, I met him later along the way and he seemed to be limping. He complained of a sore leg, fearing that he might have a touch of tendonitis. I offered him a tube of Feldene that had been recommended to me as an anti-inflammatory for this complaint and wished him well. I offered to walk with him, but he preferred to walk at his own reduced pace in order to give his leg a chance to heal. How easy it is for things to go wrong. As I continued, I marvelled at how I had avoided any real trouble up to this point but was only too aware how easily anything could occur that would prevent me from finishing the walk.

Approaching Viana, I saw it rise up from the plain. There was nothing notable that struck me about the town skyline but I very was glad to be approaching the refugio where I hoped to get a good rest. Walking along the streets of the town I passed the four-storey mansions, many of which were in need of repair. Outside each of the houses was the family coat of arms that reflected former times of prosperity.

Viana is almost on the borders of Navarra and La Rioja. The guidebook described how Sancho VII in 1219 had created a stronghold at Viana, as it was on the borders with Castile, and he granted it special status. Also, in 1507 the notorious Cesare Borgia was buried in the church of Santa Maria in Viana having being killed in the battle of Mendavia nearby. The marble tombstone to Cesare Borgia stands outside the church. Apparently the more lavish mausoleum to Cesare had been desecrated in the late seventeenth century to be replaced by the modest marble tomb in the courtyard of the church.

At the end of the main street, I came upon the ramparts of the old city and to the right, along a narrow lane-way, was the refugio. It seemed deserted. Most of the pilgrims must have decided to continue on to Logroño, nine kilometres away. However, I was determined to adhere to the guidebook's suggestion, which indicated a short walk to allow the pilgrim to relax after the previous seven day's exertions.

Inside the refugio, the beds were arranged in rows, with three or four two-tier bunks in each room. The place looked immaculately clean and in ship-shape order. I took an unoccupied room and hoped that I might get one night on my own for once. What a luxury it was to lay out all the contents of the rucksack on the nearby bed instead of having to keep everything packed tightly in the rucksack and under the bed! I hoped that no new arrival would disturb my sense of freedom and space.

Later I set off to explore the town. The sun by this time was baking the footpaths and creating an oven of the narrow streets. I hugged the shadows to avoid the excesses of the sun's rays and soon resorted to a local bar to have a bite to eat and a cool beer to wash away the dust of the journey from Los Arcos.

In the afternoon, I came across Liam having a beer at a bar further down the town and joined him for a chat. He was in a great mood. We laughed and joked for quite some time, as we exchanged our amusing instances of the camino. In the course of the conversation, Liam revealed that he planned to stay for two days in Logroño to give his leg a rest. This surprised and disappointed me; walking with a companion is so enriching and as the days proceed, a closeness develops, making the idea of separation very difficult to bear. It was such a pity that he would fade into the background especially as I knew that once Liam took a rest, it was very unlikely that we would meet again before arriving at Santiago.

The octagonal Romanesque Church of the Holy Sepulchre at Torres del Rio.

I returned to the refugio and was delighted to see that no other pilgrim had invaded my space. This meant I could leave my things spread over two beds and not worry about guarding my valuables. The beds were rather short for my large frame, but sleeping on the mattress placed on the floor was a viable option and I would be disturbing nobody.

Bernard and Rolf had arrived at Viana in the early afternoon. Together with Liam, we decided to visit Santa Maria, a twelfth-century gothic construction mid-way along the main street. However, when we reached the church at about four in the afternoon, it was firmly locked. We asked some young boys and girls playing in the square in front of the church when it would open. We were met with shrugs of shoulders and looks of indifference.

Because of the intense heat, the other three decided to seek shelter back in the hostel, but I was determined to visit the sleeping town, descending the sloping streets behind the cathedral. I walked towards the west side of the ramparts where the fourteenth-century ruins of the Church of San Pedro stood out clearly against the cloudless azure sky. The town was dead. There was hardly a person to be seen; and in the emptiness of the deserted streets there seemed to be no atmosphere of hospitality or life. In fact, the only place open was an ugly modern bar with pop music blaring out of speakers on to the sleeping pavements. There was no point in going much further since everything was closed. The idea of a quiet siesta was infinitely preferable to this aimless meandering along the narrow alleyways in the inferno of the afternoon sun.

That evening the four of us went to a local bar for supper. What amazed us all about this popular local eating place was the sheer noise that enveloped the whole place. In one corner the television was blaring at full volume, with the excited voice of a commentator describing some World Cup match. In the other section of the bar people seemed to be shouting at each other. It was bedlam. Yet, despite the rumpus, our time together sharing stories of the pilgrim route and discussing our plans for the next day was a real experience of community. In our own way, we contributed to the noise around us, but our conversation was more reflective and intimate in comparison to the excitability of the match commentator and the passion of the local Spaniards at the bar.

Towards ten o'clock, we decided on an early night, so that we would be fighting fit for the next day's walk to Navarette, 21km away. Bernard kindly invited us all to join him for breakfast in the morning so that we could bid our farewells to Liam. This was a touching gesture to mark the sense of camaraderie that had developed among the four of us over the last week. It would have been difficult to split up without marking the event appropriately; so a breakfast together seemed the ideal gesture. Normally, I took my breakfast as I walked, munching fruit, some bread and maybe some cheese washed down with good old water. I never had any desire to spend time around the kitchen in the refugios because of the crowd all attempting to boil water for their coffee or tea. But tomorrow would be different and I looked forward to the agape, the Christian feast of fellowship.

Despite the luxury of a private room that night, I found myself wide-awake at about three in the morning. My sleeping bag was far too heavy and hot. Yet when I cast it aside I found myself getting quite cold and still unable to sleep, so I dozed fitfully until five o'clock. When I knew that sleep would not return I decided to go for a shower. Up to this, I had taken my daily shower immediately after the walk and made this suffice for the next day. But this was a golden opportunity to benefit from the opportunity to luxuriate in the warm water of an early morning shower. Would that this were possible every morning, when instead I am usually rushing to quit the refugio for the day's journey!

Bernard was in the kitchen around six, busily preparing the chicory and laying out the bread and fruit. It was a real Eucharistic gathering. We were expressing our gratitude to each other for the gift of friendship. I took a photograph of the three eating, and then we parted with few words. The parting was rather sudden but understandable, in that we found it difficult to express the mixed emotions of our leave-taking. Liam, himself, was quite relaxed about staying in Logroño but I found myself quite sad. The hope was that Liam would meet us again at a later stage, though nothing was guaranteed on the camino and given my intention to follow my guidebook's itinerary, I doubted if I would meet Liam before Santiago. I hoped that we would eventually come together as a foursome at the end of the camino. But only time would tell.

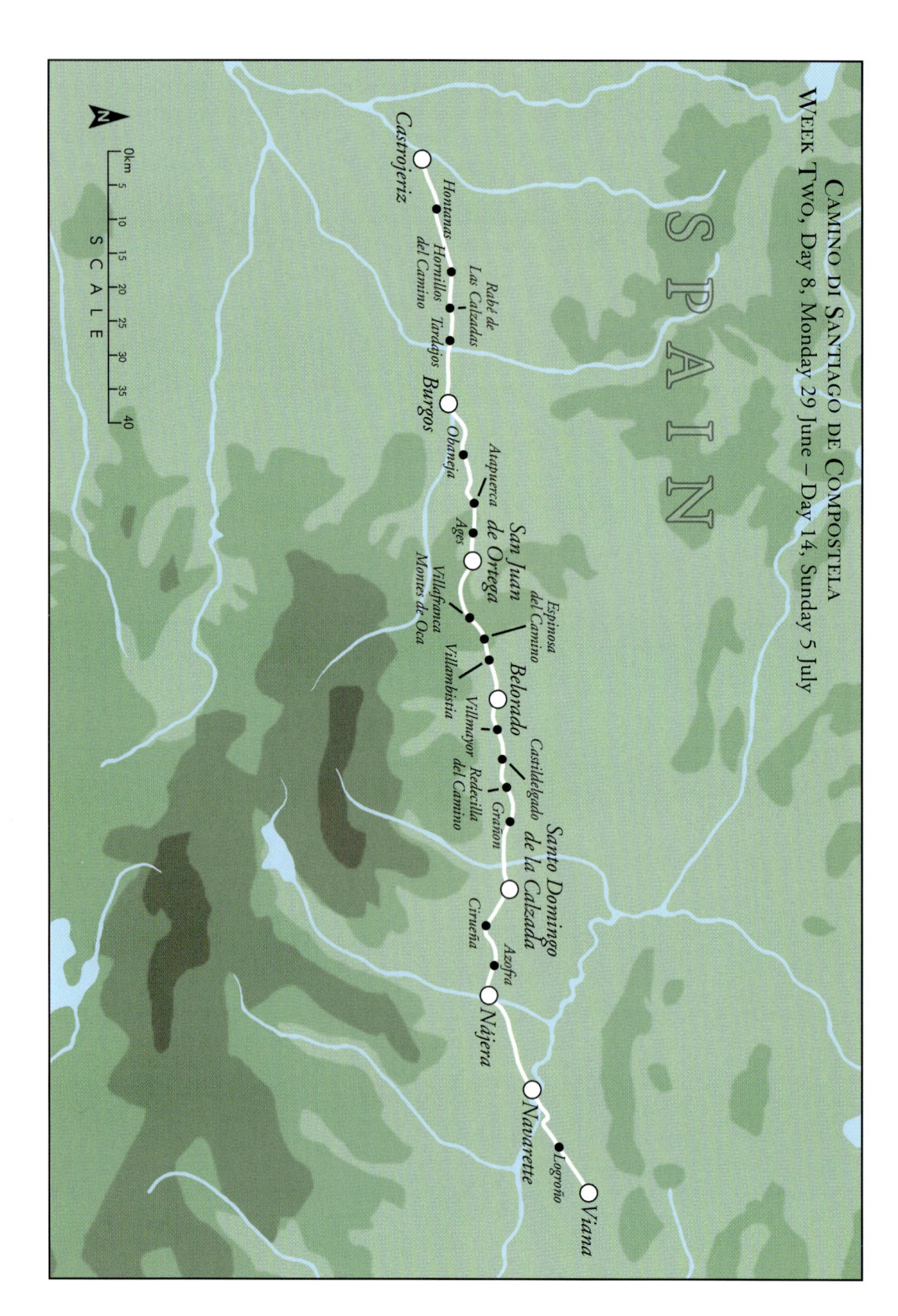

CAMINO DI SANTIAGO DE COMPOSTELA
Week Two, Day 8, Monday 29 June – Day 14, Sunday 5 July

Week Two

Day Eight
Viana to Navarette
Monday 29 June 1998

At the start of this section of the walk, I found myself disorientated on leaving the refugio. I went down along the remains of the city walls only to hear a shout from behind me. There, silhouetted against the morning sky, was the figure of a small impish pilgrim who shouted, *"Par là"* indicating the opposite direction to where I was heading. I waved back in recognition at the French pilgrim and retraced my steps beginning the descent towards Logroño.

The morning air was refreshingly cool as I viewed the vineyards that bordered the way down towards the N111 motorway that would run parallel along the pilgrim path to Logroño. The surroundings were flat and rather uninteresting, with the proximity of the motorway rather disappointing. It is always more pleasant when the traffic is well away from the camino. However, so far as I can see from the maps, the pilgrim seems often quite near the main motorways and of course it is not the pilgrim paths that have followed the motorways. They probably pre-date the latter by a thousand years or more.

To while away the time, I began re-living the events of the previous week, from when I set out at St Jean-Pied-de-Port. It took some time to identify the events of each day. Gradually, the picture came together like a jigsaw with missing parts being added as the memory dredged up the details in its own good time. What was already striking me was the rich variety of each day; the sheer novelty of the whole pilgrimage. I was experiencing a rich tapestry of life in the places I visited, the people I met and the events that happened along the way. Simply to live each day had indeed been a very positive experience, yet something infinitely richer was occurring as I reflected back on the events. It was as if I was experiencing the same events at a deeper level and in a more organic way. By creating a certain distance from each event, it allowed me to recognise themes and patterns in the weeklong experience, helping me recognise what was happening to me at a deeper level as I walked along the camino.

By far the greatest feeling that welled up in me that morning on the way to Logroño was a sense of real wonder that I had been protected from all illnesses and injuries. My prayer was one of thankfulness to the Lord for his protection and guidance. This guidance often took the form of another pilgrim shouting to me, indicating the correct route from which I had strayed. So far also, I had been protected from any serious injuries or accidents.

The approach to Logroño was an ugly sight with cement monsters of flyovers and road works everywhere. And erected quite recently, it seemed, were large metal signs indicating the camino route into Logroño and beyond into the Rioja region. These also were rather unsightly. An earthen pathway led along shanty-type buildings that lay on the outskirts of the town. At one stage, an old woman cried out some sort of greeting, offering what sounded like a stamp. I later learned that she is a real character and friend of the pilgrims and that she does, in fact, possess a fine example of a pilgrim sello, which she offers in return for a small donation. However, that day I was not in the mood for stopping at some dubious ramshackle dwelling for something I was not sure about; not a very adventurous pilgrim I have to admit. But in the early hours of the day, I was more focused on the destination than on the route, even though the sages keep suggesting that the route is far more important than the destination.

The great Puente de Piedre – the stone bridge – spans the River Ebro and leads the pilgrim into Logroño. The original bridge was much more elaborate, having been constructed by Alfonso VI in the eleventh century to create a good defensive base on the banks of the Ebro. St Dominic of the Roads and later his disciple, St John of Ortega, repaired this bridge, which had become important for the pilgrims on their way to Santiago.

Bernard was in the distance. He turned back to view the bridge and, seeing me approach, waited on the other side. He was really excited about visiting Logroño's Church of Santa Maria del Palacio, as well as the Cathedral of Santa Maria de la Redonda, apparently built around an octagonal church similar to that of Torres del Rio. However, his hopes were dashed on both counts. He found it difficult not to express his frustration at the fact that most of the churches in Spain seem to be perpetually closed.

Of course, many of the times we arrive at a church it is early in the morning or during siesta time in the early afternoon. So I never got too upset over the closure of churches. On many occasions, the exterior of the church is infinitely more interesting than the interior. It would, of course, have been nice to be able to kneel and pray within, but then I find that the countryside is my real cathedral. I often feel closer to God in the countryside than I do within the walls of an ancient cathedral.

On we went, to the famous Fuente de los Peregrinos, the pilgrim fountain; nearby this is the church of Santiago el Real. Apparently, the original one was built in the ninth century by Ramiro I after his famous victory over the Moors at Clavijo. At the entrance, there are two statues of St James. The higher one shows him on his trusty steed ready to chop off the heads of the infidels; whereas the other St James is a representation of the pilgrim.

There is no doubt in my mind that I infinitely prefer the pilgrim image to the mounted warrior. However, it was the victorious St James who inspired the establishment of the pilgrim route; sometimes good can emerge from the evils of war! Nevertheless, I find the mounted figure of St James somewhat off-putting. It reminds me of the unfortunate bellicose attitude of the Church as exemplified by the Crusades and the Inquisition, relying on force to demand allegiance of its followers and submission of its enemies. Even today, the Church can easily lapse into domination of its followers, demanding strict adherence and stifling any form of dissent. But then, so can political regimes.

We entered the Church of Santiago el Real, where all the ornamentation is linked to the Santiago myth. Just as we entered by the south door, the illumination of the retable over the main altar went out. The priest standing before the main altar had turned on the lights while he acted as guide for his select group of pilgrims, but now as his explanation came to a close, the lights faded. Although he saw us enter, he seemed disinclined to turn on the lights again for the two lonely pilgrims. So we had to make do with the light of the rose window and the other windows to make out the figures on the rich sculpted iconostasis over the main altar. Luckily, I had my binoculars and could make out the fifteenth-century statue of St James and the twelfth-century Romanesque statue of the Virgen de la Esperanza, the virgin of hope, patroness of Logroño.

Turning around, we viewed the simple design of the Templars' cross in the otherwise unadorned rose window at the west entrance. The symbol of the Templars appears everywhere along the route to remind the pilgrim of the militaristic presence of this religious order whose function in former times was to make safe the holy Christian shrines of the world in the Middle Ages.

The two contrasting images of St James on the façade of Santiago el Real in Logroño.

After this interesting tour of the Santiago shrine, we were ready for a white coffee. As we crossed the road, we stood momentarily perplexed as to where the yellow arrows had disappeared. No sooner had we stopped than a very pleasant young woman came right up to us, kindly indicating an unobtrusive yellow arrow painted on the back of a road sign. The Spanish people displayed a friendliness and a willingness to assist pilgrims that is most impressive. Often the foreign appearance of some pilgrims could frighten people; yet there seems to be an innate understanding of the spiritual nature of the quest for Santiago.

Sitting in a modern bar, sipping our white coffee, we talked about Liam and how both of us would miss his presence along the way. His sense of humour, always dry, endeared him to Bernard, Rolf and myself. It's a sense of humour best described as trans-cultural. As we sat in the increasing heat of the morning, we spied Rolf who came and joined us. He was in a good mood, obviously keen to get going on the next part of the journey; and yet to me he seemed to be wilting under the influence of the sun.

We left the café together and walked through that ugly part of the city made up of warehouses, garages and shops. On the outskirts of Logroño I encouraged Bernard and Rolf to go on ahead; I found their pace too much for me. It was also good to have some quiet time alone.

The outskirts of the city were still rather ugly with the vestiges of reinforced concrete buildings in various stages of incompletion ruining the area. Then to the right I came across a bridge that overlooked the Pantano de la Granjera, an artificial lake that was part of a local park. Some young people were playing on the bridge in the company of their parents and grandparents; this mixture of generations all united on such a fine day lifted my spirits and put a spring in my step.

Skirting the lake, I passed a monument that had been erected in 1993 on the occasion of the Holy Year. A Holy Year in pilgrim terms is when 25 July falls on a Sunday. The monument consists of a graphic design of a pilgrim in blue, red and white. It looks like a logo for the World Cup instead of one for Santiago. For me it was not very religious in tone.

As I left the park and continued into the wilderness, I saw Rolf sitting on a mound of earth and obviously exhausted. He needed to rest and take it easy for some time, so I left him in the shade and continued my way under the merciless rays of the sun. By this time, I was skirting the motorway again, high above it and walking on a beaten earth path. At a petrol station, I crossed the N120 and continued through vineyards towards Navarette, looming high in front of me. At the base of the hill leading to Navarette was the Hospital de San Juan de Acre, a fine archaeological site.

Bernard was sitting there waiting for me and taking a rest before facing the rather steep hill up to the town. It was 12.30pm as we entered the village. We noted the sign for the refugio that was situated under the arches of a most impressive sixteenth-century covered arcade. To our disappointment, the notice informed the pilgrim that the refugio was closed until 3.00pm. This would mean that we would have to wait well into the afternoon for our shower and also for the opportunity to wash our clothes. This delay can be a problem because it means there is less time for drying clothes. Since Roncesvalles, I have tried to avoid hanging the damp clothes outside the rucksack as I walked. I had lost one shirt and certainly wanted to avoid losing another.

So there was nothing more to do except visit the Los Arcos Bar next to the refugio. By this time Rolf had arrived, so the three of us were ready to sample the local fare. The young girl at the counter served us hot tortillas and she willingly engaged in conversation with us. She was very proud to let us know that her boyfriend was a young Corkman and that she intended visiting him the following summer. Although she had a smattering of English, she did not show the enthusiasm to converse in English that Europeans do when they want to upgrade their elementary grasp of the language. However, it was also obvious that she was very proud of her country and of her own contribution in making the camino a welcome place for foreigners.

We later went to visit the Church of the Assumption, and as we approached the main entrance, we saw that an elderly woman was about to lock the church for the siesta period. On seeing us, however, she beckoned to us to approach and seemed more than willing to allow us to visit the main monument in Navarette.

The exterior was a type of Baroque style dating back to the sixteenth century; the interior had a triple nave of gigantic proportions. The woman gave us a running commentary on the history of the church but our Spanish was far too rudimentary to pick up more than mere snatches of the content. She kindly put some coins in the box to pay for the automatic illumination of the magnificent altarpiece, which depicted the Assumption in gilt wood carving.

The huge baroque altarpiece of the Church of the Assumption
at Navarette dates back to the sixteenth century.

We listened to the uninterrupted flow of Spanish as she continued to demonstrate her love and appreciation of what must have been for her a thing of beauty and a place of prayer and devotion.

As we came to the end of the guided tour, the woman was very keen to show us the foot-long key that locked the main entrance to the church. It was, she appeared to be saying, the original one that had been in her family since the construction of the church, though I wondered about the possibility of this being the case. Certainly, it looked as ancient as the very stones of the impressive edifice. Also, the way she guarded the key, placing it in a special pouch and placing it in her bag, demonstrated how seriously she took her responsibility as keeper of the key.

For the rest of the siesta time, we lay down under the shade of the trees on concrete benches and relaxed, away from the unrelenting heat of the afternoon. Looking upwards, the clouds seemed to be appearing quite rapidly and covering the glorious blue sky. Before long, the skies were almost completely blocked by what looked like rain-bearing clouds. It was no longer pleasant to lie out and we made our way towards the refugio that fortunately was about to open slightly ahead of the scheduled time.

The refugio had been recently refurbished and could not have been more comfortable and suited to the needs of the pilgrim. The place was beautifully tiled and everything immaculately maintained. The bunks in freshly varnished pine exuded neatness and sheer comfort. The kitchen was equipped with every implement necessary for cooking a meal: cookers, fridge, worktops and so on. There was a variety of cooking utensils that would do justice to any family household. It was most impressive that such a service had been put in place for pilgrims of the camino who were asked to pay a mere €3.

No sooner had Bernard, Rolf and myself begun our laundry than the heavens opened and it poured down torrents. Thunder and lightening filled the sky and any hope of drying clothes went out the window where we had hoped to hang our washing. However, we were grateful that we had made it to the hostel and uttered a silent prayer for those pilgrims still on the way to Navarette.

We were prisoners for the rest of the afternoon, but this gave us the opportunity to catch up on our journals, although I am not so sure that either Bernard or Rolf took extensive notes as I was doing. They expressed surprise when they saw the size of my journal. It certainly weighed half a kilo and this would have been a considerable percentage of the overall weight that I was carrying in the rucksack. Still I was determined to keep all my notes within the covers of one volume. I wanted to have the journey formatted as a unit, rather than divided into small copybooks and then posting each one home as it got filled.

With our makeshift clothesline, we hung the laundry across the bedroom and hoped that the crosswinds would go some way to drying our clothes. It looked as if the rain was there for the rest of the afternoon. However, two hours later as suddenly as the rain started, so it eased greatly, giving me the opportunity to emerge out into the streets.

Shops were beginning to open after the siesta period so I went hunting for a local bakery for some fresh rolls for the morning. I found one and purchased half a dozen rolls. When I asked the price, the woman immediately asked for €3, and then as quickly again corrected herself and settled for half the amount. It seemed to me that she initially considered me a tourist that could be exploited; then realised I was a pilgrim who would not have the resources of the tourist. As I left the shop, I felt uplifted by the concept that the pilgrim is worthy of reverence and respect. This once again underlined for me the sacred nature of the journey.

Rolf, Bernard and myself repaired to Los Arcos Bar again for supper and enjoyed our glass of wine with the meal. On returning to the refugio, we were greeted by two women and two boys, all Spanish, who obviously had arrived in Navarette in the pouring rain when we had been visiting the town. The women were cooking a meal while the boys prepared the tables. They invited us to join them for a bite to eat but we explained that we had already had supper and were more inclined to retire for the night. As we mounted the stairs to the bunk bed area, our only hope was that when the foursome would later join us they would not be like some groups, who seemed totally unaware of the need to keep quiet when others were trying to sleep. We need not have worried.

Day Nine
Navarette to Nájera
Tuesday 30 June 1998

They say that you should make a mistake each day but not the same one. As I started out for Nájera, I was lost again and could not find the correct road to the next stage. I asked a farmer on a tractor, who pointed the way and wished me, *"Buon viajo"* (safe journey). It was then that I made up this verse to remind me what to do to avoid wandering around in a daze at the outset of each day's journey:

Before night falls
Examine the walls
And look for the arrow
That will help you tomorrow!

So I hoped that the following day I would not have the same problem, now realising the need to make some simple orientation preparation prior to setting off on a day's journey.

The local cemetery had an impressive Romanesque splayed portal that originally came from the pilgrim's hospital of San Juan de Acre, which I had passed on entering Navarette the previous day. I noticed a memorial stone on the wall of the cemetery, which commemorated the death of Alice de Craemer, an unfortunate Belgian pilgrim. No-one knows how she met her end.

Soon I was walking through flat country territory covered in vineyards. Ahead, I saw the two young brothers whom we had met the previous day at the refugio of Navarette. They obviously had passed me when I was wandering lost in town. Bernard, too, was ahead in the distance.

On I walked when suddenly I realised that I had forgotten to take my clothesline, which I had rigged up in the hostel the previous day. I had also forgotten to take a photograph of the sign at Navarette before leaving the town. Senior moments were occurring with frightening rapidity. Navarette, Navarette, what did you do to me? Still, I was on the road and I was not going to allow these minor memory lapses ruin my enjoyment of the new day.

The track ran parallel to the N120 along a pilgrim path that wove its way through the vineyards. At regular intervals, I came across mounds of stones that marked some mysterious moments in the lives of pilgrims who had preceded me. I did not understand the significant of these mounds, but I felt on occasion the desire to stop and place my own stone on one of them as a mark of solidarity with the pilgrim confraternity.

Soon I joined Bernard and we chatted together as we walked along this pleasant path. At the rate we were walking we would reach Nájera at about 10.30am. Bernard was considering walking on to San Domingo de la Calzada, which was another 20km beyond Nájera, but I was determined to stick to the schedule laid down in Lozano's book.

I advised Bernard that it was important to have the more challenging days of 30km or so interspersed with shorter ones. I have to admit that my advice to Bernard was motivated more by my concern at losing another walking companion than by a real concern for his own ability to walk to San Domingo.

Crossing the N120 again we passed the Poyo de Roldan, a small hill that commemorates the mythical victory of Roland over the giant Ferragut. According to one version of the legend, Roland went to Nájera to free the Christians that Ferragut, the Moorish knight who ruled over Nájera, had held prisoner in his castle. Roland, according to the myth, climbed up the hill that bears his name, picked up a huge stone and threw it at Ferragut, striking him on the head and mortally wounding him. Roland then entered the city and freed the Christian knights, becoming a hero to the local Christian community.

On our arrival at Nájera we had walked a mere 14km. As we crossed the bridge over the Najerilla River, we saw the two brothers and the two Spanish women whom we had met at Navarette sitting on the banks of the river below the bridge. They were having a picnic and waved to us as we passed.

Walking along the narrow streets we unexpectedly came into a square where we noticed the sign '*Albergue por Peregrinos*' (pilgrims' shelter). The refugio was open, with the guardian there to greet us and to stamp our pilgrim passport. The refugio had a large reception area on the ground floor and a balcony, which had bunk beds along the wall and a door leading into

Pilgrim donkey at Najéra is well equipped to make the 800km journey to Santiago.

another area with more beds. In all, the place could house up to 40 pilgrims. The kitchen facilities were rather cramped but adequate.

I was delighted to meet Emmanuel again; he appeared out of nowhere. I thought after Los Arcos that I had lost him but he explained that he had decided to spend an extra day in Nájera. The town had celebrated the local annual festival the previous night; instead of the rest he had hoped for, he had had to put up with fireworks and bands playing into the early hours of the morning. So he was taking another day to recover from the bedlam of the previous night and already he looked more rested and in better shape.

As I unpacked my rucksack, a rakish looking pilgrim sat on the bed beside me. He was long, thin and lean with a wide-brimmed hat hanging around his neck and a crude staff in his hand. No sooner had he opened his mouth than I knew I was meeting my first Scottish pilgrim.

"I'm Roger and I'm exhausted," he exclaimed. He began taking off his shoes and socks and indeed I could understand why he was so weary. There were quite a few blisters, some of which looked quite nasty. "I'm really an experienced walker," he went on, "and I canny understand how in the name of God I got these blisters."

When he talked about walking 40km in seven hours, I understood exactly how he had got the sore feet. He explained why he was doing the walk to Santiago.

"I'm not religious," he explained, "but I love walking, and I just wanted to have some fun."

As he was talking, he was joined by what appeared to be his girlfriend, who was French. She smiled and greeted me.

"You may not be religious but I'd say you're spiritual," I tentatively suggested.

"Aye, I am somewhat spiritual but I'm just doing the walk for a lark. And the Spanish beer isn't bad," he added with a laugh.

He introduced himself as Roger; his girlfriend was Emmanuelle. They seemed a nice couple and I looked forward to meeting them later. But I had already made an appointment with Emmanuel (my Danish friend) to visit the town together and I could see him waiting below for me to join him.

As we walked through the historic town, we chatted about our adventures over the previous few days. He was obviously enjoying the pilgrim experience and was very happy to have arrived at this point without mishap. He told me that the previous year he had begun to walk from his native Denmark to Santiago but had to call off the venture in Switzerland due to unbearable pains in his legs. He had reached the 1200km mark when he had called it a day. In many ways, this walk was chicken-feed to him.

Emmanuel told me about his parents, who were teachers of the Steiner school system of which he himself had been a pupil. Steiner was an industrialist who decided to provide for his workers an education that would prepare them for life in his factory. He concentrated on a broad-based education, with emphasis on manual skills, musical competence and general academic subjects. Each pupil was encouraged to play a musical instrument, learn cooking and knitting as well as other craft skills. Emmanuel had found the system very helpful in his present studies as a student of ecological agriculture. He came across as a most mature young man, far beyond his 19 years. His philosophy of life and general attitude would have sat easily on someone ten years older.

I had heard of the two monasteries of San Millan de Suso and San Millan de Yuso that were near Nájera and was keen to visit them. The monasteries had been built on the hillside near the caves when San Millan and his disciples lived there, in the fifth and sixth centuries. There is supposed to be a fine statue of San Millan to be seen as well as some fine examples of Arabic and European architecture. Inquiring from some locals as to the whereabouts of these monasteries, I was taken aback to learn that they were situated some 35km south of Nájera. What a disappointment!

So San Millan de Suso and de Yuso would have to wait for the next time, when I returned to the camino by car. Certainly I can see how enjoyable it would be to explore the camino by car visiting all the towns that border the main route. Just as we have in Ireland tours entitled 'Hidden Ireland', so in Spain I could see myself returning to uncover its many layers of culture.

As we retraced our steps, we came across a rather young but heavy-set pilgrim sitting beside the petrol pumps just beside the bridge over the Najerilla river. He sported a white bandage around his knee and what particularly struck me was his t-shirt with a map of Australia emblazoned on the front. We stopped to talk and, much to my surprise, I learned that he was a former pupil of the Christian Brothers in Queensland. He talked with affection of the Brothers who taught him, naming various instructors. However, as he talked I felt gratified that here was someone whose experience with the Brothers was wholly positive. How different this is from the media's portrayal of the Brothers, which sometimes seems to wish to paint them in a very negative light.

Nick was this pilgrim's name. He had been suffering from tendonitis for a few days, and had finally reached the point where he could no longer walk. So he was taking a few days rest and travelling by bus. He seemed very philosophical about the mishap, preparing to continue on the camino, albeit with the help of public transport.

On our return to the refugio, we found it quite full. A group of cyclists had arrived and assembled around the big table in the centre of the lounge area. They were in high spirits, laughing in surprise and with good humour at what different people were saying. The group comprised two French girls, an Italian boy and a Spanish and Norwegian girl. They were all full of the joys of spring, and as we entered, they invited us to join them, as they were about to have 'real coffee'.

One of the guests invited to the group was a bearded young American man who had left his job in the States and was hoping to find some form of employment in Spain for a year or so. Phil talked about which jobs he could take, admitting that teaching English would not be one of his options because of his inability to spell. How open and refreshingly honest Americans can be! Not in a month of Sundays would I freely admit to strangers that I could not spell. And yet how liberating to be able to confess to our weaknesses without any big deal.

Another case in point was the Italian, who was rather embarrassed when he admitted that he could only speak Italian when most of the group had at least one other European language. The Norwegian girl seemed, on the other hand, to be able to speak all the languages of the group assembled. She was able to switch effortlessly and seamlessly from one language to the other.

Travelling along the camino had increased my motivation to continue studying the languages I now know and to begin to attempt to broaden my repertoire of new languages. There is no doubt that knowledge of languages provides one with a wonderful entry into different cultures.

Later on in the afternoon, there was the opportunity to follow the tourist trail of Nájera alone. I wanted especially to visit the Church of Santa Maria la Real that is supposed to be the place where the kings of Navarre are buried.

Legend has it that the Church of Santa Maria la Real was built by Don Garcia, son of Sancho the Great, who was out hunting one day when his falcon disappeared into one of the basalt caves that tower above the town of Nájera. When he followed the bird into the cave, he discovered a statue of the Virgin Mary, with a lamp burning before her and a display of lilies at her feet. He decided to build a church at the spot where he found the statue.

The statue of the Virgin can be seen inside the church in an elaborately decorated niche. This fourteenth-century statue of the Virgin and Child is an exquisite piece of workmanship that portrays the Virgin and Child as regal figures reigning over all they survey. And close by is the Pantheon containing the tombs of the kings of Navarre as if to demonstrate the temporal nature of human power before the eternal power of the spiritual.

The fifteenth-century Gothic church also contains the Knights' Cloister with its well-preserved Gothic carvings on the upper parts of the arches. One could only admire the sheer delicacy of the tracery work. And not to be missed were the magnificent choir stalls, again Gothic in style and probably of the same century if not earlier. All in all, the fifteenth-century church built on the earlier eleventh-century monastery established by Don Garcia must be considered one of the jewels of the camino.

The Madonna rests in the cave around which was built the church of Santa María la Real at Nájera.

I wandered into a small plaza in the midst of a warren of narrow streets and could not believe my eyes when I saw Liam sitting down on one of the public benches. It was really good to see him. He explained how he had found a very comfortable and modern refugio in Logroño with a spirit of hospitality there that almost tempted him to stay longer if they had allowed him. But the usual rule for refugios is to allow the pilgrim to stay for only one night. From there, he had made good progress, skipping Navarette to arrive directly at Nájera that day.

He had already met Bernard and Rolf and had made an appointment with them for supper. It was now near that time, so we walked together to the chosen meeting place, where Rolf and Bernard were already waiting. I would have liked to have invited Emmanuel to join us, but he was nowhere to be seen. Moreover, I am aware that often he did not eat in restaurants, being more inclined to prepare his own supper in the kitchens. His budget was probably quite restricted.

And so the day ended with this 'reunion' with Liam. Even though I began the day getting lost and forgetting my clothesline, the conclusion was one of finding Liam once more and of sharing our reminiscences that we had had along the camino. Things were looking up.

Day Ten
Nájera to Santo Domingo de la Calzada
Wednesday 1 July 1998

I awoke suddenly. I thought that I had overslept, but on checking my watch, I discovered that it was only 5.30am. I was wide awake but rather than go back to sleep I decided to begin walking really early, as an experiment, to see what it would be like to set out before dawn.

Packing the rucksack is a noisy affair, especially as I had lined it with a black refuse sack that made a terrible din in the silence of the early hours. A woman sleeping in a bunk near me woke up with a start, furious that I had disturbed her at what she considered a ridiculous hour. The more I tried to hurry packing my rucksack the louder the sounds that came from the blessed black bag, until I almost ran out of the place as fast as I could to avoid waking any more slumbering pilgrims. I could feel the woman's frustrated ire following me right to the main door of the refugio as I exited.

The pilgrims' route at Nájera begins behind the monastery of Santa Maria la Real. Despite having checked it the previous evening, there seemed to be no sign of the yellow arrows now in the morning darkness. In blind faith, I continued up a steep road that led to a wider courtyard at the end of which began a dirt track. I was still unsure of where I was, having not seen a single arrow. So I waited for a while. The sun began to make its tentative appearance on the horizon. With some more light I proceeded; yet still I could not make out any yellow arrows. Voices behind me reassured me that I was on the right trail, but I paused to see in which direction they were going.

The group comprised a Spanish family that I had met for the first time the previous day. The father was a dour burly Spaniard; his wife was small, thin and wiry; their young son and daughter were nine and seven years old respectively. They were actually from Santiago and had decided to walk from Roncesvalles to their home during their holiday period. As they passed, the young boy saw that I was lost. He pointed to the hill somewhat in the distance and said in English, 'mountain', indicating that I should go in that direction.

Walking along the path that went among the pine trees, I continued through farmland and along the uneven track. The first village along the route was Azofra, known for having documents that attested to the existence of a pilgrim hospital in the town during the Middle Ages. I passed the Fuente de los Romeros – the pilgrim fountain. Romeros is an older term for pilgrim, linked possibly to the word Rome, where pilgrims travelled to when Jerusalem was inaccessible at the time of the Moorish occupation.

Leaving the village, I could hear footsteps behind me. It was my faithful companion Bernard. We walked together almost in silence past the cross that indicated the medieval boundary stone between the villages of Azofra and Alesanco. The ubiquitous N120 was to our right and the track ran parallel to it for quite some time. At one point we began climbing towards the village of Cirueña with its impressive copse of oak trees on the outskirts of the town.

I became aware as I climbed the hill that I was almost running up the steep incline. This was very different to the time I was climbing the hills from St Jean-Pied-de-Port, when I had struggled to catch my breath.

"Easy on!" panted Bernard. "If you continue at this pace you'll be exhausted before you reach the refugio!"

He was right. There is always the danger of pushing things too much, and then collapsing in a heap – not to mention bringing on the dreaded condition tendonitis. I slowed down considerably.

Cirueña was almost a deserted village. We had hoped to stop for coffee there, but as we went through deserted barns and came to the main road of the village, we could see no bar in sight. We walked left up the road to where there seemed to be some shops, but at this early hour, everything was closed. I went a little further on while Bernard sat down for a rest.

An old lady sweeping the ground before her open front door asked me what I was looking for. I explained that we were hoping to find a bar to get a coffee. She said that there was no bar in the village and as I made to continue the journey, she asked if I would like a coffee from her. This was amazing. Here was this frail lady asking a rather unshaven stranger if he would take a coffee from her. I thanked her, and she indicated that I could sit on the doorstep.

Bernard had stayed at the crossroads and I beckoned him to join me. But he declined and continued down the path towards Santo Domingo de la Calzada. Eventually the lady came back to the door and invited me into her house. She had prepared coffee and biscuits on a small tray covered with a delicate white crochet cloth. The coffee was in a china coffee-pot; as if I was being transported back to a modern coffee-house in Ireland. On and on she went talking in Spanish without a care in the world. I think she was talking about a niece of hers who was going to Ireland to learn English. It was a real privilege to have been welcomed by a complete stranger into their house and given such hospitality. I uttered a sincere prayer of gratitude to all those people who open the doors of their hearts to welcome the stranger and the thirsty.

As I walked along the path that led out of Cirueña, Rolf appeared. Together we caught up with Bernard who was walking along the hilly track leading to Santo Domingo de la Calzada which was by now visible in the distance.

Just as we entered the town, the sky, which for some time had looked rather menacing, now opened; it began to rain quite heavily. Luckily we were within running distance of the refugio and, on entering the impressive entrance, we found perfect shelter from the storm.

The volunteer women were still cleaning the refugio after the previous day's pilgrims, so we had a moment to relax and be grateful that we had reached our destination before getting drenched in the downpour. Because of the weather being so uncertain, I was unwilling to change my t-shirt for fear that I would have nothing dry for the following day.

At midday, Rolf and I decided we needed a more substantial meal than usual and we spied a lovely local restaurant where we had *lomo* (pork) and home-made croquettes all washed down with a bottle of Rioja wine. I found Rolf's company most enriching and he talked about his work as a teacher in his hometown of Marienfeld. The meal was taken at a very leisurely pace, and we felt very relaxed after our 20km walk that day. However, at the end of the meal we both admitted that the only place we wanted to visit at that moment was our beds. So we both retired to the dormitory, neatly divided with heavy wooden partitions each just above the height of the beds. And for an hour or so, I simply dozed as I thought of the woman's hospitality to me that day.

Santo Domingo de la Calzada is a name intimately connected with the Camino de Santiago. My Lozano guide informed me that Santo Domingo had been born in the nearby village of Viloria and studied at the Abadia de Valvanera, south of Nájera and near the monastery of San Millan which I had tried to visit the previous day. He was not accepted into the monastery, consequently becoming a hermit in the place now known as Santo Domingo de la Calzada, St Dominic of the Roads, thus highlighting his enormous contribution in building roads along the pilgrim route. He devoted his entire life to the assistance of pilgrims and in 1044 built a pilgrims' bridge over the River Oja. Alfonso VI took possession of the town in 1076, and he supported Santo Domingo in his efforts to support the pilgrims en route to Santiago. Santo Domingo died in 1109 and was buried in the village that bears his name.

The town is well-known for the story of the miracle of the roasted cock. The Lozano guidebook offers a good summary of the story, which I read with amusement:

> In the fourteenth century, a man and his wife from Santes, a part of the diocese of Cologne, were making the pilgrimage to Santiago de Compostela, accompanied by their son, Hugonell. They stopped for the night at an inn in Santo Domingo de la Calzada, where the innkeeper's daughter took a fancy to the young man, who virtuously resisted her advances. Thus spurned, she hid a silver goblet in Hugonell's baggage, and the following morning denounced him as a thief. The boy was arrested and hanged. As his parents were preparing to depart, they heard their son's voice telling them that he was still alive, as St Dominic was holding him up by the feet. They hastened to the house of the judge, who was just sitting down to dine on a pair of roast chickens, a cock and a hen, and told him the extraordinary tale. The judge retorted that the boy was no more alive than the cock and the hen on his plate. At that, the birds jumped out of the plate, grew feathers and began to flutter around and cackle and crow, thus demonstrating the hanged boy's innocence.

Inside the cathedral there is still today a chicken coop, a very decorative gilded one that contains a pair of live white chickens, a cockerel and a hen, which are changed every so many weeks. Apparently it is only since the Holy Year of 1965 that the birds have taken up permanent residence in their luxurious home. Prior to that the birds were only on display between 15 April and 13 October, the significance of which dates eludes me.

The hens in their special cage in the Cathedral of San Domingo de la Calzada.

Also in the cathedral can be found the impressive statue of Santo Domingo de la Calzada at his altar of gold; and in the panels of the altar are scenes from his life. And nearby is the mausoleum of St Dominic with a fine statue of the saint lying on his deathbed.

When I visited, the restored altarpiece over the high altar was simply stunning with the gold leaf glistening in the afternoon light. I had forgotten my binoculars but I could see that the overall impression of the huge panels of hagiography was sufficient to make one feel in the presence of something special. Obviously, Santo Domingo de la Calzada had been one of the giants of the faith in the eleventh century. Devotion to him has continued to the present day.

What particularly impressed me was the sanctuary that had been completely remodelled along modern lines. It looked as if the architects had used travertine (a white rock deposit) to create a modern space for liturgical celebrations. And although the new decoration was in stark contrast to the more Renaissance style all about it, I found the adaptations a refreshing addition.

I sat there in the quiet and coolness of the cathedral thanking the Lord once more for the privilege of being a pilgrim in solidarity with the many pilgrims past and present who prayed at this shrine.

Leaving the church, I met Liam and joined him as he searched for some raingear. He had been caught in the downpour that morning and wanted to avoid a repeat of the experience. As we hunted for a raincoat, what amazed me was the number of souvenir shops, with every conceivable souvenir of St Dominic, including, of course, the chickens in their golden cage.

I found the experience of shopping with Liam most enjoyable, as I attempted to use the Spanish I was picking up along the route. We found him a waterproof poncho and bought provisions for the next day. And I made a point of spending as long as I could in each of the

The refugio at San Domingo de la Calzada is situated along the pilgrim route through the town.

shops talking to the proprietors or shop assistants about anything and everything I could think of to prolong the conversation in Spanish. I was really getting great practice in this beautiful language. What impressed me very much was the shopkeepers' kindness and willingness in giving time to pilgrims of all nations who must, at times, try their patience. And guessing what these foreigners are trying to say must severely test their command of language.

Bernard, Rolf, Liam and myself came together that evening in a bar that advertised a pilgrim menu. On entering the narrow bar, I noticed a couple of older women who were filling a scrapbook of their pilgrim journey. They were writing their journals and interspersing the text with photographs they had cut from tourist brochures. Their total absorption in the task made me all the more determined to continue my own journal, though at times it was often difficult to find time to write a detailed account of each day's happenings. However, without the written record, the separate memories can fuse into a mishmash of vague recollections; and I knew that at the end of the journey I would be regretting that I had not made the effort to chart the salient day-to-day events. Sitting down and taking the trouble to record the day's recollections after the effort of walking for seven or eight hours gave me a renewed admiration for the Dervla Murphys and the Bettina Selbys of travel literature.

On our return from the bar, I came across the diminutive French man who had directed me in the right direction on leaving Viana. On closer inspection, I realised that he was the same pilgrim that had slept on the table in the refugio in Puente la Reina. He was about 1.6 metres tall and almost completely bald, with not an ounce of spare flesh on his frame. What he lacked in height he made up for in vivacity and energy.

On leaving the hostel that morning, he could be heard talking in the kitchen area. Now on my return he was still pouring forth, scarcely taking a breath to finish one sentence before launching into the next. Laughter interspersed his narration, given in both French and Spanish. He seemed equally fluent in both languages, so much so that I was not sure from which country he hailed. But the more I listened the more I felt that this man should be taken in small doses. The persistent chatter would truly drive me wild were he to be my companion along the camino.

Francesco was his name and apparently he was of Spanish origin, but his parents had had to flee Spain during Franco's reign because of their ideological opposition to his regime. So Francesco had lived for most of his life in southern France but had maintained links with his country of origin, especially to the Spanish language, which his parents continued to speak in the home. His French-Spanish origins made him the perfect subject for a French film crew who were attempting to keep up with him along the route. It seems that he had been invited to participate in their film about the camino, but although he accepted the offer, he spent most of his time avoiding them. He would rise early in the morning before they had the team assembled and then walk unbelievably quickly to the next refugio as if he wanted to outfox or frustrate them in their task.

As I lay on my bed, I could hear the hysterical laughter of the little pilgrim and it seemed as if he continued right into the night regaling his audience with anecdotes and jokes. At some point during the night, I ceased hearing his voice as I slipped into a profound sleep in the very comfortable pilgrim quarters in Santo Domingo de la Calzada.

San Domingo de la Calzada is a town rich in legend and memory for the pilgrim.

DAY ELEVEN
Santo Domingo de la Calzada to Belorado
Thursday 2 July 1998

After a very substantial breakfast of salami, cheese and fruit, Rolf, Bernard and I set out for Belorado. When we pushed back the big doors to the entrance of the Casa del la Cofradia, the house of the Confraternity of St James that manages the refugio, we were met with the blinding lights of the television crew. They were determined to capture Francesco that morning before he could leave unobserved. For good measure, they followed us with their cameras as we set out along the Calle Mayor towards the River Oja.

Bernard was particularly camera-shy. He had been asked by the television production team to give an interview and had declined most emphatically. He explained that he wanted to be a simple pilgrim and not get involved in discussing his very personal journey with the wider public. He was most impressive in the quiet but firm way in which he maintained his determination to remain anonymous. There was no doubt about his motivation for making the pilgrimage to Santiago. He simply wanted to complete the camino for his own personal and spiritual reasons, preferring to share his inner feelings and thoughts with fellow pilgrims instead of before a television audience who had no direct contact with him.

We crossed the 24-arch bridge that had been built by Santo Domingo de la Calzada over the River Oja and continued along the motorway N120. It was only later that I realised how important the bridge was in the history of the saint. At the time, it was simply another bridge to cross. When one imagines the plight of the medieval pilgrim who would have had to negotiate rivers in full spate without any bridges, the work of San Domingo grows in importance. His concern for, and practical assistance to, the pilgrims meant that the camino could be completed in relative safety and within a reasonable time frame.

After about two or three kilometres we cut inland and headed for Grañon where we hoped to find a local coffee bar open and take a rest over a warm cup. However, again we were to be disappointed. The town was still sleeping, with no bar to be found in this isolated village. We paused for a rest. I checked my feet, which were feeling somewhat uncomfortable. However, on examination, there was nothing untoward to be seen. Why I was feeling uncomfortable was a mystery for the moment.

It was pleasant, however, in the early morning light, to sit in the shade of the buildings in the Town Square and relax for a while. The blue sky augured well for a clear day and we hoped to arrive at Belorado before the intense heat of the early afternoon made walking rather trying.

Leaving Grañon, I took some photos of Rolf and Bernard as they walked ahead along the track towards Redicilla del Camino. The route was quite difficult to walk on because of the muddy nature of the terrain. Deep ridges of sun-baked clay ran along the route making it awkward to find a safe place to plant one's steps. The progress was very slow and tiring. All conversation dried up, because it took all our concentration to avoid slipping on the ridges or twisting our ankles in the ruts that dug deep into the track.

When we reached Redicilla del Camino we met Emmanuel sitting beside a picturesque fountain and bathing his weary feet. He had camped out the previous night and said he hoped to join us in Belorado. Certainly, his tent was providing him with a pleasant option to the refugios, where the snoring and late night conversations often made it difficult for pilgrims to get any decent sleep.

Again, our search for coffee proved fruitless in Redicilla del Camino and because of the early hour we did not get the opportunity to view the Romanesque baptismal font dating from the twelfth century. It was housed in the parish church of the Virgen de la Calle – the Virgin of the Way.

Passing the modern refugio that stands on the site of the old Hospital de San Lazaro, we continued on towards Castildelgado along the motorway. A young German who apparently had decided to walk to Santiago along the motorways without following the pilgrim tracks overtook us. He was walking quite quickly, yet I wondered how his feet would endure the unyielding surfaces of the path that flanked the motorways. Most pilgrims long for the soft surfaces of the tracks after walking for some time on the hard asphalt footpaths. But each pilgrim makes his or her choice; each pilgrim's journey is very personal and individual. So I blessed this young man as he strode away from us along the footpath.

Just ahead of him was the Spanish family I had met in Nájera; they were sitting down at the side of the road taking a break. They had an arrangement that when any one of the family wished to rest, the four of them would stop and wait. There was no question of people continuing on by themselves. It was a good example of collaboration and solidarity with the weakest member at any particular time. They were almost a model of how people should work together: moving from individualism to partnership, from competition to mutual support.

The route continued along the motorway, past a petrol station. Then suddenly I found myself ahead of Bernard and Rolf. The sun was splitting the heavens. My two companions were obviously finding the going tough. There was no sign of Viloria de Rioja, the birthplace of Santo Domingo; instead, the road continued unrelentingly. I was looking forward to Belorado where we could take a rest and finally get the coffee that we had been searching for

This Romanesque baptismal font is found at Redicilla in the Church of the Virgin of the Way.

since early morning. It was not that I was particularly thirsty or needed the coffee, but somehow when expectations are raised about obtaining any object of desire, no amount of waiting seems to diminish that desire. The postponement only seems to increase it.

Having left the vineyards and wheat fields that bordered the beaten track, the route led to the busy motorway. The traffic was frightening. Articulated trucks sped along the motorway at breakneck speed, one following the other in almost an uninterrupted line. The noise and the smell of diesel were quite overwhelming, as was the draught created by the passing vehicles, which almost blew me off the path. It was hard to believe that such a convoy was possible in what appeared to be a rather quiet part of the country.

It was a perfect moment to pray for the Lord's protection and to extend that prayer to my two companions following close behind. Being alone again was something to be savoured. It afforded me the opportunity to quietly place myself in the Lord's presence and to relish the sense of his provident care. Travelling with others along the camino has many advantages, but there are moments too when the pilgrim needs to be alone with his or her God and to create a space for the breaking through of the transcendent into one's consciousness. This was one of those moments, and as the powerful lorries roared past, I held on to my bordón and opened my heart to the Lord as protector.

At one stage I looked back and could just see Rolf in the distance, easily recognisable by his lop-sided rucksack perched on his back. There was no sign of Bernard.

Just before reaching Belorado, I turned off the road and continued along a track to the right until I came across the refugio adjacent to the Church of Santa Maria. On entering the refugio I was met by the smiling bearded hospitalero's kind words, "Welcome, pilgrim, would you like a cup of tea?"

What better greeting could any pilgrim wish for in the heat of the day! The hospitalero was Dutch; and the refugio was under the management of the Dutch Confraternity of St James. All I could do at that stage was to slump down on a nearby chair and take off the heavy walking boots. As I rested, I looked around at my surroundings.

The refugio appeared as if it had been a small theatre, with the kitchen now occupying what once had been a stage. The ground floor had tables and benches where people could sit and eat their prepared meals. On the same floor, there were showers and toilets; and in the corner, a stairway led upstairs to where the bunk beds awaited the newly arrived pilgrims.

Just as the tea arrived, the young German lad I had seen outside Santo Domingo de la Calzada emerged from the toilets and began loading up his rucksack. He said that he wanted to continue on for another 20km that would bring him to St Juan de Ortega. He was welcome to it. The stage for today had been almost 22km but a combination of rough terrain, the heat and the struggle with the traffic dissuaded me from even contemplating walking another metre.

I chatted with the guest master, each of us exchanging some superficial details of our provenance. By this time, I was feeling almost human; tea has always that effect on me. Considerate as ever, the hospitalero offered to stamp my passport and showed me to the dormitory. At the top of the stairs, I spied some single beds, situated alongside the banisters. They looked far preferable to the bunks; so, with his encouragement I opted for one of these.

Rolf arrived and was followed immediately by Bernard who seemed to be in great pain and was limping badly. His shin muscles were aching, and his left leg was appreciably swollen. Certainly, it appeared as if he would not be able to continue the camino. I had already seen people struggling with tendonitis but Bernard's plight seemed very serious. My heart went out to him, considering the time he had taken to prepare for the walk and how he had studied the route for the previous two years or more. This was a shattering blow to his hopes.

However, he himself was quite calm about the matter and said that he would try to visit a doctor in the town. We agreed that the three of us would meet for lunch so that we could hear the doctor's verdict. An hour later, as Rolf and I were sitting in the square, Bernard approached sporting a tight white bandage and walking much more confidently. He told us that he had indeed tendonitis and that the doctor advised him to rest for a few days before attempting to continue the camino.

When the doctor had completed his diagnosis and treatment and had given Bernard a prescription, he refused to take any payment. He simply requested that Bernard pray for him on arriving at Santiago. The Spanish people continued to amaze me with their consideration and generosity towards pilgrims. They have, as a people, embraced the pilgrims as people on a mission, as people who deserve respect and reverence. It seems as if the medieval welcome to pilgrims has endured through the centuries.

Bernard suggested that we exchange addresses at that stage, but we protested that it was too early to make that decision. We hoped that a rest during the afternoon might resolve the predicament; we agreed that we would meet that evening together with Liam, who had not yet appeared on the scene.

No sooner had we agreed on a time to meet that evening than we spied Liam turning the corner into the square where we were seated under the shade of the restaurant umbrellas. Liam was also suffering from a sore leg, and when he described the symptoms, we suggested that he visit the chemist to get Feldene. Bernard also encouraged him to visit the doctor and gave him the directions to the surgery. I accompanied Liam to the chemist, and we succeeded in getting the necessary anti-inflammatory. Eventually, he decided to repair to bed for the afternoon to allow his leg to rest and recover.

That afternoon, I explored the town of Belorado. The town is built around the River Tiron, with a bridge spanning it, which was built by St Juan de Ortega, a disciple of Santo Domingo de la Calzada. On a limestone outcrop that overshadows the town, remain the ruins of a castle that once defended the frontiers of Castile.

The people of Belorado refused to pay the annual tax to the church at Santiago de Compostela, the '*voto de Santiago*', imposed by Ramiro I after the victory of Clavijo in recognition of the role St James played in the battle. When the king of Leon tried to force them to pay it, the elders claimed that they were not under the king's jurisdiction. The dispute continued until 1408, when an agreement was reached and the document detailing the elements of the settlement is kept in the Casa Consistorial.

The Church of Santa Maria was a welcome shelter from the heat of the afternoon. On entering, I immediately felt the coolness of the calm interior, finding peace and quiet within. Over the altar is the impressive stone retable with the two images of the apostle: the Moor-slayer on the upper central panel and, underneath, the simple pilgrim sporting the bordón with his hat in hand. Around those two central images were two scenes from the life of St James.

As I sat there, I prayed that my fellow companions, who were experiencing difficulty at that moment, would find the healing and strength to continue their pilgrimage. It was a heartfelt prayer for their welfare, tinged with some understandable desire on my part to have them as companions along the camino.

Belorado Town Plaza has the Church of Santa Maria with the stone altar dedicated to St James.

On leaving the church, I passed through the narrow streets that led to the town square. As I rounded a corner, I came across a shop that sold hand-made shoes. The worn stone of the original building was unadorned; and a simple window and door comprised the façade of the shop. Above was the name of the shoemaker.

In the window were displayed high-quality shoes of exquisite beauty, expertly crafted and delicately designed. Even the display was impressive in its simplicity and beauty. I wondered why someone would decide to establish such a specialised business in this small town of a few thousand inhabitants. It appeared to me that the craftsman would have been more at home in the wealthy streets of Madrid or Barcelona. Yet, here in Belorado, with a population of hardly two thousand, was a shop that sold high-class footwear.

I could see the shoemaker working away in the back of the shop. He was holding a shoe in one hand and what appeared to be some shape or form of cutting implement in the other. His concentration was complete as he began to cut away the excess leather. Although tempted to enter and engage in conversation with the craftsman, my lack of any real flow in the Spanish language made me reluctant. So I simply marvelled at the man's commitment.

That evening, as I waited in a restaurant in the main square for Bernard, Rolf and Liam, a woman I had seen periodically during the week approached me. She introduced herself as Frieda and hailed from Norway. For a pilgrim she was dressed amazingly well, in a long flowing silk blue dress with floral patterns and matching blouse and scarf. Apparently, she had two or three such co-ordinated outfits that she alternated after each day. Fair-haired and slight with an engaging smile, she would have been in her mid to late fifties. Having been to some educational conference in Ireland a few years previously, she showed great enthusiasm about everything Irish, describing the various places she had visited.

My three companions approached, and with a certain degree of reluctance, I continued listening to fair Frieda. Liam, Bernard and Rolf joined us and as they did, the waiter inquired if we were ready for our evening meal. A certain awkwardness ensued, and without too much enthusiasm, we invited our fifth companion to dine with us.

During the meal, Bernard said that he was thinking of getting the bus to Burgos where he would await us. However, he was still hoping that a good night's rest would improve the situation and not necessitate such a drastic measure. Liam too decided to rest in Belorado for an extra night so that he would avoid straining the already swollen muscles. We exchanged addresses at the table in the presence of this new arrival to our group. It seemed amazing that she could not see how she was intruding into a circle of special significance between people who had already formed a certain bond. She appeared oblivious to what was happening; and as the evening came to a close, I felt disappointed that our parting could not have been ritualised properly.

It looked very likely that our 'group' would be halved for the rest of the camino. Yet I found myself imagining the best scenario: Bernard's difficulties would be resolved without delay, and Liam would recuperate as quickly as possible. The eternal optimist had kicked in.

Day Twelve
Belorado to San Juan de Ortega
Friday 3 July 1998

I was awakened by the sound of movement nearby, and I was amazed to see Bernard almost fully dressed and obviously intent on continuing the journey to San Juan de Ortega. He whispered that he had slept well and that he hoped that the rest and sleep had contributed somewhat to healing his leg. Instead of resting in Belorado for the day, he thought that he would take the next stage very slowly, in the hope that nothing serious would occur to his already weakened leg. I wished him well as he quietly loaded his rucksack and descended the stairway to the main entrance of the refugio. It was about 6.30am. Soon after, I decided to face the new day, and towards seven I was leaving the refugio.

Conscious of the fragility of my own physical state, I was very careful to walk slowly at first. Never having been physically fit, I felt very grateful that I had been spared any real problems to date. Even as this thought came to me, fear raised its head with all sorts of images of what could happen to me along the camino. If people twice as fit as myself were having difficulties, it was likely that my turn would come. And yet, despite such gloomy thoughts, my spirits were quite high in the cool of the morning air.

Feelings of well-being swept over me. As I walked along the camino, I began reciting the morning offering several times. Each recitation deepened my gratitude for the gift of a new day and filled my heart with a sense of privilege. The words: 'May I spend each moment of the day loving you with all my heart and soul and strength' challenged me to see how practically I was doing this and would continue to do this for the day. While this is easy to say, the practical expression of this dedication often presents challenges that are very down-to-earth and demanding. Stanis, a friend of mine, often said, "Words are cheap; it takes money to buy bread." It is so easy to think fine altruistic thoughts; the doing of the same becomes more difficult.

Continuing to pray, I began reciting the Hail Mary in various languages. From English to Irish, from French to Italian, I slowly repeated the phrases of this ancient prayer that honours Mary, the mother of Jesus. Again, the recitation was not the mechanical mouthing of words from my youth. Instead, I reflected on the significance of the words, indeed changing some of them as I continued along the way.

I remember doing a retreat in France in the mid-eighties. Having heard of a famous preacher, Pere Callerand, who had established a retreat centre near Besançon, I decided to make my annual retreat there.

Pere Callerand had been a prisoner of war in Germany while still a seminarian. When he was freed from incarceration, he decided to dedicate himself to promoting devotion to Mary, who he felt had protected him during his imprisonment. So he established a centre of spirituality, La Roche d'Or, which over the years became a place where thousands of retreatants came to hear his conferences on the scriptures.

In preaching on the role of Mary, Pere Callerand made the observation that the conclusion of the Hail Mary had been composed during the time of the plague, when the idea of death was foremost in the minds of the faithful. Consequently, they viewed death as a moment of fear, when they could be condemned to eternal punishment for their sins. And so they prayed: 'Pray for us sinners, now and at the hour of our death.'

Pere Callerand proposed an alternative ending that would highlight the unique position of Christians in the plan of God. And so in his version it became: 'Pray for us your children now and at the hour of our re-birth.' This appealed far more to me in that it stressed our relationship of love with the transcendent instead of one with sinfulness and also pointed to death as a re-birth instead of a final termination.

And so in Irish, English, French and Italian, I repeated the ancient Marian prayer as I walked along the track that ran parallel to the N120. The vegetation was quite lush and often made me forget the nearby roadway. After about four kilometres was the town of Tosantos, with its hermitage of la Nuestra Senora de la Pena dug into the hillside and which houses a twelfth-century Romanesque statue of the Virgin. On I continued past the hermitage, imagining what it would have been like to live as a hermit in the twelfth century, indeed in any century. Somehow, the romance of living totally dedicated to prayer and fasting was lost on me. All I could imagine was the deprivation involved without envisaging much of the benefits of such a life.

On reaching the cemetery at the small village of Villambistia, the plastic bag hanging from my rucksack broke, spilling its contents onto the road. This forced stop enabled me to rest for a moment and to sample one of the oranges I'd bought in Belorado the previous day, now rolling along the path in every direction. Having captured the escapees, I packed them in the rucksack and took a while to enjoy one as I sat on a low wall in Villambistia. Certainly, oranges seem to be the most refreshing fruit for a pilgrim in the heat of the day. The adjacent fields of wheat that bordered the path were still very unripe and green. How different this was from the wheat fields that abounded on the journey to Los Arcos. Regional climatic differences could be seen in the time it takes for the wheat to ripen in each area.

Crossing the motorway, I entered Espinosa del Camino, where San Indalecio is venerated as one of the seven apostles who accompanied St James on his evangelising mission in Spain. At this stage, Villafranca Montes de Oca was visible in the lower ground along the banks of the River Oca. The descent was gradual. Approaching the main road, I could see a bar. Outside the bar against the wall was a pilgrim's rucksack. I looked forward to meeting someone with whom perhaps I could share the remaining part of the walk. I did not want to be alone all of the time.

I had enjoyed the time alone from Belorado where I was able to pray, reflect and simply be with my own thoughts. For me, however, the ideal way of being pilgrim was to have the early part of the day alone with my God and then to have the opportunity to share the journey with other pilgrims for the latter part of the day.

On entering the bar, I found Bernard sitting somewhat forlornly at a corner table. He smiled bravely but it was obvious that things were not going well. He explained that his leg was giving him great pain and that he was finding it very difficult to walk. He asked me to stay with him for the rest of the journey and to support him en route. His request was done so humbly and simply that I could not, nor would have wanted to, refuse. And so we rested for quite a while talking about what we had seen along the route from Belorado.

I checked my own feet because I had felt some discomfiture just before arriving at the bar. One of my nails was rubbing against a toe and this required some simple surgery before setting off once again.

We passed the Church of Santiago and noticed how one of the bells seemed to have frozen at a right angle to the bell tower, as if suddenly at a point in history, time had stood still. The bell had become a symbol of the paralysis that had crept into the religious faith and practice of many people in Europe during the twentieth century. The brickwork of the tower was clearly visible amid gaps in the plasterwork and in obvious need of repair. Overall, the church gave that appearance of abandonment.

A small dwelling on the outskirts of Villafranca de Oca along a busy motorway.

We began to climb the Montes de Oca, a rather steep climb along what was once one of the most feared stretches of the pilgrims' route. The fear was due both to the climb and to the fact that this stretch was often infested with ruthless bandits who would stop at nothing to wrest any valuables or money from a passing pilgrim. The climb was also made difficult because of the heat of the day.

We travelled slowly through the holm oaks and the pine trees along an ever-ascending route until we came to a pilgrim fountain of Mojapan where we rested until Bernard could give his leg some respite. He was finding the going tough, but he put on a brave face and he suggested that we take up the route again without delay. The ascent continued until we arrived at the Monumento a los Caidos, the monument to those who had died during the Civil War. As we viewed the surrounding countryside and the motorway to our left, we heard voices. To our horror, we saw Francesco, fast approaching in the company of four other pilgrims. We could also hear him as he expounded at the top of his voice about who knows what. He bounded along with the tiniest of rucksacks on his back – it could hardly have weighed more than five kilos. He passed us with a loud salute and continued talking incessantly to the group, which seemed to be amused with his monologue. I thanked the Lord that he did not stop!

Further along the path that was now descending, we suddenly came across the TV crew that were filming pilgrims along the route. We stopped and chatted with them as they explained how pleased they were to have found Francesco. Talking about the programme they were producing made me want to see the final edition and when I expressed my interest, the producer, Jean-Pierre Beauvenaut, promised that he would send me a copy if I wrote to him.

The team comprised five members, all travelling in a large Range Rover with their photographic equipment in the back of the four-wheel drive vehicle. They were most friendly and appeared to be very enthusiastic about the project. They talked about how they had met many types of pilgrims, starting out from Le Puy en Velay in France and travelling through Spain. Obviously, they had become enthused by the spirit of the camino, and I had no doubt that their programme would present the camino in the most positive of lights. Before we left them, they offered us a taste of brandy and wished us every blessing as we continued along the route to St Juan de Ortega.

The guidebook mentioned that the route from the Valdefuentes hermitage to St Juan de Ortega was a distance of six kilometres; it felt a lot longer. The heat of the day and the monotony of the remaining track contributed to this sense of a never-ending path. Bernard was limping quite badly at this stage, and it was obvious that he was suffering quite a bit. I was quite relieved, therefore, when the sign St Juan de Ortega appeared in the distance.

I used the excuse of getting a photograph of myself before the sign to let Bernard have a final rest before we entered the village. As we rested, Rolf appeared afar off and waved to us as he approached. He had found the heat of the day quite difficult and his face was covered with perspiration from the exertion of the walk. However, he was in good form and very solicitous of Bernard.

We continued into St Juan de Ortega, which consisted of a long row of buildings with a church at the east side of the town. The town is named after its founder, St Juan de Ortega, who was born in 1080. On his return from Jerusalem, where he had gone on pilgrimage, he became a follower of St Domingo de la Calzada and was subsequently ordained. He built churches, roads, bridges and hospitals for the pilgrims to Santiago and he built the church in St Juan de Ortega, dedicating it to St Nicolas of Bari, whose miraculous intercession had saved him from drowning in a shipwreck on his return from Jerusalem. St Juan de Ortega is buried in this church where his reclining figure can be seen on his tomb. He also established a monastery of Augustinian monks that flourished during his lifetime but later declined.

The refugio now occupies what was formerly the Augustinian monastery. Emmanuel, Roger and Emmanuelle, his girl friend, were sitting outside the refugio while to their right there were two old Spaniards at an open door. When we found the refugio closed, I approached the two old men and began talking to them. They appeared to be the hospitaleros, and as I chatted away to them, they seemed to thaw out, inviting me in to book my room and to get the passport stamped. Maybe they had been nervous of the younger pilgrims and it took someone nearer to their age to give them confidence.

We were shown to our bunks that were in a room upstairs and looking onto a quadrangle below. The place was spartan in its furnishings, with no hot water in the showers and signs forbidding the washing of clothes in the bathroom. However, anything was worth it to get away from the heat of the sun and to clean up after the 24km walk.

Refreshed, I met with Roger, Emmanuelle and Phil, the young American I had first met in Nájera and who was intending to stay in Spain for some time. It turned out that he worked as a fund-raiser for one of the universities in America and had taken a year out to explore Europe. In the end, he decided to walk from Le Puy en Velay to Santiago, a distance of more than 1600km. I recognised him as the pilgrim who was drawing very clever cartoons in the pilgrim book in each of the refugios. In each cartoon, he drew himself, a bearded pilgrim, and sketched the setting or circumstances in which he found himself at that particular moment. I always looked forward to seeing his sketch for the day.

We went to the local bar at the other extremity of the village from the church and had a beer and a tortilla for lunch. Bernard and Rolf had decided to cook for themselves. Following lunch, Phil, Roger and Emmanuelle were very keen to watch the World Cup match, but I left them and went to visit the church instead.

The exterior of the church was simple in its design, with the façade divided into three parts: the entrance on the first level was surmounted by a second level, comprising a rose window and crowned by the plain tympanum. To the north of the church a very simple three-storey arched campanile created an overall austere impression. On entering, one is struck by the very ornate railed tomb of St Juan de Ortega in comparison with the bare simplicity of the rest of the church.

San Juan de Ortega's tombstone in the eponymous village that commemorates the saint.

Some of the capitals are quite exquisite; and apparently, each equinox (21 March and 22 September) a single shaft of sunlight strikes the capital that shows the Annunciation, the Visitation, St Joseph's Dream and the Nativity. This occurs at precisely 5.00pm solar time, and apparently the light gives the illusion that the Holy Spirit is alighting on Mary's middle.

A sign in the church said that a pilgrim Mass was celebrated each evening at seven o'clock followed by a supper offered by the parish priest. I looked forward to attending this Mass after a good rest in the afternoon.

The Mass began on time in the main chapel, which was rather shabby. By this time, many pilgrims had begun arriving so gradually the small chapel filled up. The priest entered. I was surprised to see that he was one of the old men I had first met on arrival in St Juan de Ortega. He looked more like a farmer than a priest, with deep lines running down his face that seemed to indicate many hours spent in the fields picking grapes rather than a life of study and pastoral ministry.

No sooner had the Mass begun than a pilgrim stood up in the central aisle with his arms slightly raised towards the altar. He was dressed like Jesus Christ in a red long-flowing garment and in his bare feet. There was an intense look to him that indicated either sanctity or insanity. I must admit I was more inclined to judge him in the latter category. This was the first person I had met on the camino who came across as psychologically unbalanced. In many ways, I would have expected to have met more suchlike, as religious events sometimes attract those for whom religion touches what is most fragile within the psyche.

Following the Mass, the priest, Don José, announced that all pilgrims were invited to gather in the refectory and to bring what each one had by way of food for a communal meal. We came together at 8.30pm and found Don José in the process of preparing his famous garlic soup. For years, he has offered pilgrims this service in recognition of the spiritual journey that each one was undertaking. The soup consisted simply of salted water, bread floating in the boiling water and lashings of garlic. The taste was rather terrible but the idea was so inspiring that I forced myself to take some; and it seemed to be appreciated by most of the pilgrims – obviously garlic enthusiasts. More importantly, the meal offered all pilgrims the opportunity to chat about the camino and tell their individual personal stories. A real sense of solidarity pervaded the gathering, and the gesture of Don José in bringing pilgrims together enhanced the Eucharist that we had already celebrated.

The next day would bring us to Burgos, one of the bigger cities along the camino. My friend Lori from Italy had given me the names and address of a Spanish couple that our mutual friend, Davide Gandini, the author of *Il Portico della Gloria*, had met on the camino when he was a pilgrim a few years previously.

I phoned Alfonso and Isabel, introducing myself as friends of Lori and Davide. The conversation was difficult because of the language barrier but they kindly offered to meet me the following day and to show me around their city. This was an opportunity not to be missed; and we arranged to meet at the refugio in Burgos at 2.00pm. I was delighted that I had managed to make myself understood and was further relieved when I learned that Isabel spoke some English and some Italian. The day would not be too linguistically strenuous.

As I replaced the phone card in my wallet, I found to my consternation that my Visa card was missing. A moment of sheer panic gripped me; I had a vision of having to ring Dublin to cancel the card. All the composure of the day was instantly replaced with confusion and panic. I examined every pocket of the wallet but there was no sign of it. Reluctantly I resigned myself to the fact that it was gone and was just planning to make the phone call to Ireland when I saw the card falling from the folds of my shirt. Obviously, it had simply fallen from the wallet as I took out the phone card. I felt my breath being expelled with gratitude that a crisis had been avoided. What a relief!

Still, it made me think how much I was relying on money and financial support to make the camino. Many pilgrims had very limited resources and had to rely on the charity of others along the way.

As the day came to a close, I became aware of the fragile nature of the pilgrim way. Physical disabilities, like those of Bernard and Liam, and ordinary mishaps like losing credit cards, all contribute to a sense of the unexpected that renders the pilgrim dependent on the Providence of God. Smugness or feelings of self-sufficiency have no place on the camino.

Day Thirteen
San Juan de Ortega to Burgos
Saturday 4 July 1998

Before we set out the next morning, Don José invited us to breakfast, where he gave us dried bread and coffee. It intrigued me why he had not offered any butter or jam, both of which were on the sideboard. But beggars can't be choosers; so we ate our fill of the dry bread and savoured the good-tasting hot coffee. Bernard set out first and despite his bad leg, he was nowhere to be seen as I followed his track. I always took things very gently in the early morning in order to warm up the muscles and to avoid any strain. Maybe this is why Bernard was having trouble. Any time I saw him walking, he seemed to stride out as if he were a two-year-old instead of a retired person.

It was a lovely morning; rather chilly but ideal for walking. I found myself repeating the morning offering, the prayer of the pilgrim that I had learned at Los Arcos and some Hail Marys. Not a sound was to be heard, except for the song of some unidentifiable birds.

Rolf soon caught up with me, and we made our way across a raised plateau through bushes and pine trees. The sun was beginning to make its appearance in the morning sky. There was little conversation between us; yet we felt comfortable simply being together along the route.

Gradually the track descended towards the village of Ages, a sleepy hamlet with very ancient adobe and wooden buildings, some of which appeared to be about to crumble. They had doubtless been in a similar state for 50 years. Rolf paused to take photographs of one just as it was catching the slanting rays of the rising sun and appeared golden in the morning light.

The countryside was majestic in its early-morning colour, with the corn blowing in the breeze, swaying like dancers to a silent tune. The asphalt track continued on for about two kilometres into the village of Atapuerca. Here in 1992, some prehistoric human remains had been found and given the nomenclature 'Atapuerca Man' as possibly the earliest example of homo sapiens in Europe.

Rolf noticed a bakery at the far end of the town, and we made for it to sample some fresh bread. The door was closed, but we could hear the noise of baking tins being banged against tables and of people moving within. Knocking on the door, we heard a voice that seemed to invite entry. Pushing in the door, we saw a woman open the oven and with a big wooden spatula withdraw a freshly baked baguette, so hot that it had to be handled with gloves. She handed over one of the recently baked loaves that were lying on the table nearby. It was still quite hot but looked most appetising. Having paid a few cents to the lady and thanked her for her patience, we emerged from the bakery and sat at the side of the road where we used the bread to make salami sandwiches for our early-morning snack. We shared some fruit and drank water that we had got in St Juan prior to departure. Breakfast had never been so good!

As we were enjoying our second breakfast, we noticed two pilgrims to our left who were continuing up the Sierra de Atapuerca. They seemed to be almost running instead of walking. We knowingly smiled to each other, convinced that we would probably pass them out somewhere before they reached the top of the hill. In fact, we had hardly gone half way up when we met them sitting down and looking rather exhausted. One was a fine-looking woman, tall and thin with fair hair and the other, a youth, was much younger with round-rimmed spectacles and his hair in a short ponytail. He could have been her son.

A gentle climb led to the plateau, which was covered with fields of wheat whose golden hue contrasted with the rich blue of the cloudless sky. We followed the barbed wire fencing

Cross outside Atapuerca where the prehistoric 'Atapuerca Man' was discovered in 1992.

and continued on along paths that sometimes were difficult to follow, being hidden by the wheat that invaded the very paths. However, the telltale landmark of the quarry and telephone posts kept us in the right direction towards Orbaneja.

The bar at Obaneja was a welcome stop for a coffee, and there we met Bernard who was nursing his leg. He informed us that he would spend a few days in Burgos because he now realised that the shorter rests were not having any appreciably ameliorating effect on his leg. He was quite resigned to halting for some days even though there was some disappointment in his voice. I eventually left Bernard and Rolf chatting in the bar, as I was anxious to arrive in Burgos on time so as to meet Alfonso and Isabel.

The journey led me to a bridge that crossed the A1, a busy motorway crowded with speeding articulated trucks that created a din that could still be heard long after crossing the bridge. A train emerged from behind some buildings on the outskirts of the town, the first train I had seen to date on the camino. Eventually I reached the outskirts of Burgos and found myself walking along a footpath that ran along the main thoroughfare into the city. I kept walking through industrial estates along the Vitoria Road, keeping an eye on the yellow arrows that had not failed me so far. The route through the outskirts of Burgos was ugly enough.

At one point, I saw Emmanuel sitting outside a church near a junction. He looked exhausted. We talked for a while, and from what he said I could see that he hated the cities and was fed up with the long walk along the concrete path of the motorway. He said he needed time to gather his forces before making the last stage into the city.

As I passed Burgos cathedral, I was overwhelmed by the sheer detail of the Gothic edifice, which dated back to the thirteenth century. The combination of flying buttresses and intricately carved spires created a latticework effect that gave a sense of delicacy and majesty. Fernando III laid the first stones of the Gothic edifice in 1221; the cathedral was consecrated 40 years later. And although work continued on the building until the sixteenth century, the whole cathedral gives the impression of architectural completeness and continuity.

There were artists everywhere along the road, each painting the cathedral from their own vantage point; each using their own preferred medium of expression: oils, watercolours, sepia and so on. Around each artist there were three or four admirers, yet their presence did not seem to distract the artists, who went on working feverishly on their masterpieces.

On I continued, past the cathedral and the church of San Nicolas until I came to the major seminary of St Jeronimo that stood majestically behind high walls. It must have been built for hundreds of seminarians and I wondered what it was being used for now when the number of vocations had fallen dramatically. It would have made a great hostel for pilgrims. Reflecting on the availability of a disused seminary for use by other people and for other purposes made me wonder about how free the Church can be in situations of change. Often, a seeming paralysis grips the ecclesiastical institutions in moments when there is obvious need to adapt to changing circumstances. Change is always difficult, especially for institutions, and the Church is no exception to the rule.

Before arriving at the refugio, I stopped at a fruit shop to obtain supplies for the next day. As I examined the fruit, I spied a beer in the fridge and decided to reward myself for all my effort in the heat of the sun. The queue at the checkout numbered about half a dozen. As I waited in line, I decided to drink the beer to slake my growing thirst. How refreshing the chilled beer felt. Never did a beer taste so good. Reaching the cash desk, I offered the empty can so that the laser could check the bar code. The man at the checkout exclaimed:

"That was my beer in the fridge, it wasn't for sale!"

The look of shock was clearly visible on his face. The customers spontaneously broke out laughing, and despite the shopkeeper's surprise, he saw the funny side of the incident, laughing and joking with the shoppers. What was said by way of banter, I could not understand. I was taken aback initially but found myself laughing with the other customers. My profuse apologies were assuaged by the semi-comic assurance that a pilgrim has certain privileges – that sometimes even extend to drinking the shop owner's beer!

From there, the route led to the bridge over the Rio Arlanzon that runs through Burgos. I entered a park where the refugio was situated. It consisted of a number of log cabins clustered around a central office. The welcoming staff were most friendly and hospitable, creating an atmosphere of real support to the pilgrims, who often arrived tired and disgruntled after the long walk along the footpaths of Burgos. They stamped my pilgrim passport and assigned me a bunk in a nearby cabin. All around the cabins there were tables for picnics and scattered in the grounds were tents for those camping.

No sooner had I unpacked and taken my shower than I spied a couple talking to the staff at the central office. It had to be Alfonso and Isabel. I approached them and their smile of recognition confirmed my conjecture. We introduced ourselves and they invited me to accompany them on a tour of the city. I explained that I would be with them once I had completed my laundry rituals. Alfonso laughed. It reminded him of the time when he had accompanied Davide Gandini on the camino a few years previously, when he too had had to attend to his laundry first before ever thinking of eating or resting.

We drove first to the hill overlooking Burgos, where Count Diego Rodriguez Porcelos had founded the town in AD 884. The defensive towers ('burgos') give it its name and made the town so important that at one time it became the capital of Castile. Burgos is also the name of the immediate region that includes Belorado, St Juan de Ortega and Castrojeriz.

The view of the city was spectacular. Alfonso and Isabel were obviously very proud to show off the various sites that could be identified from this vantage point. We next went to a café overlooking the town, where we sampled the local beer. By this time, I was starving and about to take some of the tapas on the counter only to be told that we were about to eat lunch at the couple's home. I was so grateful for their generosity both in giving the time to show me the sights of Burgos and then inviting me into their home.

We started with a shrimp cocktail, accompanied with a beautifully crisp chilled white wine. The main course consisted of black pudding stuffed in peppers, a local speciality; it tasted exquisite. The main thing I had to avoid was eating too much and drinking too much of the rosé wine. The meal concluded with special biscuits, again a speciality of the region, and strong hot coffee. It was truly a gargantuan feast! By the end of the meal, I was ready for a siesta, but they were keen to show me more of the town. Politeness demanded that I acquiesce to their invitation.

The visit to the Gothic cathedral was most interesting, though I have to say that the rich interior was almost too much for me to take in after the meal I had just enjoyed. The *escalera dorada* (golden stairs), the portals, the rose window and the Capilla de Santiago, which houses the statue of St James the Moor-slayer – all these passed before me as in a haze. What particularly kept me walking around this immense monument was the cool temperature that pervaded throughout, in stark contrast to the heat of the afternoon sun outside.

On emerging from the cathedral, we had a look at the Arch of Santa Maria, which forms an impressive gateway into the city across a bridge over the River Arlanzon. The town is crammed with history, much of which could not be viewed in an afternoon's walk. So Alfonso and Isabel strolled along the narrow streets pointing out some of the more notable features and indicating where I could return to visit on my next pilgrimage.

Arch of Santa María in Burgos, which was designed by Francisco de Colonia in the sixteenth century.

They particularly wanted me to see the Monasterio de las Huelgas Reales. Lozano's guidebook informed me that the monastery was founded by Alfonso VIII in 1187 for the Cistercian nuns of royal or aristocratic families. Apparently several Castilian monarchs are buried there, including the founder, Alfonso VIII, whose wife Eleanor Plantagenet, the daughter of Henry II of England and of Eleanor of Aquitaine, ended her days in the monastery as a member of that enclosed community.

As it turned out, however, we did not get the chance to visit this spectacular convent. The time for prayer had arrived, and the doors of the monastery closed. Nothing was going to interfere with the spiritual lives of the sisters. I will have to return some day to view the cloisters and the many fine chapels that the monastery boasts of. Even from the exterior, a sense of magnificence informs this ancient but still vibrant monastic settlement.

It was approaching five in the afternoon, and Alfonso and Isabel had to take their leave. Before we parted, they offered to take some of my excess baggage to post home to Ireland. Their generosity and kindness deeply moved me; I will be forever grateful for their amazing

Las Huelgas Convent in Burgos was founded by Alfonso VIII in 1187 for the Cistercian nuns.

hospitality to a pilgrim whom they had never met up to that day. Once more, the spirit of the camino was clearly palpable in a concrete expression of welcome and support.

I returned to the refugio, hoping to meet Rolf, Bernard or Liam. None of them was to be seen, and although the place was thronged with other pilgrims, I felt truly alone and uncomfortable among strangers. To escape the feeling of isolation, I went again towards the cathedral area to write my journal and, in the adjoining square, I sat at a bar and wrote my notes for the day. This moment of quietness afforded me the opportunity to reflect again on the blessings of this day and on the kindness of ordinary people.

Opposite me there was a large sign promoting an art competition due to take place that day, in which artists had to paint a picture of the cathedral within the day and submit it for adjudication to a panel of judges by six o'clock. This explained the scene that had met me as I entered Burgos. By now the artists would have completed their masterpieces, and all that remained were the adjudication and the prize giving.

There appeared to be a carnival atmosphere in the square, so I finished my journal and sauntered along the banks of the river. It was obvious that the people of Burgos were celebrating some festival. There were bands of all types playing their music to the delight of the onlookers. Bands from Brazil mixed with those from France, Germany and even Scotland.

The skirl of the bagpipes could be heard from quite a distance and eventually I saw the lone piper dressed in the traditional kilt and sporran.

There were children everywhere running through the crowds and pestering their parents to buy them ice creams and toys and to pay for rides on the merry-go-rounds. Young couples walked hand in hand along the riverbank or stopped to embrace and kiss under the shade of one of the many trees.

The mime artists drew the biggest crowds, as people waited to drop some cents into their boxes. One mime artist was covered in terracotta clay, giving the impression he was an ornament. When he received his donation, his slow, jerky movements amused the crowd no end.

Towards seven o'clock, I decided to return to the refugio to catch up with my two companions, but on crossing the bridge over the river, I passed a modern church and decided to get to Mass. The next day would be Sunday, and there was no guarantee that there would be Mass available along the route or indeed on arrival at Castrojeriz. (It would be quite easy to miss Sunday Mass along the route: I set off walking early each morning before the churches opened and continued walking during Mass times, to finish the walk before the extreme heat of the early afternoons.)

The Carmelites were in charge of the church. As I entered, the Mass was about to begin for the very large congregation, who were in great singing voice. Although it was difficult to understand the readings or the homily, I was glad to be there and to have taken some time for prayer. During the quiet moments, I prayed for Alfonso and Isabel who had opened their home and hearts to me and had gone out of their way to make me welcome in their hometown. I prayed that they would be especially blessed for their kindness to me and I thanked the Lord for his protection during the day.

Back at the refugio, I found the place alive with young and old people all mixing together and bonded by the common hope of arriving at Santiago. The 'Jesus figure' from the Mass in St Juan de Ortega was very much in evidence and surrounded by new-found disciples! A folk group performed both religious and secular songs with great fervour.

At each of the tables there were many pilgrims, most of whom I did not recognise. But there was neither sight nor sound of Rolf or Bernard.

Over in one corner I spied Frieda and Phil, the American cartoonist, and as I picked them out, they beckoned me over to join them. They were about to begin their evening snack and invited me to partake. However, that Lucullan feast at midday meant that I could only nibble at a sandwich as I listened to their stories.

Frieda has taken the bus for most of the journey to Burgos. She explained that she had found the route monotonous and un-pilgrim like and had had no desire to walk along the motorway into the town. While I sympathised with her reasoning, I had made the decision that, God willing, I would walk every part of the camino on foot. And although I had no problem with Frieda's decision, I would later find that some pilgrims took exception to any pilgrim who did not complete the walk as it should be done.

Night was falling and although I had not yet seen Bernard, it was time to turn in early so that I could be ready for the morning's long journey to Castrojeriz. This stage of the camino would be the longest of the entire walk; and I wanted to be well rested for the endeavour.

The refugio was filling up with pilgrims who had the same idea of an early night. Most of them were Germans, it seemed, and the ones near my bed explained that they were beginning their walk from Burgos, having given up walking at Burgos the previous March because of heavy rains and impossibly muddy tracks.

As I lay on my bed, I wondered about Liam who was probably still at Belorado, nursing his tendonitis. Bernard, too, would be leaving the camino for some days and I knew that I would miss him as a companion. Only Rolf remained of the three companions who had met for the first time at Larrasoña almost two weeks previously. I sincerely hoped that he would be able to continue to the very end. Yet even as I thought of having to complete the camino alone, I never felt more determined than I did at that moment. Tomorrow would be a very long walk, however.

Day Fourteen
Burgos to Castrojeriz
Sunday 5 July 1998

At the crack of dawn, I was awoken by the movement of the Germans in my bunkhouse, obviously keen to get started on the first day of their pilgrim walk. When I emerged from the refugio, I saw Rolf arranging his gear and ready to go; he too had planned to leave early.

He told me that Bernard had arranged to stay for a few days in Burgos and had booked himself into a small hotel in the town. He had gone to the famous Hospital del Rey to be treated for his tendonitis. All that was needed was rest, the doctor informed him, and Rolf told me that Bernard was determined to give his leg a chance to heal so that he could continue the camino later. I had wanted to wake him to say goodbye, but Rolf said that he had expressed the wish to sleep on in the morning. Probably he did not want to make a fuss or to find himself awkwardly trying to say farewell.

Rolf and he had dined the night before and it seemed that at least, on Rolf's part, the separation had gone smoothly. Emmanuel, who caught up with us as we leaving the town, explained that he had left a note for Bernard, wishing him the best. On hearing this, I felt ashamed that I had not thought of a similar kind gesture to my travelling companion. Nothing could be done now but I was impressed with the sensitivity of Emmanuel, someone less than half my age and twice as thoughtful.

The morning air was very cool. I stopped to put on the fleece just as I had done when leaving Pamplona at the foot of the Sierra del Perdón. Rolf continued on while I took the opportunity of being alone to greet the Lord on Sunday, the Lord's Day. Bernard was very much in my thoughts as I imagined him sitting in the refugio lamenting the fact that he had had to abandon the camino, at least for the moment.

Some of the yellow arrow signs were not that clear, and after crossing the Malatos bridge over the River Arlanzon and passing the Hospital del Rey, the route cut across the railway and through high grass that bordered a path running through vegetable plots. Rolf was ahead but I was not convinced that we were on the right path. Yet he seemed to be forging on without hesitation. On we went until we reached the N120, where Rolf stood waiting. He obviously sensed that I had not been sure of the route and I had missed one of the signs at a strategic point just after the railway bridge.

We continued along the road until reaching Tardajos, where we discovered a café open on the main street despite the early hour. We stopped for hot chocolate and *magdalenas* (fairy cakes), and while we sat there in the early morning light, a constant stream of pilgrims came and went from this café run by an obviously enterprising lady who knew her market.

Leaving the N120, we turned left along an asphalt road that led to Rabé de las Calzadas, two kilometres away. For the next nine kilometres we travelled on a country road and on through cornfields. The day was getting very warm even at this early hour. It was going to be a challenging walk.

After another three hours walking in the heat of the day, we arrived at Hornillos del Camino, a one-street village that was beautifully kept with houses that must have been centuries old. All was silent in the village except for the low sound of a radio or television programme. In the distance there was a sign indicating a bar from where, no doubt, the sounds were coming.

Hornillos del Camino is a village consisting of a single street, which is the pilgrim's way itself.

The bar was the ideal spot to take some shelter from the sun and despite the blare of the television in the lounge, we were only too glad to rest ourselves before facing the next part of the journey. We asked the young waitress for tea and a sandwich. Deciding to order a second helping, we almost regretted it. She took ages to find more bread and ham, and as we impatiently waited, we calculated that it would take quite a few more hours before reaching our destination.

One of the Germans I met in Burgos entered the bar, looking as if he were about to collapse. With his head down and his rucksack thrown down beside him, he ordered a coke and drank it down with an earnestness that was frightening. I wondered if he would ever complete the camino considering how exhausted he looked after one day's walk. There was no sign of the rest of his group.

As Rolf and I left Hornillos del Camino we found ourselves on a track that was rather barren although occasionally there were some fields of wheat to be seen between patches of sunburnt land. The sun continued to beat down on us unmercifully as we trudged our way. Still, despite the heat, we felt in great spirit, sustained as we were by the tea and sandwiches.

After about four kilometres, we noticed a sign at a fork in the track indicating a refugio 200 metres to the left at a place called Sambol. What really prompted us to stop for a rest was the sign, which mentioned a pool and a bar as part of the refugio.

What we saw eventually was a small almost eastern-style 'mosque' at the side of the track. Just as I was about to enter the refugio I heard a voice say, "David, what kept you? You must have been dawdling!"

There, hanging over the parapet was Kristen, smiling at the look of incredulity written all over my face. I could not believe my eyes. She was dressed in the same baggy trousers and simple top, with her shoulder-length hair just covering her neck.

She should have been back in Madrid by now, and I had presumed that our paths would never have crossed again. But there she was, smiling and enjoying the moment of meeting once more. Apparently, she had walked for less than ten days when she began to have trouble with her feet. Disappointed, she returned to Madrid and took to her bed to rest. As she lay there, she could not get the idea of failing to complete the camino out of her head. She had decided to resign from her teaching job and returned to where she had abandoned the camino. Now she was looking forward to completing the camino and experiencing again the life of the pilgrim route.

We chatted for some time, exchanging stories of the camino and adventures along the way. I thanked her for the money returned, and it was then that Naomi, her friend, told me how Kristen had left Pamplona that morning and gone for an hour and a half along the route until she remembered that she had forgotten to leave the money. Without thinking, she had turned back and walked five kilometres to Pamplona to post the money on the notice board of the refugio where I had found it on my arrival there. What a girl! I decided not to reveal to Kristen how disappointed I had been initially when I found the money on the noticeboard without the note. My initial judgement of her that morning in Pamplona as someone who was dependable had been confirmed.

There was quite a crowd of young people gathered there in Sambol. Nick, the young lad I had met at the petrol station in Nájera, had re-joined his group, which included his girl friend, Naomi, a fellow Australian. He seemed in great form and his medical problems seemed to be a thing of the past. Having lost an enormous amount of weight, he looked really healthy.

A young English student called James offered me an ice cream and, while Rolf decided to swim in what was no more that a large trough, we chatted about the camino. He seemed particularly interested in the monasteries and churches along the camino, and prior to beginning the pilgrimage had obviously studied quite a bit about monasticism. He came across as very intense and somewhat self-conscious, but this did not prevent him from initiating the conversation in the first place.

The young people pressed me to stay with them, seeing as the heat of the day was so unbearable for walking. They intended remaining in the shade of this oasis until the sun went down and then they would continue the journey. I was momentarily tempted to suggest this to Rolf, but I knew that he would be keener to finish the walk in one stretch, and I felt a certain loyalty to him because he had been a companion so far. There was no way that we were going to be separated at this stage. I certainly would have enjoyed chatting some more with Kristen but decided to join Rolf, who was preparing to depart. So, with a promise to meet them in Castrojeriz, we set off on the journey while the sun beat down relentlessly. As it turned out, the young people must have stayed at Sambol, for I never saw them at Castrojeriz that evening.

We continued climbing for a brief period, and then continued along the plateau through rather barren land that had unusual mounds of stones known as 'majanos', according to my guidebook, the significance of which escaped me. Then we began descending towards Hontanas, which derives its name from the Latin 'fontanos' meaning a fountain. The town appeared almost by magic as we came to the edge of the plateau.

Hontanas, a name that is derived from the Latin 'fontanos', meaning fountain.

On entering the town, we were greeted by an odd-looking character, who invited us into his refugio. The place appeared very dilapidated, and when we crossed the threshold and our eyes became accustomed to the dark interior, we could see that the inside was even worse. There were some tables covered with oilcloth with a faded pattern and a few chairs around each table. The bar counter served as a display for various types of tapas. At the back of the counter were rows of dusty bottles. And pinned to the walls were postcards that appreciative guests had apparently sent him from their home countries.

The host was a small man, whose jerky and excitable movements made me feel rather disinclined to stay. There was also something pathetic about his attempts to offer us a sample of tapas to eat. Reluctantly, I agreed to take a slice of tortilla and some iced water. Rolf took the same. As we ate, he began demonstrating how wine should be drunk in Spain. He held the traditional wine container, which consisted of a leather satchel with a narrow spout at the end. He threw his head backward and with the bottle held at arm's length, he began pouring the wine through a narrow spout into his mouth! The narrow trickle of wine he then moved up to his forehead; the wine trickled down his nose and into his mouth. He was better than any circus performer. But there was something sad about the performance and I became uneasy about staying there for long. So we paid for the snack and continued our journey.

We passed the official refugio a hundred yards down the road. A municipal swimming pool nearby looked particularly tempting in the unrelenting sun, but time was passing and we were still nine kilometres away from our destination. The walk skirted the surrounding sunburnt hills that were almost devoid of any vegetation. We followed in single file the track that looked down on the road below. On the other side of the road, vines were neatly laid out in parallel rows and an occasional farmhouse broke the monotony of the red earthen soil.

I was beginning to feel very tired and thirsty. Moreover, my feet were beginning to experience a burning sensation that was quite painful, making it very difficult to walk. By this time, the track was rapidly descending towards the road and before long, we had reached a place where we stopped for a short rest and a shared an orange. Our water was almost gone by this time, having had recourse to the water bottle quite frequently since Hontanas.

We stopped beside San Anton, the ruins of a fourteenth-century monastery and hospital, and I could see the spire of the church of Castrojeriz in the distance; above the town stood a ruined castle. We breathed a sigh of relief that the longest stage of the camino was almost finished.

We passed the collegiate church and continued to climb up the steep road that led to the town. On and on we trudged, wishing to see some sign that would indicate the refugio but it seemed that we would never reach it. Eventually, we passed another church and came to the refugio just as we were about to give up hope. It was almost at the extreme end of the village, the only consolation being that our route the next day would take us immediately out of the town without having to walk its entire length again.

We were given a marvellous welcome by Anna, a warm and friendly woman from New Mexico. She felt for us who were obviously suffering from the long walk and suggested that we dissolve salt in water and bathe our feet in it. She was ready to get the salt and basins but was then inundated with other pilgrims who seemed to have appeared from nowhere. So we had to make do with the usual shower and trust that the feet would recover without the salt.

As it turned out, the other pilgrims were a group of cyclists on the camino. Anna had to explain that preference is given to foot pilgrims; they would have to wait until 7.00pm, after which time foot and bicycle pilgrims have equal rights. She explained the rule most sympathetically, but it was easy to see that she empathised with the tired cyclists just as she had felt for us.

Although the hostel was a higgledy-piggledy warren of floors and rooms, it was very suitable for pilgrims in that there was a decent amount of space between the bunks and everything was immaculately clean. I found a bed near the window overlooking the surrounding countryside and began my rituals of washing body and clothes. It was a relief, at last, to have arrived at our destination. Never did a bed look more inviting after the struggles of walking almost 40km.

Resting on the bed afterwards brought a sense of real peace after the ordeal of the long walk. As I lay there, I reflected on the people I had met along the way. Neither the exhausted German nor any of his group was anywhere to be seen. Kristen, Nick, Naomi and James would only be thinking at this stage of setting out for Castrojeriz, having enjoyed the cool of the quaint refugio. And the strange man of Hontanas was probably waiting to trap more unsuspecting pilgrims into his dark den where he could perform his trick. They came before my eyes as I lay slipping between consciousness and sleep.

Later in the afternoon as I sat in the shade of the unrelenting sun writing my journal, I was joined by the German woman whom I first saw with her son trying to run up the Atapuerca mountain outside St Juan de Ortega. Edith was nursing badly sunburnt legs that had been

The twelfth-century Church of Santa Maria del Manzano at the entry into the town of Castrojeriz.

exposed to the terrible heat for the entire walk. She was wearing the skimpiest of shorts, and the backs of her two legs were almost raw. She was joined by her son Sabastian who assisted her in smoothing cream on the affected parts. I could hardly bear to look at her face, contorted with sheer agony, despite the best efforts of Sabastian to be as gentle as he could. It was difficult to believe that she would have walked for so long under the sun without some protection.

In contrast, I had been covered from head to foot to avoid any such danger of sunburn. My cap has a big flap at the back to protect my neck, the shirt is long-sleeved and the trousers full length. And although it appeared rather incongruous to be wearing almost winter clothing in the heat, I was certainly not going to risk the danger of sunstroke. I wondered how Edith would sleep that night. It certainly would take her some days to recover from the sunburn.

That evening, Rolf and I dined in a lovely small restaurant near the refugio. The evening meal at the end of each stage of the journey is always special; it provides the pilgrim with the opportunity to share something of one's life story and to listen to the variety that characterises each one's personal journey. We found ourselves having two bottles of wine between us. As we came to the end of the meal, we were not too steady on our feet as we made our way to the refugio.

We had achieved a mighty feat that day and were ready for an early night in preparation for the next day's walk. We had been walking for 14 days and had covered over 300km. Tomorrow I would be at the start of the third week. There were still some 500km to go, but today it was understandable that we would experience a real sense of achievement after the long trek from Burgos to Castrojeriz. Sleep came quickly despite the surrounding noise of the happy pilgrims.

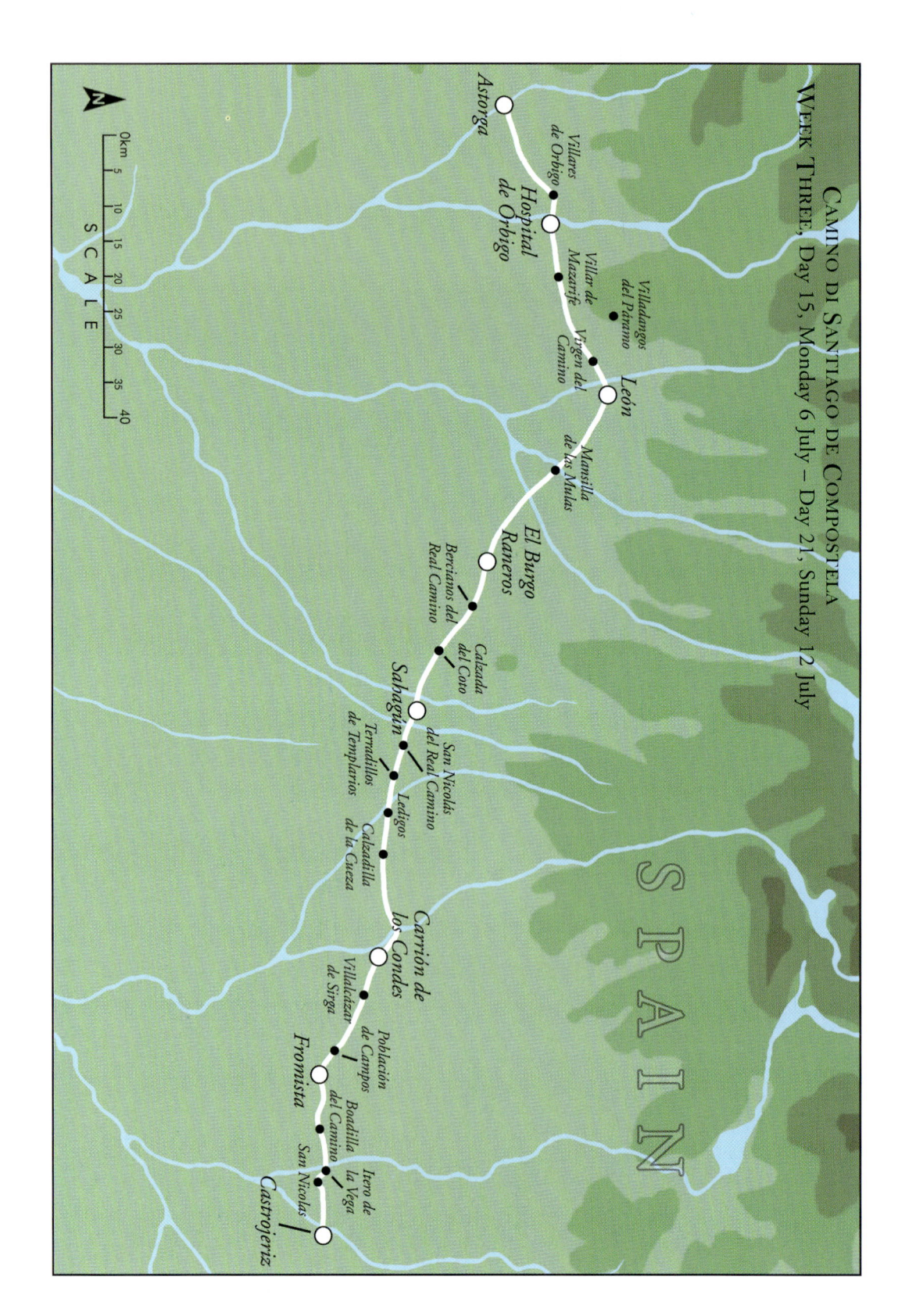

Camino di Santiago de Compostela
Week Three, Day 15, Monday 6 July – Day 21, Sunday 12 July

Week Three

Day Fifteen
Castrojeriz to Fromista
Monday 6 July 1998

The sound of Gregorian chant awoke me. As I lay on the bed in the darkness, the majestic voices of the monks chanting part of the Divine Office of the Church seemed to be coming from below. The recording of the chant was a novel and most suitable way to wake the pilgrims to a new stage in the camino. What an appropriate way to begin the day in a place where nearby the monks of San Anton in the fourteenth century would have probably chanted the same liturgical setting as I was hearing at that moment!

Breakfast was a lavish affair, and all provided gratis by Anna, the hospitalero. Apples, biscuits with butter and home-made raspberry jam and fresh coffee were freely available to all the pilgrims. What generosity she had displayed in providing such a spread when most refugios offer nothing more than kitchen facilities for pilgrims to make their own breakfast. I felt, therefore, obliged to leave a more generous contribution to defray the costs of running the refugio. The normal amount requested was in the region of €3 but in this case, a more generous contribution was in order. As I left, I felt better for having experienced the care and concern of someone who obviously considers the role of hospitalero more a vocation than a job.

I started walking very slowly, almost at a snail's pace, out of the village and across the road. Having reached a bridge, I turned around to look once more at Castrojeriz that had been so hospitable to me. The scene was breathtaking with the early morning sun, rather pale and indistinct, creeping from behind the hill overlooking the village and casting its rays on the outline of the ruined castle and the buildings at the highest point of the village. No postcard could do justice to the beauty of the scene; certainly my camera could not capture the beauty that made me stand for quite some time admiring it.

The route led over another bridge, which spanned the River Odrilla that was almost completely dried up. The track rose steeply up the Mostelares hill until reaching a plateau. I came across stone mounds and types of crosses, which appeared more like astrological rather than Christian symbols.

Rolf was well ahead and walking at a brisker pace. This provided me with the opportunity to become aware of the Lord's presence and to have my conversation with Him at the beginning of the day. The quietness that surrounded me brought an indescribable sense of peace and joy as I surveyed the cultivated plains that stretched for miles ahead of me. It was good to be alive in the beauty of the mild morning air and to have the strength and health to be able to walk the pilgrim path.

Just before the Puente de Itero bridge spanning the Pisuerga river lies the remains of the St Nicolas' Hermitage. I remembered that Lori, my Italian friend, had recommended that I visit this church that had been restored by the Italian Confraternity of St James under the direction of Professor Paolo G. Caucci von Saucken. So I decided to call into the refugio in order to greet my Italian colleagues. Having spent ten years in Italy, from 1980 to 1990, I have maintained a love of the Italian language and I never let an opportunity pass without at least attempting to have a conversation with a native speaker.

Pilgrims gather together to share stories, food and wine.

"Buon giorno a tutti quanti!" (Hi, everybody!), I exclaimed and was greeted with a similar response together with much laughter and surprise. The Italian volunteers there would not have had too many of their compatriots calling in on this mid-point refugio between Castrojeriz and Fromista. I had only met one Italian so far along the camino. I wondered why people would stop here rather than continue to Fromista. There were, however, quite a few Italian volunteers in the refugio; they seemed busy preparing for an invasion of pilgrims. Already there was a scattering of mainly German pilgrims who seemed ready to stop there for the day. I had arrived just in time for coffee, and I was delighted to see that they were preparing it the real Italian way. No sooner had I sat down and introduced myself than one of the staff shouted, *"C'é una lettera per Lei!"* (There's a letter here for you!)

I could not believe my ears. But sure enough, the volunteer handed me a letter that I immediately recognised as coming from Lori, my Italian friend. That was why she suggested that I call in at San Nicolas. As I opened the letter and read the message wishing me every blessing and expressing support in overcoming the pains and aches, I felt really moved at her thoughtful gesture. Tears were not far off, this time tears of gratitude for the wonder of friendship and the kindness of such a good friend.

For the rest of the camino, I kept the letter in my journal as a source of support and inspiration. Lori had done the walk two years previously. I felt very much in solidarity with her and with those Italians who had rested in this beautifully restored twelfth-century place of pilgrimage. The visit to San Nicolas was one of the highlights of the camino for it was there that the treasure of friendship was experienced in a moving and affirming way.

Crossing the impressive eleven-arched Romanesque bridge over the Pisuerga river, Rolf and I entered the province of Palencia, having left the province of Burgos as we crossed over.

On our journey towards Itero de la Vega, Rolf talked about his love of Italy and of the holidays that he had spent with his family walking in the Tuscan Hills. Like many a German, he had almost made Italy his second home and in so doing, had followed the example of Goethe, one among many literary figures who considered Italy a land of rich culture and history.

As we approached Boadilla del Camino, we stopped at a welcome fountain that provided us with refreshingly cool water where we could drink and replenish our flasks. Continuing into the village, we followed the yellow arrows, which seemed to lead to a restaurant. Passing the restaurant, we came back to the fountain and discovered to our annoyance that the owners of the restaurant had painted yellow arrows to ensure that pilgrims passed their establishment instead of heading directly for Fromista. I was furious with them for trying by subterfuge to lure the weary pilgrim into their establishment. It was a mean trick that backfired because personally, even were I hungry, I would have refused to succumb to such a marketing ploy. It took some moments before we could re-orientate ourselves on the proper track, turning right just at the church and in a westerly direction towards Fromista.

The track that led to Fromista ran parallel to the Canal de Castilla, an eighteenth-century construction that was still in perfect working order. Apparently, the canal serves not only to irrigate the area for the cultivation of corn but also to transport it to the various nearby villages and towns. The water is also used to run the mills that grind the corn. The word Fromista, according to some writers, comes from the Latin word 'frumentum' meaning wheat, which would make sense considering the fields of cereals surrounding us. Others, however, say that Fromista is a Visigoth proper name.

Walking along the canal allowed me to admire the engineering feat of bringing water through a series of pumps and sluice gates to all parts of the surrounding land, now covered with ripening wheat. What actually amazed me was the absence of any sign of vandalism or litter. At regular intervals there were locks that regulated the flow of water from one channel to an adjoining one and not one seemed to have been interfered with. And while comparisons are odious, I found myself thinking about the canals in Dublin and how frequently they can be, in some parts, littered with rubbish of every kind or indeed, vandalised.

The heat of the sun was, by this time, oppressively energy-sapping; the soles of my feet began to burn and ache. But just as I was about to stop for a rest, I came to the junction of the canal with the railway and the main road leading into the town.

The refugio was situated in a small square, and luckily, Rolf and I managed to get beds. Had we arrived 15 minutes later, there would have been no chance, for out of nowhere pilgrims began arriving at a great rate. My friends from Sambol arrived en masse and were disappointed to discover that the refugio was already full. The only alternative was to seek accommodation in a pensión nearby. There were, however, many pensións in the town because it was a place of historic interest, and before long, everyone had found a place to sleep.

It would be fair to say that the refugio in Fromista was the worst I had so far encountered. The water in the showers was cold and the welcome from the hospitalero was equally gelid. His main concerns were to check our passports, collect our money and warn us to be in our rooms before ten o'clock at night. After the long walk in the heat of the day, the pilgrims found his attitude very difficult to take and he almost succeeded in destroying the normal friendly spirit that exists among pilgrims on the camino. However, the pilgrim spirit can overcome even these obstacles and once we had dealt with the hospitalero's pecuniary concerns we escaped from the hostel into the warm sunshine.

The square was full of pilgrims, all intermingling and sharing stories about their journey. Kristen was there and we chatted for a while together with an older English guy, Adrian, who

The Canal de Castilla was built in the eighteenth century to transport cereals and irrigate the land.

had joined the Sambol group. He was carrying recording equipment with him to make a radio programme for the BBC. He had already interviewed quite a variety of personalities on the camino and seemed confident that the end result would provide listeners with a good insight into the effects of pilgrimage on the lives of those who venture out in the spirit of trust. The experience of listening to others telling their stories caused him to personally challenge his own motivations and afforded him the opportunity to examine his own life path. A former teacher and group facilitator, he seemed to be at a crossroads in his life and was taking the time of the pilgrimage to discern what he really wanted to do professionally in the future.

Adrian talked quite a bit about his personal life, although it would not be appropriate to disclose his thoughts, as many details shared among pilgrims are for the camino only and are given in confidence. This agreement of confidentiality is not demanded explicitly by pilgrims, rather something that develops along the route.

Fromista is famous for the Romanesque Church of San Martín. The guidebook provided me with very precise architectural details, which I was able to see for myself on this occasion. The exterior was particularly impressive, with its circular stair turrets on the west side and the octagonal dome rising from the transepts. There was also a series of 315 carved corbels, each one different, running around the eaves. There were human figures, animals, flowers and monsters all carved with amazing skill. The typical Romanesque windows and multi-lobed but simple doorways went together to create a harmony in stone that could not be easily equalled. Moreover, the bright sun beaming directly on the red stone cast vivid shadows to highlight the windows and entrances to the church.

San Martín Church at Fromista is one of the finest examples of Romanesque architecture.

Detail of one of the carved capitals in the Romanesque Church of San Martín at Fromista.

The interior was especially notable for the carved capitals that I tried in vain to photograph. My simple camera could not capture the play of light and shadow on the beautiful carvings. The rest of the interior consisted of a three-aisled nave leading to a triple apse and was beautiful in its simplicity and lack of ornamentation. The only surviving part of its original decoration was a thirteenth-century Christ but the focus on this one figure highlighted the centrality of the person of Christ in the entire edifice.

Just after the shops opened in the afternoon and during the time when most in Fromista were indoors sheltering from the cruel sun, I went to the local supermarket to buy rations of fruit for the next day. No sooner had I entered the shop than I was joined by a pilgrim dressed in a full-length white habit gathered around the waist with a large pair of rosary beads and on his feet a simple pair of leather sandals. He looked the part; he was tall, and with his neat beard, white habit and the sandals of a mendicant friar, he could have stepped out of the Middle Ages. Never had I come across such a sight, except perhaps the Jesus figure of San Juan. But this man seemed most normal despite the similar apparel.

I later met him with the rest of the Sambol group in the square near the refugio. We were sitting outside a bar under the shade of umbrellas, drinking cool beer. There he was sitting with a group of young people around him. Apparently, he had set off from Austria and had walked all the way to Fromista in the habit and sandals. He travelled extremely lightly and carried no money with him, preferring to depend on the charity of the people of the towns through which he passed. All he had by way of support was a letter from his bishop encouraging people to assist him on his spiritual journey. So, he never paid in the refugios and relied on pilgrims and locals to provide for his nourishment.

Normally, I would consider someone who undertakes such an extreme form of pilgrimage rather strange and eccentric. But this young man came across as most balanced, ready to discuss with our group the motivation for his decision to walk to Santiago as a penniless pilgrim. He was preparing for ordination and had decided to take some time out to discern what was God's will for him. He hoped that the time spent walking would provide him with the space to come to a well-thought out choice. The audience that he held spellbound seemed to resonate with his search for meaning in life. Because he seemed to speak most of the European languages, he was able to clarify points to the various nationalities whose Spanish may have been rather rudimentary. When I went to examine the pilgrims' book in the refugio later, I noted too that he was a gifted artist. He had designed a beautiful logo for himself, consisting of a foot and scallop shell interconnected. Obviously, this was an exceptionally gifted young man; I felt sure that he would discover the will of God for his life before reaching Santiago.

That evening Rolf and I went searching for a place to eat. By chance, we happened upon a group of ladies chatting outside what appeared to be a normal house but which had a sign beside the main door indicating that it was a restaurant. We introduced ourselves, and the plump woman in the centre of the group assured us that she was serving a meal at seven. It was 6.30, so we went across the street to what turned out to be a cheese museum that also served beer and spirits. The museum was closed but the bar was open. The beer tasted good and cost just slightly over half of what we had been paying in the bar opposite the refugio during our conversations with the Austrian monk.

Rolf told me about his first day of pilgrimage; how he almost got lost in the mist having left St Jean-Pied-de-Port and climbed towards Bianorre. He shared very openly his feelings about that stage of the pilgrimage, and I felt privileged at his honesty and openness. The more I walked the more I realised how sacred it is to walk with a pilgrim. Pilgrims are prepared to reveal so many sides to their character that they prefer to hide under normal circumstances. The pilgrim path encourages openness and honesty; many respond to this invitation to self-revelation. This challenge was particularly difficult for me as I am inclined to reveal only the good bits and hide the more difficult aspects of my life. But I was learning.

The evening meal was served in the restaurant part of the family home, and we were the only clients at that early hour. We were served a fish soup followed by steak and chips. Dessert followed, and all the courses were accompanied by wine. For this abundant repast we were charged €8, the cost of four beers at the overpriced bar opposite the refugio. We were amazed that the woman could provide this most wholesome food at an unbelievable price. Fromista redeemed itself after the initial negative experience of the inexperienced hospitalero.

The night proved very challenging. Because of the heat of the day, I decided to sleep without any covering. As the night wore on, however, the temperature dropped, until I found myself getting cold and unable to sleep. Again, my sleeping bag proved to be too heavy, so I had to choose between catching a cold and shivering or sweltering under the weight of duck down.

More irritating was the level of snoring that erupted soon after I began to sleep. The sheer volume was incredible. It came from a Brazilian pilgrim who was sleeping on the top bunk across the room from me. He seemed to inhale a massive volume of air, hold it for what seemed an interminable length of time only to then expel the air in a rush that created a loud sigh. The volume seemed to be rising continually; before long he had awoken almost everyone in the room. People began grumbling, until some uninhibited Spaniard shouted at the top of his voice and thumped the bed where our poor unfortunate Brazilian was sleeping. He awoke with a start and seemed very upset at the rumpus he had caused. I later discovered that he was even more upset than he appeared to be at that moment. Prior to embarking on the pilgrimage, he had undergone some operation on his nasal passage to rectify his abnormal snoring. Obviously it had not worked.

Despite the difficulty of sleeping, I found myself eventually slipping into a deep slumber after a day full of adventure. And the letter from Lori was, without doubt, the highlight of the day. May the Lord bless her for the gift of her friendship and her kindness over the years.

Day Sixteen
Fromista to Carrión de los Condes
Tuesday 7 July 1998

I was disappointed that Rolf left without me in the morning. It was strange, as for most of the walk we had been together and I wondered what had occurred for him to begin walking without a greeting at least. From my point of view, nothing untoward had happened between us, and I still remembered the meal we had shared the previous evening and how each of us had talked so honestly and personally about things that mattered in our lives. Not wanting to presume that anything serious had come between us, I banished any doubts and set off on my own to Carrión de los Condes.

On reaching the main junction leading out of Fromista, I was uncertain about which route to take. I had forgotten to check my way on the previous night, something I had done faithfully since Naverette. Luckily, Emmanuel and James came along to point me in the right direction. I joined them on the C980. About three kilometres along, we entered the small village of Población de Campos, a farming community. We continued through the village along the street called 'Calle Francesa', which indicated that this route was part of the original 'French Route' from Le Puy en Velay.

Crossing the road again we walked along the River Ucieza and close to neighbouring fields. I marvelled at the ease with which Emmanuel and James seemed to glide along the route almost effortlessly. In order to keep up with them I had to exert myself quite a bit. James especially seemed like a thoroughbred and in the course of the journey, he revealed that he would often make a detour of anything up to ten kilometres to visit a church or monastery. It was taking me all my time to follow the route as laid down in my *Practical Guide for Pilgrims,* and I had avoided any detours along the way. That said, there had been occasions when I would dearly have loved to have visited nearby shrines and places of interest. But I had to remind myself that my eyes were on Santiago, and I did not want to get sidetracked from this main objective.

While we walked alongside the fields, we could see various hermitages to our right and left. What struck me most forcefully was the frequency of such structures along the route. There seemed to be one or two along almost each stage. They would have been built at a time when faith drew people to abandon the 'world' and devote themselves to a life of total dedication to the Lord.

As I looked at these buildings, I became increasingly aware of the Lord's call to devote my own life to prayer and to deepen my relationship with the Lord through prayer. Those who became hermits answered this call with singular passion. I felt the challenge to do likewise, albeit as someone who would not withdraw from the 'world' but would live 'in the world' as a Brother. I was only too aware that the call to monastic living could be for some people a 'fuga mundi', a flight from the world, but I knew that no-one could live this type of life for long if they did not have a real vocation for it.

We eventually arrived at Villalcazar de Sirga or Villasirga for short. The main feature of this village is the Romanesque Church of Santa Maria la Blanca. This was built by the Templars around the thirteenth century and was still used as a place of worship under the direction of white-robed monks.

I found myself strangely uninterested in staying inside the church. The famous stone statue of the 'Virgen Blanca' (White Virgin) left me unmoved. Maybe the decapitated head of the infant in her arms took away from the overall effect. The Virgin is supposed to have cured pilgrims who were returning from Santiago still uncured. I simply did not find myself attracted to the church, and although I found myself praying as I walked, here in the church I felt as if I were in a museum.

The graceful pillars in the Church of Santa María la Blanca at Villalcazar de Sirga.

The café opposite was more inviting, and seeing many pilgrims beginning to gather inside made me want to see new faces and meet with old friends.

Francesco was there with his four friends, holding court. He shouted over to me, *"Buenas!"* – the shortened version of 'buenos dias!' He introduced me to one of the walkers who was French but living in Germany, having married a German. Dominique was a woman in her mid-forties and judging from her physique, she was well used to hiking. Athletic in build, she exuded health, strength and athleticism. While very pleasant and friendly, I noted an inner steeliness and determination that could face any difficulty. She would be well able to take care of herself, I thought.

There was a group of elderly Germans, who, I learned, were travelling along the pilgrim route by car. Each day, three of them would walk all or some of the stage while the other drove and then they would alternate drivers on subsequent days. They seemed to be thriving on the experience, and I found myself admiring the initiative of these retired men and women who had ventured out on a very different kind of holiday.

James went off with one of the robed religious to get his passport stamped; Emmanuel had decided to rest a while in Villasirga. Consequently, I took off alone along the C980, so that I would be in Carrión by the middle of the day. Walking along the roadway, I was passed by a group of cyclists who shouted a greeting or so I thought. It was only as I reflected on the words and gestures that I realised that they were telling me to walk on the other side of the road. I had forgotten that the traffic system is the opposite of what it is in Ireland, so I crossed over to the safer side.

Walking along the road, I felt so strong and fit that I considered skipping Carrión and continuing on for a few hours. However, prudence won the day, reminding me of the sound advice of pilgrims who had preceded me that it was unwise ever to go beyond the advice of Lozano, author of *A Practical Guide for Pilgrims.*

The first building of historical interest in Carrión is the thirteenth-century Convent of Santa Clara, which is supposed to have sheltered St Francis of Assisi during his pilgrimage to Santiago. I noted its position and resolved to pay it a visit later on.

A little further on there was the church of Santa Maria del Camino, which stands beside the walls of the town. And further again along this road was the refugio apparently run by the priest of the parish of Santa Maria del Camino.

On entering the refugio, I was met by Phil, the American cartoonist, who was sitting in a low chair and drinking a can of beer. He had a bucket of cold water before him with more beers immersed in the cold water. He held out a cold beer, offering me one, and invited me to join him. What a considerate thing to do. Although I had not had much contact with Phil up to this point, I was touched by his kind gesture.

Having spent some time with Phil and having recovered from the fatigue that crept up on me, I approached the hospitalero, a thin, sharp-featured woman who appeared tense and anxious as she rushed around more or less aimlessly. Once she stamped my pilgrim passport, she brought me upstairs to the dormitory, which was immaculately clean. The beds were perfectly laid out in ordered lines; the floor sparkled as if it had been polished that morning. Nothing was out of place. As she showed me to a bed, she pointed out to another pilgrim that she could not place her shoes on the windowsills. No wonder the place was perfect. She insisted that everything be kept tidy right from the beginning. For the weary pilgrim, this was a real nuisance, but I admired her dedication and devotion to keeping such a neat and orderly refugio. After a wash, a snack and a sleep, I went to visit some of the sites of Carrión.

In the eleventh century, Count Gómez Díaz built a monastery over the relics of the martyr San Zoilo. This was joined to the Cluny monastic movement through the monastery of Sahagún, 40km away and on which it depended. The monastery was famous for its cloister, and I was keen to see this Renaissance piece of art.

On crossing the bridge over the River Carrión, I saw the monastery to the left. A notice indicated that it was under restoration. Nearby, however, was the Hotel Zoilo, which, I presumed, could provide access to the cloister. As I neared the entrance, there were groups of soldiers, troop carriers and a number of tanks. A notice indicated that a peace conference was taking place. Obviously, peace needed to be defended with tanks parked strategically at the entrance, with soldiers everywhere. I entered the hotel and made directly for the conference hall that looked out on the cloister. Just as I was about to enter the hall, a hand held my elbow, and one of the managers told me that access was restricted for the duration of the meeting.

As I was in the hotel, a five-star establishment, I decided to have a drink. Something mischievous in me wanted to see how a pilgrim in simple garb would be treated by such a high-class hotel. In fact, the staff could not have been more gracious; to my surprise, I found that the cost of a coke was cheaper than what I paid in the bar opposite the refugio in Fromista!

Retracing my steps, I came to the remains of the Church of Santiago, which stands in one of the streets along the pilgrim route. Apparently the original church had been pillaged and burned by the Napoleonic troops in the early nineteenth century. The portal shows Christ on his throne holding what appeared to be the bible and a sceptre, surrounded by the apostles and the symbolic representations of the evangelists.

The medieval bridge over Rio Carrión leads to the Benedictine monastery of San Zoilo.

Teresa, the Spanish girl who had been my guide in Estella, was standing, lost in wonder and admiration before this glorious work of art. She had a notebook in her hand, in which she would periodically note some idea or thought that came to her during her private meditation. Eventually, she noticed me standing beside her; she smiled and talked about how much she adored the portal of the Santiago Church. I found myself really in awe of her and her single-minded approach to the pilgrimage. She seemed totally engrossed in the camino and more inclined to journey on her own rather than in a group. Had I had better Spanish I would love to have been able to discuss her pilgrim journey, but this was not to be. We saluted each other and went our own ways.

Eventually I met Rolf at the refugio. He told me that he was going home. Apparently, his wife had not been well, and for the last few days, he said, he had been contemplating abandoning the walk to be with her. In fact, he had already discussed things with Bernard in Burgos and now felt that it was time to return to Germany. I felt sorry for him because I knew how precious these days had been for him and how much he was entering into the spirit of the pilgrimage. At the same time, he was at peace, knowing what his priorities were. His wife came first and his daughter Ciara.

Walking the pilgrim route helps clarify our priorities. How, often in the day-to-day routine of life, we can allow many things to come before the people that we hold dear. The urgent can take over from the important; we can find ourselves devoting our time and energies to what is not essential. How many times does the husband find himself working himself to the bone for his family until he realises that he has neglected to communicate both with his wife and children? So he achieves success in business to the detriment of family life. Or how often a wife can invest all her energies in bringing up the children, in arranging for their education

Detail of Santiago Church at Carrión de los Condes showing 'Christ in Majesty'.

and social development, in the process forgetting that her priority should be deepening her loving relationship with her husband, thus creating a caring home. How easy it is for me, as a religious, to get lost in the striving for success in teaching and being busy about many things to the neglect of my relationship with the Lord and with my Brothers.

Rolf was very calm about his decision and, although disappointed that he was interrupting the camino walk, he was determined to return one day to complete it. I felt hugely in admiration of his inner freedom to leave what had meant so much to him without becoming too downhearted. We walked around the town and decided that we would dine together that night. I thought that the evening meal could provide us with the chance to say our goodbyes.

As we approached Santa Chiara, I met Nick and Naomi who invited me to dine with all the pilgrims in a local restaurant. I felt I could not refuse them again, having left them for Rolf at Sambol. So I agreed that Rolf and myself would join them. No sooner had I left them than I met Frieda; in the course of the conversation I mentioned to her the evening arrangements. I saw Nick and Naomi frantically gesticulating to me not to invite her. Obviously, she had been her awkward self with them too, and they had no wish to spend an evening with her. However, the damage was done: Frieda had enthusiastically 'accepted' the invitation.

When I told Rolf about the change in arrangements, I realised that I had made the wrong decision in agreeing to join the larger group. He did not express any disappointment with the change in plans but I knew that mingling in the large group could not compare with a more personal tête à tête where he might want to discuss his family situation in more detail. I felt torn by the decision I had made. On the one hand, I did not want to refuse the friendship of those young people with whom I would spend the rest of the camino; yet here I was on the verge of separating from Rolf, my companion of over two weeks. Mingling with a big crowd simply did not seem that appropriate for the occasion of his departure.

In fact, the evening meal turned out to be a disaster. I found myself sitting opposite Frieda, together with Francesco and Dominique, his French-German companion. Rolf sat with the German contingent that had miraculously reached Carrión. Nick, Naomi, Kristen and James were on a third table immediately behind me. So, having agreed to eat with the young people, I found myself with people with whom I had really nothing in common.

They say that good decisions lead to positive outcomes. Here it was evident that I had made a *bad* decision, and all because I had not been firm enough in the first place. I had allowed the fear of disappointing people with whom I would meet over the next few weeks to prevent me from being faithful to a friend who had supported me along the way. A sense of regret and disappointment dominated me for the evening. Self-criticism overwhelmed me, and although I tried to carry on a normal conversation with my table companions, I felt somewhat upset.

After the meal, the entire group packed into a crowded café to watch some of the France-Croatia (I think these were the teams) World Cup match. But my heart was heavy, and I decided to return to the refugio alone. This was the first time on the camino that I felt lonely and disappointed with myself.

There was a message for me when I returned to the refugio. It was from Tim, one of the members of my community in Dublin, who had telephoned earlier on in the evening. Sabastian, the young German and son of Edith, had taken the call, telling Tim that I was not to be found. However, the fact that Tim had been in contact raised my spirits. I would return the call tomorrow when I arrived in Sahagún.

That night I found myself beside the snoring Brazilian and hardly slept a wink. Thoughts of Rolf's departure were running through my mind, as were thoughts of how stupid I had been to allow myself to deviate from my agreement to have dinner with Rolf on his last evening of the camino. I would miss Rolf just as I missed Bernard.

I spent some time praying for my departing companions. The Italians have a phrase, *'Partire è un po' morire'*, which means 'Leaving is a little like dying'. And so I entrusted these fine companions to the Lord, asking him to protect them and their families. And my prayer was that eventually I would begin to make better decisions myself instead of being swayed by the expectations of others. One day I would get sense!

I felt in a sense that I was beginning the camino again. For up to this point I had not walked for any length of time with anyone else other than Rolf, Bernard and Liam. Where Liam was then I could not say, but I hoped that he had succeeded in healing his leg and would eventually meet me in Santiago. Bernard, too, could possibly make it to Santiago, though I felt that this was a remoter possibility. Time would tell.

Day Seventeen
Carrión de los Condes to Sahagún
Wednesday 8 July 1998

The stage from Carrión to Sahagún is 37.6km, the second longest stage in the camino. An early start would give me the chance to complete most of the walk before the heat of the early afternoon. However, I reckoned that it would take about ten hours to arrive at Sahagún. The guidebook said that the stage could be divided into two parts, but that would have entailed adding another day to my 31-day schedule. I was not keen on this because I wanted to keep to the plan of a stage a day so that I would have the option of walking to Finisterre at the end of the Santiago walk.

I left the town along the N120 and crossed the bridge, passing the monastery of San Zoilo. Being dark, it was therefore difficult to make out any yellow arrows. The Guardia Civil (Spanish Police) passed by in their jeep and slowed down to see who was walking along the roads at such an early hour. I inquired from them the direction to the camino; they pointed ahead, saying something about left and right, but it was impossible for me to understand what they were saying.

As I was about to stop and examine the map once more, Phil the American joined me along the road and seemed confident of the route. As we walked together he shared how he had begun his pilgrimage in Le Puy en Velay about six weeks or so previously. For the first week, he had suffered a lot from blisters but had persisted despite the pain and discomfort until his feet were almost immune to them now. Certainly, he walked very quickly; it became quite difficult to keep pace with him.

At the ruins of the Abbey of Santa Maria de Benevivere, an eleventh-century Augustinian monastery, we turned off the asphalt path and onto what are the remains of the 'Via Traiana' that once went from Bordeaux to Astorga and which now stretched for more than 13km from Sahagún to Calzadilla de la Cueza. At this stage, I urged Phil to go ahead at his own pace; I felt he was being held back by my more leisurely approach, and so he left me with best wishes for this long stage to Sahagún.

Alone, I reflected on my leave-taking with Rolf that morning. He was obviously sad to be finishing his camino but assured me that he would return some day to complete it. He was also looking forward to seeing his beloved wife and daughter, which anticipation lessened his disappointment at leaving Spain. He could not have been more supportive to my continuing the camino, and I felt his encouragement as he waved to me shouting, *"Ultreya!"* as I took my leave that morning. I would miss him greatly.

As I walked along the pathway that was bordered by farmland, I began to feel extremely tired and almost dopey. Whether the lassitude came from the lack of sleep or from the fact that I had taken two Feldene during the night to offset inflammation, all I knew was that I could not continue walking. A strong sense of powerlessness rendered me incapable of literally putting one foot in front of the other. I could not understand what was happening to me but I knew I had to stop. I sat down on a stone and decided to take a rest for a while. But even this did not seem the appropriate solution, and I had to find a place on the grass borders of the track to lie down to get a real break. As I lay down, a feeling of exhaustion came over me; I wondered would I be able to walk for much longer that day.

I closed my eyes and allowed myself to drift into a state of semi-consciousness. The sounds of birds could be clearly heard around me as well the distant drone of some tractor or farm machinery. But it felt as if I was falling into a pool of unconsciousness where I could remain for the rest of the day. I made no effort to resist these feelings, simply allowing myself be enveloped in this not unpleasant torpor. I felt my chest rising and falling as I inhaled and exhaled the fresh morning air.

Perhaps only a quarter of an hour elapsed, during which time I heard some pilgrims passing without stopping. As I opened my eyes, I could feel myself regaining energy; the sense of helplessness seemed to have dissolved as quickly as it had appeared in the first place. However, I remained lying for some time as I watched the sky becoming brighter with the rising of the morning sun. Only when I began to feel impatient to continue along the camino did I get up and begin to walk very slowly along the old Roman road.

If anyone had seen me at that stage, they would have said that I was walking as if in a daze. But I was determined to take things very slowly and to avoid rushing. Rushing would only lead to a general collapse.

The words of a Jesuit, Tim Hamilton, came to me at that stage. He had been working with a group of us a few years before in planning for the future of the Christian Brothers' Province in Ireland. We had an enormous amount of work to get through in a very short amount of time and were beginning to feel rather anxious that our progress was alarmingly slow. He warned, "We have no time to lose, gentlemen, so let us go very slowly!"

I had already seen pilgrims rushing along the camino, invariably overtaking them along the route when they had to rest after exhausting themselves. So I knew that I would only make Sahagún if I took things gently. Rushing would be counter-productive.

Eventually I reached Calzadilla de la Cueza and entered a bar at the edge of the hamlet. Francesco and Dominique were having their breakfast, and they beckoned me to join them. It was tempting to simply buy mineral water and continue walking towards Ledigos, but I resisted that temptation and forced myself to rest a while and chat to the couple; or rather listen to Francesco who seemed to be suffering from what psychologists call pressure of speech. He talked without taking a breath, more by way of a monologue than any real conversation. However, at that stage I simply glad to sit and listen without having to make any effort to talk.

When the drone of Francesco's voice began to irritate me it was time to take my leave and continue along the motorway past Ledigos, which seemed to have nothing of real interest that would merit a stop.

At Terradillos de Templarios, the green patch of grass just at the entrance to the village was a tempting place to rest. Already, a group of cyclists had made it their resting place. I sat on the grass enjoying the softness of the earth beneath and the shade of the trees nearby. Again, I lay down and relaxed after having already walked 27km since Carrión. The gentle breeze cooled my weary feet, which I had liberated from my heavy boots and thick woollen socks. Eventually I sat up and began talking to the Spanish cyclists.

The leader of the group spoke English and was very friendly, introducing himself and his group and showing genuine interest in where I was coming from. The group were cycling to Santiago and had begun in Roncesvalles five days previously and were hoping to finish the route within another few days. They came across as a congenial bunch of people, and I regretted that I would not be meeting them after Sahagún. Before leaving, they offered me some sweets, which out of politeness I took. Sweets seem only to increase my thirst and generally I avoid them at all costs. But their offering symbolised a simple gesture of friendship between pilgrims along the way. In accepting, I was entering into the spirit of communion that becomes so real at times as people walk together.

Just as I was leaving Terradillos de Templarios, Dominique and Francesco arrived, and

The church in Ledigos is dedicated to St James and houses a statue of the saint as a pilgrim.

with a wave, I quickened my pace. I needed space and quiet for a while for the next sections of the walk. Francesco could only be taken in small doses. Much of the journey went through cornfield after cornfield, as I passed through Moratinos and on towards San Nicolas del Real-Camino.

As I entered San Nicolas del Real-Camino, it seemed as if all the men in the village had come out to view a pilgrim passing. They were seated near the Church of San Nicolas, where, I'd hazard a guess, they spent much of the day passing the time. I wondered where their wives were, and almost immediately knew that they would have been indoors preparing the lunch or doing household chores. It was obvious that the 'division of labour' was still very much in evidence in that rural society.

San Nicolas, after whom the village is named, is the patron saint of pilgrims and travellers. So, as I passed the church I prayed for Rolf and Bernard and Liam, that each would be protected in their separate journeys.

The nearer I got to Sahagún, the more my feet hurt. That burning sensation had returned and, although I had stopped almost religiously every two hours or so to rest my feet, walking was becoming increasingly difficult. On examination, I discovered that a small blister had appeared at the side of my big toe. This was the first blister I had got in almost 400km, and although it was not too preoccupying, it would need careful attention to avoid any form of infection.

The route crossed the N120 and continued over a recently constructed cement bridge that spanned another motorway. I stopped once more to eat an orange and rest my burning feet. The journey was almost finished and my feet were protesting that I had walked too far.

Sahagún could be seen in the distance; immediately below me was the Ermita de la Virgin – a shrine to Our Lady – in a park area with copses of poplars scattered around. Walking

Outside Sahagún, a stone marks the region of Palencia and points the way to Sahagún itself.

through the park, I discovered I was lost. There wasn't an arrow anywhere, and it took a false turn before I found the way ahead. This lack of signage increased my frustration, making me more impatient to get to the refugio.

Along the path, a couple were picnicking on the banks of the Rio Valderaduey. They offered me something to eat but I declined, being anxious to care for my blistered feet as soon as possible. No sooner had I left them than I regretted not having accepted their gesture of hospitality. Who knows what I might have gained from such a meeting with the local people of Sahagún. The pilgrim route is a school – and I was often a slow learner.

The refugio in Sahagún is situated in the recently restored Church of La Trinidad. It is also the Centre for Studies into the Pilgrims' Route to Santiago. This is where Millán Bravo Lozano had worked on his pilgrim guide, first published in 1993. This same guidebook, which I had hanging in a plastic pouch around my neck since St Jean-Pied-de-Port, had brought me to Sahagún and had provided me with all the historical information that went to make my journey so rich and interesting. I would love to have met the author in person, but such a meeting would hardly have been possible on that Wednesday afternoon.

The facilities at the refugio were all that one could hope for. The large dormitory was divided into sections for greater privacy, and the beds could not have been more comfortable. The shower and cooking facilities were simple but modern, providing for every need. It was a real place of welcome and rest after the long walk from Carrión.

I treated the blister with the old needle and thread technique that my Italian friends had taught me. It consists of passing a needle through the blister to allow the liquid to escape and leaving the thread to hang on either side of the punctured blister. Cutting the thread on either side of the blister and removing the needle, disinfectant is liberally applied to the thread, which absorbs it into the blister. A plaster is placed over all this to keep the wounded area safe from infection. This would ensure that I would be able to walk without too much difficulty the following day.

After washing and resting for an hour or so, I went to the local bar across the plaza to write up my journal and send postcards. The cold beer was exquisite after the heat of the long walk. Sitting there in the terrace of the bar, which allowed me full view of the refugio, was an ideal vantage point from which I could see the pilgrims arrive.

The Romanesque and Moorish influences can be seen in the Church of San Tirso in Sahagún.

I saw Emmanuelle and Roger making their way to the refugio. When I shouted out to them I could see that they were flabbergasted that I, the nineteen-stone pilgrim, had arrived before them. It was a real case of the hare and the tortoise. I took some sinful pleasure at my accomplishment, though I knew that at any stage I could find myself in trouble. However, the victory of the moment was sweet.

Sahagún seems to have been a monastic settlement from the ninth century and was further developed by Alfonso VI, friend of Santo Domingo de la Calzada, who turned it into a thriving Cluniac monastic settlement.

Too tired to visit the town in any great detail and finding the museum of Santa Cruz closed, I limited myself to visiting the impressive church of San Lorenzo, which holds the sarcophagus of Alfonso VI. The Mudejar style of the church, with its Gothic features, creates a sense of real antiquity on the exterior. The interior was rather bare and museum-like.

Later I telephoned Tim in my community back in Dublin and was fortunate to find him answering the phone. We chatted for a short time, yet even those few minutes made me aware of the value of community support along the way to Santiago. I was truly grateful for his kind gesture in ringing me, and as we talked, the support and interest that the entire community had shown me from the outset impressed me greatly. So, even though I was on my own on the camino, I knew that I had Brothers with me as I journeyed.

I learned later that others in the community had phoned at different times along the camino, but not having Spanish, they could not get their message across. The schedule I provided them with did not correspond exactly with the stages that I was in fact reaching, and often their call preceded or followed my arrivals.

It was now nearly seven o'clock and my stomach was telling me that it was time for supper. The first few restaurants I tried had their first sitting at 9.00pm. The Spanish eat notoriously late, but this was the first time that I had encountered restaurants where such a late hour was de rigueur. This was most unsuitable for a pilgrim who at nine o'clock should be preparing to turn in for the night. The early start in the morning necessitates an early night; eating a meal at a late hour would only prevent sleep. Eventually, however, I found a simple café in the Plaza Major, right in the centre of Sahagún.

I was the only pilgrim there at the time but when I was halfway through dinner, an athletic man in his fifties sat next to me and ordered a meal. He wore the trappings of a cyclist: the coloured jacket, the tight fitting Lycra shorts and the cycling gloves. Chatting with him, I learned that he had walked to Santiago a few years before from his home in France, a walk that had taken him 54 days. This time he had decided to attempt the same journey by bicycle. Interestingly, he had preferred by far the walking to the cycling. The former allowed him to reflect as he walked and to meet many pilgrims; cycling was more physically demanding and more a solitary affair. Talking to him that evening provided him with the opportunity to share his story of the cycle towards Santiago. As he continued, I felt pleased to have offered him the chance to talk with a fellow pilgrim along the camino.

As I was about to leave the restaurant, Frieda arrived and joined me at my table without any invitation. She had walked some of the route from Carrión to Sahagún and, like me, had found it quite difficult. She was also hungry, having discovered the difficulty of finding a restaurant that catered for the pilgrim.

The waiter arrived, and she began asking about the various items on the menu. As he described each dish, she showed positive distaste, complaining that she could not eat what he suggested. When the waiter said a dish was poached, she would want it grilled and vice versa. It was comical and tragic – and annoying. How the waiter maintained his composure was a miracle of the camino. He continued going down the list of possible choices, with Frieda crossing out the previous dish because it was too oily or dry or without a particular sauce. I excused myself without showing indecent haste. I simply could not stand the carry-on of the petulant Frieda.

Back at the refugio, a group of pilgrims were watching the semi-final of the World Cup, where France beat God knows what team. My interest in sport is not great, but it was good to be sitting with such companions as Roger, Gabriel, James and Emanuel – as if I were part of a big family.

Rolf would have arrived home by this stage, and I hoped that his return would have brought support and comfort to his wife and child. I hoped too that Bernard was getting over his injuries and that Liam had rested and was on his way. I missed their company.

I wondered whom I would meet along the way the next day, but I was sure that the right people would appear at the right time. While I hoped that Frieda would not appear too soon on the horizon, I realised how unkind that was. I wanted to be friendlier to her but I feared that this conversion would take a long time to come about.

The day had been tiring. But I found myself satisfied that the second longest stage of the camino had been completed without any major dramas or personal injuries.

DAY EIGHTEEN
Sahagún to El Burgo Raneros
Thursday 9 July 1998

A good breakfast is always a help in beginning the day on the camino. So in Sahagún I took my time to relish the bread, cheese and yoghurt that I had bought in the local supermarket the previous day. Hot coffee helped me to wake up in preparation for the day ahead.

During the breakfast, I examined more closely the Spanish family that I had met in Nájera for the first time. The father was big and burly with an intimidating face that precluded any arguments. His wife, in contrast, was small, thin and rather quiet; the children seemed unaffected much by the powerful presence of the father. I doubt, however, if they would disobey him. They sat in almost total silence as they attempted to wipe the traces of sleep from their eyes.

Crossing the bridge over the Cea river, I saw the place called the 'Field of Charlemagne's Lances' where poplars grow in abundance. The story goes that when Charlemagne was on the eve of a battle with the Saracen caliph, Aigolando, his troops camped at the side of the river and the soldiers stuck their spears in the ground beside where they slept. The next morning many of the soldiers found that their spears were covered with bark and had set down roots in the ground. This was a sign that those whose spears had begun to grow and form leaves were the ones who would be martyred during the battle. That day forty thousand Christians were killed including Milon, Roland's father.

The actual distance to El Burgo Raneros is only about 18km and on very level ground. It would probably only take about five hours to complete. The track to El Burgo Raneros – created in 1991 as a tree-lined path – goes from Calzada del Coto to Mansilla de las Mulas, a distance of 32km. Strangely enough, despite being described in my guidebook as tree-lined on

En route to El Burgo Raneros along a specially constructed path flanked by trees.

both sides, the route is only lined on the south side of the pathway. The trees at this stage were only saplings; it would take a few years before they would provide shelter.

Along the path, there were some kilometre markings that indicated I was in the region of León. The border between León and Palencia is situated just beyond San Nicolas del Real Camino and just before entering Sahagún. Also interspersed along this raised pathway were benches, offering pilgrims a resting-place along the route, a thoughtful gesture.

As I walked, I began reflecting on the reality of celibate living. My encounters with Kristen over the last few days had awakened in me the desire for intimacy; and the attraction that I felt for women highlighted the challenge of celibacy in religious life.

As a vowed religious who has taken a vow of celibacy, these feelings of desire for sexual intimacy, however natural, often create in me an inner feeling of loneliness and isolation.

Celibacy is a vow that grows out of the conviction that a life dedicated totally to God, following the example of Jesus of Nazareth, is a life of infinite richness and potential. By deciding not to marry, I have made the decision to devote my life to the service of the Lord in whatever way he guides me. Celibacy is meant to free my heart to love many people and to be available to serve them in great freedom and love. But does it?

As I walked along the camino, I felt the desire for closeness to women particularly. I looked back over my life and thought of the relationships that I had, and have at the present, with women. Sometimes the relationship was and is one of real friendship. At other times, it was or is one of desire for sexual intimacy. When it is the latter, the challenge of the vow of celibacy becomes very real and very difficult.

In recent years, there have been many scandals in Ireland surrounding priests and religious who became sexually involved with women. The outcome of this breaking of the boundaries between the minister and the person of the opposite sex has rocked the church, bringing misery to many people. Priests and religious of both sexes who enter into sexual relationships tarnish the image of priesthood and religious life, which leads to much cynicism among the laity.

And yet, the feelings of sexual attraction are so strong and primitive that the decision to forego such pleasure requires maturity, a well-developed conscience and psychological health. The desire for intimacy with women is something that I have struggled with over the years. As I walked along the track, I began asking myself relevant questions. Am I happy with my celibate living? Do I consider that my relationship with God and my desire to dedicate myself totally to Him or Her is sufficiently strong that I can deal with feelings of loneliness and unfulfilled sexual desire?' Although I wanted to answer in the affirmative, I found myself feeling empty and lonely on this monotonous path to El Burgo Raneros.

Continuing along the flat, unchanging route, I reflected on how the call to celibacy means living in real intimacy with God. There is no way I could live a life of celibacy without depending totally on a relationship with God that is all encompassing. This only happens when I enter into a life of real prayer, devoting time each day before the Lord and deepening my relationship with my God. Jesus Christ thought that this was so important that he forewent relations with women. True, he had many very close friends who were women – and indeed, they seemed to be more faithful to him than all of his apostles – but he did not commit his life to any one of them. He remained free, so that he could be completely dedicated to his mission.

The challenge facing me was to integrate sexual desires that cannot, and should not, be denied into an effective life that is liberating and loving. Prayer, I knew, was the key. The vow of chastity can only find its fullest expression when I am open to the presence of God in every aspect of my life and at each moment of the day. Prayer consists of being aware of the presence of God in my life, as well as in all the people and events of my life, then responding to this presence with love.

The Good News of the Gospel is that a life fully lived in total connection to the Lord brings the fullness of happiness and peace. And fully living it necessitates moments of sacrifice and denial. But what life does not involve these same two things? I could see that the challenge for me was to stay with the choice I had already made and live it more fully in the future.

Such deep thoughts were interrupted with my arrival at El Burgo Raneros. I initially found it difficult to find the route to the refugio. It took several detours before I came across it along the main street. The refugio was named after Domenico Laffi, an Italian priest who, in 1673, set off from his native Bologna to make the camino to Santiago.

I was the first to arrive at the recently restored refugio. In all probability, I would find myself alone, as most pilgrims would prefer to go to Mansilla de las Mulas rather than merely walk the short distance to El Burgo Raneros. However, no sooner had I washed the body and the clothes than Francesco and Dominique arrived. These were followed closely by my German friends from Burgos, all of whom were going to stay put.

After a light lunch with Francesco and Dominique, I decided to sleep for the afternoon. The walk to Sahagún the previous day had taken more out of me than I realised and I knew it was time to listen to the body and give it a rest.

El Burgo Raneros appeared to be a very small hamlet with few services. There was no place of significance to visit, so the afternoon passed without me hardly moving from the refugio. Moreover, it was sweltering hot and nothing was going to entice me to venture out for any lengthy period.

Strangely, as evening approached, I discovered that most of the pilgrims were of Germanic origin and as we gathered in the restaurant, I found myself surrounded by Teutonic sounds that were foreign to me. Luckily, Francesco and Dominique sat at my table, which at least afforded me the opportunity to converse in French during dinner.

But as I sat talking to them, I realised that if I continued at this pace along the camino, I would find myself struggling with the Germans for the rest of the route. They appeared very pleasant, yet the language barrier would make life rather difficult. There and then I made a decision to skip the next stage of 18.5km to Mansilla de las Mulas and make for León, about 35km away. I hoped in this way that I could come in contact with pilgrims whose prime languages might be English, French or Italian.

That evening I learned that the four German pilgrims who had begun the

The Church of San Pedro at El Burgo Raneros, which houses a Romanesque statue of the Virgin.

camino in Burgos were teachers in primary and secondary education. They spoke some English and appeared friendly and willing to make an effort. However, I still felt it would be better to take two stages the next day in the hope of finding pilgrims with whom I could communicate more easily.

The woman who owned the restaurant where we ate turned out to be a most generous and welcoming host. During the meal, she went out of her way to ensure that everyone was enjoying themselves and at the end of the meal, she offered a cocktail of Marie Brizard and Cognac to each pilgrim together with a postcard with the pilgrim stamp of the restaurant on it. She had obviously entered into the spirit of the camino, considering it part of her mission to welcome the pilgrims with hospitality and generosity.

Just as we finished our meal and I was returning to the refugio, a young woman passed by the restaurant with what appeared to be an artist's kit held under her arm. She was an American pilgrim who spent much of her time sketching scenes along the route. Some of the pilgrims knew her and said that she would often spend some hours in the middle of the day working at her art and then arrive at the refugio towards evening. She obviously had her own rhythm along the camino.

The experience of having such a short walk that day was most beneficial for body and mind. As evening came, I found myself feeling completely rested and relaxed, in total contrast to how I felt on arrival at El Burgo Raneros that morning. Listening to the body is vital for any pilgrim who wishes to complete the camino without too much difficulty. Trying to force oneself to walk when one is feeling exhausted only leads to eventual trouble. And so far, I had avoided any serious problems. This was no guarantee for the future, of course, but all I could do was take things a day at a time.

That night I slept soundly up to about midnight when the loud snoring, both in my small room and next door, shattered my slumber. The noise was so loud that I found it impossible to get back to sleep. Consequently, I took my mattress and blankets and moved downstairs to the dining area. There, on the tiled floor, I placed my mattress near the entrance to the refugio, where sleep once again was possible.

I knew that I would be ready for the unscheduled longer stage to León on the morrow and I looked forward to meeting other pilgrims in the next refugio. Hopefully, I would be better able to communicate with them.

Day Nineteen
El Burgo Raneros to León
Friday 10 July 1998

Just at the outskirts of the village, there was a large pond from which could be distinctly heard a cacophony of croaking frogs. It was only five in the morning. The sun was not yet beginning to make its appearance and it was only from the light of the almost full moon that the route could be barely made out.

The same tree-lined path continued parallel now to the León-Palencia railway line and through rather unchanging flat countryside with nothing to break the monotony of the route.

The quietness of the morning provided a good opportunity to spend some time in prayer and meditation. Walking along this unchanging path, the prayer that was foremost in my mind centred on the challenge to live fully the commitment to celibacy. The predominant feeling during the morning walk was a sense of loneliness and isolation. Whether it was simply that the route appeared so desolate that morning or whether the thoughts of the struggles I have had with the vow of celibacy and loneliness were simply crowding into consciousness, I found myself feeling rather low and began wondering why this should be. Surely a life lived in dedication to the Lord should bring joy and happiness?

Henri Nouwen, one of the foremost spiritual writers of the 1990s, wrote about the journey from loneliness to solitude. He pointed out how people often try to fill the loneliness within with many types of distractions. Material goods, entertainment and various addictive substances are often resorted to in an attempt to dull the pain of loneliness. But, he insists, the very experience of loneliness serves to invite the individual to move from this feeling of pain to a new level of intimacy. Only when we are prepared to bear with the pain of loneliness, he says, can we begin to taste the experience of solitude where the person comes in touch with the inner core of their being. Solitude involves coming to accept our deepest feelings without seeking to flee from them or suppress them.

So I prayed that my experience of emptiness and loneliness would translate into moments of enlightenment, when only God's love would fill my life and I would realise that the only person who can transform that emptiness is the Lord. Everyone wants to be loved and to love. That is a universal need. The Good News of the gospel is that only God's love can displace existential longing. Many seek this love in human relationships, but no human love can ever compensate for knowing God's love in our hearts.

The journey to Mansilla de las Mulas was a great opportunity to allow my solitude to grow and develop. There were no sites to be visited or any people along the way. The route continued uninterrupted without any distractions. And in the emptiness of the early morning I asked the Lord to walk with me in the moments of aloneness, so that my fear would be replaced with trust, my loneliness with solitude.

The refugio in Mansilla de las Mulas is situated along one of the narrow streets of this historic town. Although I intended to by-pass this stage, I was attracted to the newly renovated refugio that succeeded in maintaining its historic character. On entering the refugio, I was met by the most lively and vivacious of hospitaleros. She exuded life and her infectious smile brought sunshine to the sun-starved narrow street. She enthused about the new refugio and of Mansilla de la Mulas, encouraging me to visit the town before leaving for León. Were it not for the need to get to León before the real heat of the day, I would certainly have followed her advice. But simply being in her company for that half-hour was a real tonic after the quietness of the journey from El Burgo.

The route to León was rather confusing initially, but generally, it ran parallel to the ubiquitous N120, occasionally crossing the motorway and then returning to the other side. It was only for the last few kilometres, when the route joined the motorway, that the strain of the long walk made itself felt.

The pilgrim entrance to the city was traditionally through the Puerta Santa Ana and I passed the eponymous church as I entered the city. The walk through the city became a real torture. The sun beat down unmercifully on the pavements, reflecting the heat back onto me as I made for the refugio.

For the pilgrim there was now a choice between staying in some enclosed monastery or in the recently established municipal refugio, both in the city centre. I chose the municipal refugio simply because it appeared closer at hand and was advertised everywhere along the route. Pilgrims later told me that the monastic setting was infinitely preferable and, in fact, far closer to the centre of the city.

The enrolment at the refugio was very bureaucratic and off-putting. The staff seemed more interested in getting the pilgrim to fill up forms than welcoming them after a long walk. No sooner had I arrived at the refugio than I regretted not continuing as far as the monastery. However, I was too tired to go further.

Having found a local bar, where I ate, the need for a good rest became high on the agenda. Returning to the refugio, I discovered that a bus was about to depart to take pilgrims around the various sites in León. But bed was a far more attractive alternative at that moment. A good hour's rest in the quiet of my room was all that I needed to restore my energies and enthusiasm before embarking on a visit to the city.

León, with a population of 135,000, is an ancient city dating back to Roman times. In the tenth and eleventh centuries, it was considered one of the most important cities of Christian Spain. On the original site, a Jewish ghetto grew up but was destroyed in the twelfth century. The city grew and developed in the fourteenth century, when defensive walls were built; and its history is both glorious and tragic.

I made for the Basilica de San Isidoro, which, like Fromista, is considered one of the finest Romanesque buildings along the pilgrim route. It dates back to the twelfth century when it was constructed to house the relics of San Isidoro, Bishop of Seville. The guidebook recommended a visit to the Pantheon, built in the crypt where 23 monarchs were buried, as well as a visit to the casket containing the remains of San Isidoro. There was also the illuminated San Isidoro bible dating from AD 960. But a Mass was being celebrated in the basilica, and given that the time was after 7.00pm, it seemed preferable to make for the cathedral without delay to see the famous stained-glass windows.

All I could do was to stop for a moment outside the basilica and admire the two south doors with the magnificent statuary executed by Master Esteban, who also decorated the Puerta de Platerias at Santiago Cathedral. From there, I went to the Cathedral of León.

This twelfth-century Gothic cathedral is considered a 'miracle of luminosity' by Lozano, author of my faithful guidebook. On entering the immense three-aisled nave, I was almost taken aback by the sheer colour of the windows. Apparently there are over 100 of them, and each is vividly coloured with patterns of stained glass. Sitting down to admire this exuberance of light, I found myself overcome by the brightness of the colour. What I did not realise was that the windows were the more traditional stained glass depictions of biblical scenes. But in the brilliant sun, all I could see were the shafts of multi-coloured light that streamed into the huge space of the cathedral. It was as if they were modern designs in a medieval monument. It was only on a subsequent visit to León that I saw the

Statue of St James that forms part of the portal of the twelfth-century Gothic cathedral at León.

windows under more subdued lighting and realised how traditional, albeit impressive, they were.

Leaving the cathedral, I noticed four Spanish girls who had been walking the camino for the last week or so. Although we had never talked, they seemed most friendly and given that I was alone, I approached them simply to greet them. They said that they were from Catalonia and had spent the last ten days walking the camino, hoping to conclude it the following year. Many Spanish people, and indeed people from other countries, cannot take a month's holidays, so they do the camino in stages over a number of summers.

The girls talked about their experiences of the camino over the previous ten days; obviously it had meant a lot to them. Their open expressions and smiles further confirmed for me the conviction that the camino to Santiago is a transformative experience that offers the pilgrim the opportunity to deepen their spiritual life in a way that few other experiences do. These four young women would never be the same after the time they spent together along the pilgrim path. They would be returning home renewed and looking forward to the final stage next year.

León is certainly a tourist trap, with all kinds of souvenir shops, cafés and ice-cream parlours. Remembering that Francesco, the talkative French-Spanish pilgrim, had recommended that I taste *leche meringado*, I entered one of the ice-cream parlours and ordered a cone. Leche meringado is a mixture of vanilla ice cream and meringue. The taste was exquisite, and on this hot day, the cone was a beautiful way to cool off. Any pilgrim should make an obligatory stop in León to sample this local speciality. Sauntering down Calle General Franco, I felt like a tourist, mingling among other tourists from every nationality under the sun as I licked my leche meringado.

I passed occasional fellow pilgrims, and although they were strangers to me, I felt united to them in an indefinable spirit of solidarity. There are no real strangers on the camino. All are united in the common purpose, and even passing and saluting without talking to them creates a sense of oneness with the wider world of pilgrimage.

Returning to the refugio, I came across some of the volunteer hospitaleros playing Ludo with the children of the Spanish family of four from Santiago. It was enjoyable to sit with them as I wrote my postcards and completed my journal for the day. The laughter and banter did not interfere with my concentration though I often stopped to enjoy the verbal skirmishes between the children and the volunteers.

Towards 9.30pm, the father came to bring the children to bed. It was obvious that the children would have preferred to stay, and the boy began to protest. But all the father had to do was to look at him sternly; not only did the children stop in their tracks but a hush fell on the entire group – not a man to be crossed.

With two players missing, the volunteers invited me to join the Ludo team. For another hour or so we played, squabbled and laughed around the board game. All my initial prejudice about the hostel was replaced by admiration and gratitude to the many volunteers who worked so hard at making the pilgrim welcome and included in everything. I had made the right choice of refugio after all.

And from the moments of loneliness that had oppressed me that morning, I found myself feeling grateful for the gift of people and friends. I felt so privileged that so many people had come into my life over the years and even on the walk, with the likes of Bernard, Rolf and Liam. And so to the God who provided such people in my life, I uttered a silent prayer of thanks.

Hostal de San Marcos at León is the headquarters of the Order of St James of the Sword.

DAY TWENTY
León to Hospital de Orbigo
Saturday 11 July 1998

The bridge that crosses the Bernesga river is called the Puente de San Marcos, and is located beside the Hostal de San Marcos. San Marcos used to be a monastery and hospital and was established in the twelfth century while the present structure was built in 1523 by the Order of St James of the Sword as its headquarters.

It was about six o'clock as I crossed the bridge at the dawn of a new day. Negotiating the route out of León was rather mystifying, though the arrows were quite plentiful. It seemed as if the pilgrim was being invited to walk through the ugliest parts of León's suburbs. The route passed very dilapidated housing areas and wound its way towards the Sanctuary of the Virgen del Camino through an area of rubbish dumps and broken down lorries and disused warehouses. What a contrast from the beauty of the cathedral and of the Basilica of San Isidoro!

Eventually the route led to the church of La Virgen del Camino, a modern structure dating back to the early 1960s, which replaced the original seventeenth-century sanctuary. The modern statues covering the façade each measure six metres high and weigh 700 kilograms. The work of the Catalan sculptor José María Subirachs, this ensemble of the 12 apostles and the Virgin Mary offers a fresh interpretation of the role of Mary in the life of the Church. Unfortunately, once again the church was closed. I promised myself that I would someday travel the pilgrim route by car, so that I could ensure that the churches would be open when I visited them.

The modern sanctuary of the Virgen del Camino on the outskirts of León.

At the cemetery gates diagonally opposite the sanctuary, there was a sign indicating that the pilgrim could take one of two routes. One was described as the 'Camino Frances'; the other pointed to the motorway. My aim was to reach Villadangos, so I decided to take the Camino Frances, which led me out into the country and away from the N120.

The day was splendid, with the blue sky overhead and the countryside spreading out before me. The joy of creation prompted me to reflect on God's love and of his choice of me to be his servant, his brother. The idea of God's protective love, which had guarded me from so many pit-falls, filled me with a sense of joy and peace. God was offering me a love that no human love could compete with, and though I still struggled with the human need for physical intimacy, I knew at that moment that what I needed most to do was to surrender to God's love without any human intermediary.

Two pilgrims walked ahead of me and soon I reached them. Caroline and Michael were a young German couple who had just begun the camino at Sahagún and hoped to walk to Santiago.

Caroline was small and vivacious with frazzled reddish hair and glasses. She exuded vitality and life. When she heard I was from Ireland she cried out with delight for she had just finished a year in Galway University the previous year as a history student. She talked of her experiences of hill walking in Connaught and how amazed she had been to find that the mountains had no real way-marks. She found the experience very un-German and had loved everything about it.

Michael was more reserved but very gentle and pleasant. He had just successfully completed a course in cabinet making, having produced an ash table for his final exam. Now he was about to embark on his three-year journeyman apprenticeship. During this time, he would not be able to visit any place within 50km of his home. This was the continuation of the medieval guilds' approach to teaching trades where the young apprentice becomes the journeyman.

They were a very friendly couple and as the Irish saying goes, *'Giorraíonn beirt bóthar'* (two people shorten the road), meaning that conversation makes one forget the length of the journey. Soon I found, however, that they were walking somewhat faster than my normal pace and rather than risk a blister I had to allow them to continue ahead of me. I hoped I would meet them later in the day.

It dawned on me by this time that the route I had taken would probably not end up at Villadangos, as the track was not running parallel to the main road that passed that town. All I hoped was that I would not have to make too great a detour.

Eventually I arrived at a hamlet called Villar de Mazarife, which had at the entry to the town a beautiful mosaic showing the coat of arms of Villar. A group of Spanish pilgrims were taking pictures at the mosaic and enjoying the moment's rest. I asked one of them to take a photograph of me; rather impatiently he said he would when they were finished taking their own. He seemed rather ungracious and abrupt but nevertheless he finally took a picture of me before the sign.

Nearby was a building that housed both a small museum of the area and a shop selling pilgrim souvenirs. A quaint old-timer ran the museum and shop as well as dispensing a very impressive sello for the pilgrim's passport. Before deciding to get my passport stamped, I went to view the refugio. I was still of two minds whether to stop at Villar or proceed to Villadangos.

The refugio was a miserable place with hardly a decent bed in the room. But what particularly put me off was the cold stare and lack of greeting from a group of six Spanish pilgrims whom I hadn't seen up to that point. It would have been most unpleasant to pass the night in their company. It was obvious they wanted the place to themselves and were determined to freeze out any intruder. It worked perfectly!

The signpost pointed to Hospital de Orbigo, 12km away and mid-point between Villadangos and Astorga, where I would be stopping the next day. It appeared preferable to go to Hospital de Orbigo rather than go back to Villadangos, which was about eight kilometres to the east.

A local bar provided a welcome stop for a bite to eat and something to drink. Three cokes and a cured ham sandwich were enough to give me the energy to continue along the Camino Frances. But the heat was mounting, and the idea of arriving at the refugio was more attractive than the actual walking at that stage. It was one o'clock, the time at which I would be normally nearing the end of the walk. But I had a few more hours to go.

I was particularly aware of having no map of this section, and after an hour's walking, a feeling of real dread came over me. Was I on the right path? Should I have taken a turn to the right? I had not seen a yellow arrow for ages and wondered if I should turn back and go towards Villadangos after all. Feelings of frustration and anger welled up in me against the people responsible for placing the sign outside León that indicated the two trails to Villadangos.

Rounding the corner, I came across three teenagers chatting together on motorbikes and inquired as to the correct route. Initially they seemed dubious and then pointed in the direction ahead adding that I should take the next turn to the right. I wondered how much they actually knew and as I was about to turn right I saw, for the first time in ages, the scallop shell sign that is sometimes used instead of the yellow arrow. The sign pointed straight ahead and not right, as the youngsters had indicated.

The countryside was heavily farmed with all types of vegetables growing in the fields nearby and trees along the distant horizon. But again, my mind was more on arriving at the refugio than on contemplating the beauty of nature. I was in strange territory; without the correct map, it was impossible for me to relax and enjoy the surrounding countryside. I was afraid of losing my way completely.

The village that appeared suddenly around a corner filled me with joy, and though I discovered almost immediately that it was not Hospital de Orbigo, I welcomed the sign that pointed to a bar. On entering, I was taken aback. The entire bar was filled with men sitting in groups of three or four, all talking animatedly. There must have been at least 50 customers. Silence immediately fell on the group when I opened the door.

"Buenos Dias a todos!" (Hello, everybody), I shouted with confidence, only to be met with reluctant rejoinders of 'buenas', almost muttered. It was as if I had broken into their secret meeting without permission. I ordered an ice-cold coke and then bought a chilled bottle of water to refresh me for the remainder of the journey. As I drank the coke, I was wondering what brought so many men together at three o'clock in the afternoon. It was either a card school or a meeting of the local trade union or a political party. But it was very strange to see such a gathering, even during siesta time. Certainly, I was not going to solve the mystery, for it seemed that the men were going to wait for my departure before continuing their business.

The final two kilometres before the famous bridge leading to Hospital de Orbigo were very tiring in the afternoon sun; but crossing it lifted my heart greatly. I had arrived. A sign indicated that the key to the municipal refugio and the stamp for the pilgrim's passport could be obtained at the local bar, something that caused me to smile. Who could resist buying another drink in this heat!

The bridge at Hospital de Orbigo is one of the most famous
bridges of the camino, dating back to the fifth century.

Another sign indicated that the refugio was 500 metres further on; the longest 500 metres I had ever walked! It was situated along a tree-lined track that bordered a camping and caravan park. At this stage, I was dreaming of a shower and a good rest, away from the sun.

The refugio was almost deserted. It appeared that little work had been done to maintain it, and yet it had all the necessities – a bed, a shower and somewhere to wash and dry clothes. And after ten hours walking, my feet were beginning to protest. At this stage, any place was acceptable.

After a good sleep, I made my way back to the bar for supper. Behind the bar was a restaurant and already there were quite a number of people eating. Some appeared to be pilgrims, though I failed to recognise anyone. Others were obviously from the camping site.

The meals for pilgrims are usually very good and very reasonably priced. For €8 the standard menu includes bread, wine and a choice of three starters, main dishes and desserts. This time, however, the waiter brought a glass of wine instead of a bottle. When I complained, he brought out a bottle but I suspected that it was not the same one from which he had taken the glassful. He seemed also to be annoyed that I should complain. The trout was overdone and the chips were cold. However, I was hungry and hadn't the energy to further complain. It was also, I suppose, inappropriate for me as a pilgrim to be giving out, when I thought of the Austrian white-robed religious whom I had met at Fromista who was travelling without money.

Towards the end of the main course, a sizeable part of one of my teeth fell out. In fact, it was a huge filling that had suddenly come loose. I reflected on the precarious nature of the pilgrimage. Would I begin to have a toothache? Where would I find a dentist? I could think of almost nothing worse than trying to concentrate on the pilgrimage with an aching tooth. Even though I had gone to some length to prepare for the camino, there are always unscheduled accidents. This one impressed upon me the uncertainty of the enterprise, underlining once more the need for the Lord's protection.

Returning to the refugio, it was consoling to find that the place was almost deserted, my room being still unoccupied by anyone else. There appeared to be only two other people in the refugio. I introduced myself to Carmen, a Spanish-French person in her middle-to-late fifties. She spoke to me in French, and I looked forward to meeting her again on the walk in order to practise my language skills.

The other pilgrim was Carlos who had begun his camino at León and was hoping to arrive in Santiago within nine days. Without any guidebook, he had no idea of the various stages between Hospital del Orbigo and Santiago. He was a very pleasant young man in his thirties and appeared very athletic, though I wondered would he ever be able to walk in nine days what my guidebook indicated would take eleven.

Carmen and I spent time with Carlos, detailing the route of the camino and the locations of the refugios. He was most grateful for this assistance; and already I could see that he was beginning to experience the spirit of mutual support that had characterised the camino for me right from the very beginning.

Night was fast falling, and as I lay on my bed in the silence of this isolated refugio, I looked back over the day and thanked the Lord for his protection. There had been moments during the day when I felt lost and certainly very tired; now as I lay down, completely rested, I was filled with a sense of peace and tranquillity.

I thought of Caroline and Michael, wondering where they were at this stage. They had been good company and I hoped that I would meet them over the next few days. I was curious as to what had motivated them to undertake such a walk. Maybe in the days to come

I would discover more of their story. They were so open that I felt confident they would love to share their experiences.

And I was curious about the man who had reluctantly taken my photograph. Who was he and what had made him so impatient when I asked him to take it? Maybe I would never know, but reflecting on the events of the day underlined how little, in fact, we know about anyone as we walk through life. We pass people by and maybe speak a word to them, yet how very few we come to know in any deep way.

I was looking forward to the adventures of the next day. What had amazed me so far in the camino was that on no occasion yet had I felt any disinclination to face another day. Despite the moments when I had been very tired at the end of a day's walking, I had always risen the following day refreshed and ready to embark on a new adventure. And there was no sensation of pain in the damaged tooth.

Day Twenty-One
Hospital de Orbigo to Astorga
Sunday 12 July 1998

Walking along the Calle Mayor, I passed the remains of the old hospital on the left and the Church of San Juan on the right and made my way along the main street, then named 'Camino de Santiago'. It was not clear in which direction the camino went. The signpost seemed to be pointing left but the map indicated to the right. A group of five young Spanish girls arrived soon after at the same spot and they too began discussing which route to choose.

Taking my chances, I went according to the map and continued along an asphalt track towards some small village in the distance. Soon after I became aware of the voices of the girls following closely behind and as they passed, I was amazed to see that they were saying the Rosary as they walked. These girls would hardly have been more than 15 or 16 years of age, yet here they were expressing their faith unashamedly and in a way that just seemed so natural.

As they passed, it was obvious that one of the larger girls limping quite noticeably. She was the one carrying the biggest rucksack and she was definitely struggling. At Villares de Orbigo, two kilometres further on, as they paused, they seemed to be arguing quite heatedly about the plight of the limping companion. Obviously, some decision had to be made and this was causing division. On I went, wondering what the outcome would be.

The track now became a path that began to climb up Monte de la Columba through holm oaks and open fields. The early morning was quite cool, which made the climb much easier and more enjoyable. It is always more pleasant to be away from motorways and tar-covered roads that are so hard on the feet. The earthen path was almost like a carpet. Looking around I could see Hospital de Orbigo some way back in the distance, and ahead were the oak-covered hills that would lead me to Astorga.

Two of the Spanish girls passed me at break-neck speed as if they were fleeing the others of their group; close on their heels came a third girl who caught up with them and began remonstrating with them to return in support of the injured party. The original two were having none of it and while one returned, the first two girls continued along the path. It seemed the unity that had existed between them as they said the Rosary had sadly dissipated, leaving them disunited and hurt.

Just as I was working my way through the scrub and holm oaks of the forest path, Carlos overtook me. He was perspiring profusely and yet appeared in fighting form. He looked really enthusiastic and with a brief salutation, he left me, as he hoped to be able to reach Rabanal that day, a distance of 36km. With luck, he would make Santiago in the time allocated to him. As he moved off at a steady pace, I prayed that he would fulfil his ambition.

Having climbed for a short period, the plateau was reached; in the distance could be seen a cross. This granite cross, situated on the hilltop from where Astorga could be viewed, is dedicated to the fifth-century Bishop of Astorga, St Toribio. At the very spot where the cross stands, Toribio is supposed to have shaken the dust from his sandals when he was rejected by the diocese. It was a good place for me to rest, and already a few local farmers were sitting there, discussing animatedly some local issues. They willingly agreed to take my photo with the cross behind me and the view of Astorga in the background.

A couple of young pilgrims hand-in-hand along the camino route.

Astorga is a walled city dating back to Roman times; some parts of the walls still survive to this day. The entrance to the town was originally through the Puerta del Sol that still has some of the original decoration. To the right is the church of San Francesco, indicating that he was supposed to have stayed in Astorga. At one stage in its history, Astorga had around 20 pilgrims' hospitals, underlining its importance in the past as a stopping place along the pilgrim route.

The refugio was closed, with a sign saying that it would not open until 3.00pm. It was only 11.00am, and I didn't want to traipse around the city with my rucksack. The hospitalero, who was in the process of cleaning the refugio, kindly agreed to allow me leave it on one of the bunk beds. This provided the opportunity to view the accommodation, which I could see was terribly cramped. The room was quite small and dark; the bunk beds were arranged in rows, with little space to move in and out between each bed.

Carlos and Carmen shouted to me from outside a bar across the plaza as I was making my way towards the cathedral. "Where's your rucksack?" Carmen wanted to know.

"In the refugio – for the moment anyway, " I told her, not yet sure whether I would stay there.

"Wait for me while I do the same!" Carmen was off in a flash to leave her rucksack too in the refugio.

While waiting for her to return, Carlos and I talked about the camino. He was in good shape and was feeling very confident that he would finish in the nine days available to him. Then, before Carmen returned he excused himself, insisted on paying for the beers, and set off for the next stage. In this way, he was thanking us for our assistance to him at the Hospital de Orbigo. I hoped he would make it.

Carmen returned, still with her rucksack. She had taken one look at the refugio and decided that she was going elsewhere. As luck had it, she got the name of a private refugio run by the Missioneras Apostolicas de la Caridad, the Missionary Sisters of Charity. She suggested that we both explore the possibility of alternative accommodation.

Without too much difficulty we found the private refugio and, having considered the other, cramped accommodation, we decided to pay the €20 for bed and breakfast. This was almost ten times the price of the refugio. I had mixed feelings about paying, but when I saw the room, my scruples vanished immediately.

The place was immaculate. Each room was en suite and had two beds. The Sister said that we could have a room each on condition that we were open to accept another pilgrim of the same sex into our rooms. While not madly enthusiastic about the arrangement, it was infinitely preferable to having 20 other pilgrims snoring during the night. The idea of possibly having a room to myself was very attractive.

As Carmen and I were looking for a place to eat, she met two Spaniards whom she knew. I recognised the man as the one who took my photo somewhat reluctantly at Viller de Mazarette. They invited us to join them for lunch at a restaurant they had found a few moments previously. It turned out to be the same place where we had taken our beer with Carlos.

Javier and Nuria were both from Madrid and had walked from there to join the camino at Burgos. They were both inspectors of olive oil; we would call them quality controllers. Nuria had quite a bit of English but her companion Javier had practically none. So the only language common to most was Spanish and therefore I muddled through the meal with them, and was very glad of their company.

They chose the expensive menu, while Carmen and myself took the menu of the day. What surprised me was that the young couple didn't eat everything but didn't offer us any of the leftovers either. Maybe that is the custom of the Spanish; to me it appeared somewhat strange. However, our time together was most amiable and I looked forward to meeting them along the camino.

The afternoon was far too oppressively hot to walk around the town, so we retired to our pleasantly cool rooms for a good siesta. What a luxury: to relax in one's own room on clean white sheets and simply doze off without a sound or the laughter of pilgrims. Sleep came easily.

When I had finished my journal for the previous day and the morning's walk, I invited Carmen to visit the city. She spoke fluent French, and this made the company all the more enjoyable. Although she appeared rather nervous of being a pilgrim, I was able to assure her that she would have no difficulty along the camino. At that moment, I suggested that it might be reassuring for her to have a companion along the route for the next day or two and I was happy to oblige with this. She jumped at the offer, further confirming her real anxiety about travelling alone. My hope was that after a day or two she would be able to continue on her own.

The construction of Astorga cathedral was begun in 1471. Its façade consists of two great square towers with more Romanesque features than Gothic, although the interior is essentially Gothic. From the towers to the central part of the cathedral, which covers the nave, a double set of flying buttresses creates a sense of lightness and movement. The interior has an air of

Gaudí's neo-Gothic palace in Astorga houses the Museum of the Ways, the pilgrim route.

gracefulness by virtue of the tall thin columns of the narrow triple-aisled nave. There was a delicacy – an almost fragility – about the entire construction.

We got our passports stamped at the kiosk at the entrance to the cathedral and asked the staff where one could get Mass. As it was Sunday, I was keen to celebrate the Eucharist, as was Carmen. They pointed to a church nearby, and on arriving, we heard the usual group of women reciting the Rosary before the Mass. The priest who celebrated the Eucharist was most reverent and although I could only catch snatches of the homily, I could see that he was delivering his sermon with sincerity and passion. This made my Sunday a day of unusually rich spiritual nourishment.

Beside the cathedral is Antonio Gaudí's neo-Gothic Bishop's Palace. This is an amazing piece of architectural fantasy that left the Palacio de los Guzmanes of León in the shade. Much of Gaudí's work can be seen in Barcelona, where I had visited the Sagrada Familia cathedral and some of the houses he designed, not to mention his park. The Bishop's Palace appeared very modern, as if it had been only recently built. It had, in fact, been completed in 1913. Inside there is a Museum of the Ways, dealing with all the routes that lead to Astorga, including the pilgrim way. However, it had been closed since early evening.

Carmen and I decided to eat very lightly, having had our substantial meal in the middle of the day. Sitting in the square in front of the magnificent façade of Astorga Town Hall was awe-inspiring. The two-spired symmetrical building, with the clockwork figurines that strike the hours on the clock in the central part of the façade, created a sense of perfect harmony on that lovely evening in the square.

The façade of the Astorga Town Hall houses the beautiful clock from where a pair of mechanical dolls emerge on the hour to strike the bell.

One thing, however, that struck me about Astorga was that it seemed to lack a sense of the pilgrimage. Some indefinable atmosphere pervaded the streets that gave me the impression that the local people were more interested in making money than in welcoming pilgrims. The town had a totally secular ethos. Somehow, I felt that one day in Astorga had been enough; I pined for the more rustic atmosphere of the smaller towns.

Sitting there at the close of the day was most relaxing. I decided to taste the *mantecadas* (butter buns) for which Astorga is famous. Although glad to have sampled them, I couldn't see what the fuss was about; I found them disappointing. Their appearance was better than their taste. Not so with the day, however. For me, I had found it a most enjoyable time and despite the commercial aspects, I was pleased to have visited the town's monuments.

We left the square looking forward to the luxury of our own bedrooms. Luckily on our return there had been no further pilgrims seeking accommodation, so we still had a room each. No sooner had I put my head to the pillow than I was fast asleep, having reviewed the day and looked over the plan for the next day's walk.

Out of the farther reaches of my consciousness, I began to hear noises. It took some time before I emerged from my sleep to the sound of laughter and noise. Initially, it was not clear from where the sound was coming, but eventually, fully awake, I realised that there was a group of people next door who seemed to be celebrating something. I could not believe my ears. Not only had I abandoned the municipal refugio to avoid such noise but I had also paid ten times the amount. And here was a situation far worse than any I had experienced so far.

I lay for a while, hoping the noise would diminish. Instead, it seemed to increase until I had the impression that the people were totally drunk and completely oblivious of the time of day. Anger and frustration overcame me as I hammered on the walls. The noise stopped for a moment, but so sooner had it ceased than it began once more. What a night it was! I thumped on the thin wall, and once more the sound lessened. But nothing was going to stop these thoughtless pilgrims.

For the next hour or so I had to put up with the racket. What made me even angrier was the realisation that I hadn't the courage to storm out of my room and complain to the management. It was strange, but I felt that had I been able to insist on silence, I would not have felt so angry.

Eventually I slept, though all the good of having a room to myself had been ruined by the inconsiderate behaviour of the pilgrims. I had no desire to meet them in the morning nor indeed at the next refugio. Sleeping in Astorga had been a bit of a disaster. Tomorrow would hopefully be better.

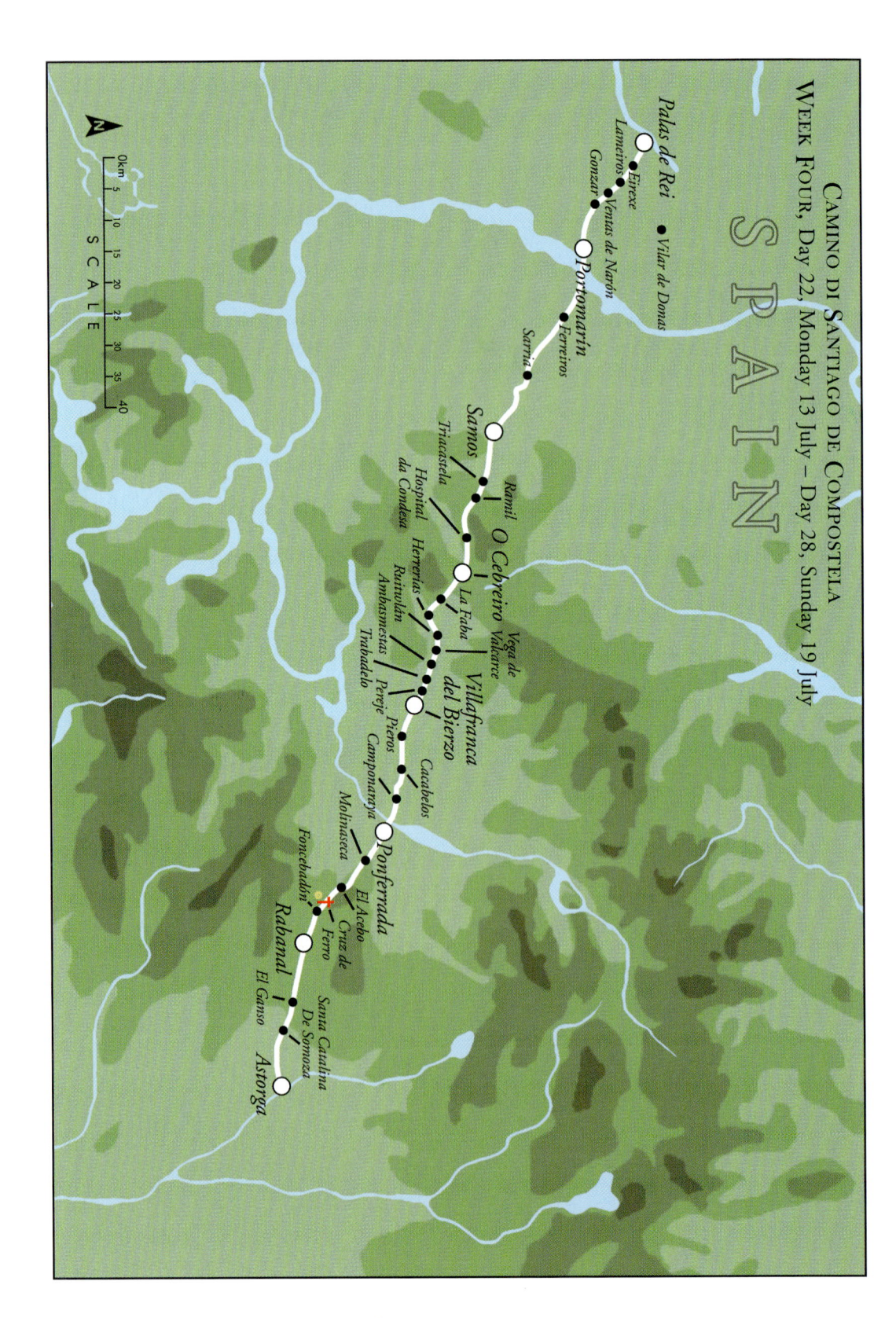

CAMINO DI SANTIAGO DE COMPOSTELA
WEEK FOUR, DAY 22, Monday 13 July – Day 28, Sunday 19 July

Week Four

Day Twenty-Two
Astorga to Rabanal
Monday 13 July 1998

The convent-refugio offered a great breakfast of fruit, bread, cheese and coffee, which to some extent compensated for the disastrous previous night. Carmen, on the other hand, had slept well and had been totally oblivious of all the noise that had gone on. She was now rested and felt less anxious about the camino. Although somewhat tired, I looked forward to this new day.

We took one of the minor roads towards the west of the town, continuing along the road past the hermitage of Ecce Homo, a medieval dwelling that had been restored in the nineteenth century. To allay Carmen's fears about getting blisters and pains, we travelled very slowly. As we walked, we discussed prayer and spirituality. She had done much work in this area over the years, and I found it refreshing to hear her discuss her journey from agnosticism to faith. As she talked, I felt privileged to be listening to someone prepared to share their inner spiritual life.

Having just undergone a thirty-day retreat the previous summer, I knew the value of having someone listen to my struggle with faith, prayer and God. And here I was on the other side of the process, listening to another as they discussed their faith journey.

When we arrived at Santa Catalina de Somoza, we met Nuria and Javier in a bar, taking breakfast. They asked us if they could join us for the rest of the journey and personally, I welcomed the additional company. Although the route was along a road under repair, the surface was still not tarred, so we could enjoy the softer earthen path underfoot.

As we passed the small hamlet of El Ganso, we could see some of the houses that were thatched like in Ireland. This type of roofing is apparently very ancient and gave the place a real atmosphere of antiquity. As we went through the village, we were overtaken by a lively young Spanish couple who were part of a parish group making for Santiago for 25 July, the feast-day of St James. I noted they were wearing very light footwear and wondered how they would fare in the long run. They seemed to be positively running along the track; it was unlikely, I felt, that they could maintain such a pace for very long.

I was finding the pace set by Nuria and Javier rather testing too, and as we came to the right turn for Rabanal El Viejo, I requested that we pause while I examined my feet. I found that there was some redness appearing on my right foot but luckily, there was no sign of a blister. We rested for about a quarter of an hour and then within a further 30 minutes, we were entering Rabanal.

Rabanal is an ancient stopping place for pilgrims and is mentioned in Picaud's account of his journey to Santiago. It was the last stop before the pilgrims began the big climb up to Monte Irago. The approach to the town along old cobbled streets and many dilapidated buildings gave the village an air of bygone days.

The refugio at Rabanal had been lovingly restored under the auspices of the English Confraternity of St James and has the reputation of being one of the more hospitable refugios along the camino. The refugio is named after Gaucelmo, a hermit of the twelfth century who built a hostelry and a hospital for pilgrims along this dangerous stretch of the camino.

These ruins at El Ganso were originally thatched cottages for the local inhabitants.

On arrival at the refugio, I was taken aback at the number of pilgrims congregated outside awaiting its noon opening. There must have been 30 pilgrims gathered in small groups, all eager to get to the showers and washing facilities.

As noon approached, some of the pilgrims became nervous about ensuring they got a place, and I found myself being pushed out of the line. There was a difference of opinion with a pilgrim whom I felt had skipped the queue. She felt very aggrieved that any such inference should be made and strongly denied it. I could see that relations between us were strained.

There was another group of about ten people who wanted to block-book places but they were told that no such arrangements could be made. There was no doubt, however, that groups do try to fill up the places, and this badly affects the lone pilgrim who is more likely to be the one who has travelled the longer distance.

The hospitalero who greeted us was Georgie, an Australian cyclist pilgrim who originally had been walking the camino until she suffered with pains in her legs. Rather than give up completely, she had decided to travel by bicycle. She was an assistant hospitalero. The official hospitaleros were Roger and Julia, who proved to be a truly remarkable team.

I first noticed Julia as she was treating the young Spanish girl wearing light runners who had passed us along the route. I could hardly bare to look at the soles of her feet, which seemed to have lost all their skin. This poor girl must have continued walking even when she felt her feet hurting. Carefully and gently, Julia bandaged her feet, putting disinfectant and other ointments on them first, then arranged for her to stay for an extra day in the refugio so that her wounds could heal somewhat.

Julia had originally been a pilgrim herself having started at Le Puy en Velay some seven or

The Rabanal refugio was restored and is now maintained by the British Confraternity of St James.

eight weeks previously. When she arrived at Rabanal, she discovered that Roger's assistant had left for England unexpectedly, leaving Roger alone in the refugio. So she decided to abandon her camino and remain for the rest of the season as a helper to Roger. Not many pilgrims would have sacrificed the experience of completing the camino to help others along the way. I would not have done it myself, I have to admit.

Nuria and Javier joined Carmen and me for lunch before they announced that they had decided to continue walking for a further 10km. This disappointed me, as we were only beginning to get to know each other and I really liked them as a couple. Yet, I knew that they had to follow their own pace along the camino. There was always the hope that we would meet again, though nothing was guaranteed. We took photographs of each other and then they left.

Towards four o'clock, Roger and Julia offered afternoon tea to a small group of us who were lolling around the refugio. The tea was served in true English style together with some tasty Spanish cakes. This lovely touch created such a feeling of welcome and hospitality not matched since Castrojeriz.

As I began exploring the town, I came across the local parish Church of Our Lady of the Assumption but it was locked. Then I noticed an old woman standing nearby and inquired in my broken Spanish when the church would open. She smiled and shouted something unintelligible up to a neighbour's bedroom. There was a muffled reply, and it took a good five minutes before an old lady emerged from the main entrance of the house carrying some keys.

From the way she conducted the very personal tour of the church it was obvious that the people of Rabanal were immensely proud of their ancient building. Although the interior was in dire need of repair, with sections showing evidence of damp, and other parts needing general restoration, there were signs too of care and devotion in the hand-made altar cloths and floral decorations. The oldest statue in the church was that of St Blaise, the saint associated with pilgrims' health. But pride of place was given to a crucifix that had been lovingly restored by the old woman's husband. Overall, the tour of the church represented a moving gesture of simple but profound faith on the part of a deeply religious woman. Towards the end of the guided tour, she pointed to the donation box. Considering her kindness in offering me such a complete tour, I was more than glad to oblige.

With a new-fired zeal to promote devotion to Rabanal, the kind woman then invited me to follow her down the road where we came upon the hermitage of San José situated at the entrance to the village. There, some recently arrived pilgrims joined us for the tour.

From my elementary understanding of Spanish, it seemed that she described how a local merchant had made so much money from his business with pilgrims along the route that he decided to erect a shrine to St Joseph. The altarpiece was in sparkling gold, with images of St James, St Joseph and St Barbara; the rest of the monument was almost in a state of collapse.

One of the pilgrims became inexplicably agitated and angry at the state of the monument, criticising both the poor woman and the people of Rabanal. He became so volubly annoyed that it seemed as if he was somewhat unbalanced. The lady took him very gently aside, explaining how applications had been made to the authorities for funding to restore the monument. This did not apparently assuage the pilgrim's agitation. Eventually, I left the scene, the woman wisely having brought the tour to a premature end. Who knows what had unhinged the young pilgrim – he certainly needed help.

The walk along the camino can be frightening at times. The fact that for hours on end one can be alone with one's thoughts, having no-one to share them with, can cause people to become somewhat disquieted. The ancient hermits who went into the deserts described these moments of mental anguish in terms of wild and devilish creatures attacking them and filling their minds with all sorts of temptations. Being alone can be peaceful; it can also open up areas of anxiety that become heightened when alone. And no-one is exempt from such frightening thoughts. The young pilgrim who became agitated in San José may have been working out some personal agenda as he walked along the way. I hoped that he would come to some resolution.

For the previous few days, I had been again struggling with the challenge of the vow of chastity. There had been moments when the pain of loneliness had been so strong that it seemed an impossible vow to keep; all I could concentrate on was the renunciation that resulted from it. What I was giving up predominated my thoughts and prevented me from realising other aspects of the vow. It took quite some time before I came to an understanding of the complete nature of its meaning. Only gradually could I once more recognise the basis for this commitment to chastity.

The love God has for each of us is so infinite that he invites some people to base their whole lives on responding to it. Rather than form a lifelong relationship of love with a partner, the religious is called to devote their self to the love and service of the poor for the love of God. Putting God first and before all other relationships is the challenge to the consecrated person. Loving a husband or wife, and in this love reflecting the love of God, is the vocation of the married person. Both are challenging and fulfilling. Each is different.

I met Julia, Phil and Carmen later in the evening, and we decided to go for supper in the local bar. Julia impressed me not only by her generous act of interrupting her walk but also because she genuinely reached out to the pilgrims in a very practical fashion. She talked about walking through France, and as she talked, I began to feel a certain longing to walk someday from Le Puy to Santiago. Phil too chatted about his experiences from Le Puy. As I listened to both of them, I appreciated once more the real value of the camino where stories are exchanged and lives shared.

During our meal, a Dutch man asked if he could join us. Marius had walked from his home town of Breda in The Netherlands and had been over ten weeks en route. From what he was saying, I could see that he had preferred his walk through France and was somewhat disillusioned with Spain. Probably this was due simply to the fact that he had been away from home for so long. But I looked forward to discussing the matter further with him.

My bedroom for the night was in the library of the refugio. A goodly selection of books on the camino was available and certainly I would loved to have had the time to study some of them. Already my own such collection was growing, and I longed for the time that would allow me read some of the more important ones. My curiosity was growing.

Towards noon, I was forced to leave the library because of the high-decibel level of snoring that would have woken the proverbial dead. A move to the entrance of the refugio allowed me to slip into a sound sleep after a most enjoyable day.

Day Twenty-Three
Rabanal to Ponferrada
Tuesday 14 July 1998

Bastille Day, 14 July, saw Carmen and myself setting out in the early morning along a path that led after about 200 metres to the road. Looking back at Rabanal del Camino, I saluted the English Confraternity of St James who had reconstructed the old parish house making it into a most welcoming place for pilgrims of all nationalities. They deserved the greatest praise for the way they reached out to the pilgrims. Roger and Julia had been more than generous with their time, taking care of all pilgrims without exception. It had been a privilege to meet them both.

The road was rising rapidly, and Carmen was feeling uncertain as to whether she would be able to stay the pace. At this stage, I was beginning to feel slightly suffocated by her presence and would have liked to have been alone in this early morning time. For me, this period should be an opportunity for solitude and a time to pray in the quiet of the rising sun. Even at home, I find myself rising early to meditate and nothing pleases me more than sitting in the chapel listening to the silence, often only broken by the sound of birds and the distant sound of the early morning traffic.

And yet, I knew that Carmen would have found it almost impossible at this early stage to go it alone. When faced with the example of Julia, who sacrificed herself completely to assist pilgrims, I could do no less than walk with Carmen.

We were climbing quite a steep road towards the top of Monte Irago when we turned into the deserted village of Foncebadón. As early as the tenth century it had been an important stopping place for pilgrims. Now it boasts only dilapidated buildings, the occasional scrapped car and broken-down pieces of farm machinery. It was eerie walking through what would once have been a thriving place, crowded with pilgrims. Now there was only Carmen, a few stray dogs and myself.

Leaving Foncebadón, we carried on uphill and passed a drinking fountain. As we walked around a curve in the road, we came to the famous Cruz del Ferro. This is one of the most well-

Foncebadón ruined church where records indicate the presence of pilgrims in the tenth century.

known and ancient of monuments along the camino. It consists of a simple iron cross, attached to a wooden pole some five metres high, which is stuck into a mound of stones. Pilgrims from every part of the world carry a stone from their own native land and deposit it on the mound when they reach the cross.

Originally, my guidebook informed me, the placing of a stone on these sorts of mounds was an ancient tradition of pre-Roman times. They were called 'mounds of Mercury' after the god of travellers. It was Gaucelmo, the hermit of the twelfth century, who Christianised the monument with the addition of the cross. By placing a stone at the foot of the cross, the pilgrim was meant to be participating in the suffering of the crucified Lord. Unfortunately, I had forgotten to bring a stone with me from Ireland and had to be content with unearthing one from the local vicinity.

Quite a crowd of pilgrims had gathered at this spot, both to get photographs taken of themselves on top of the mound placing their stone and simply to relax and meet other pilgrims. Phil was sitting drawing as usual. He had already sketched a very good cartoon in the visitors' book in Rabanal depicting his bearded self, lost in a long line of pilgrims, all trying to enter the refugio. Here, once again he had the bearded pilgrim, himself, standing on top of the mound and holding the flag as if he were Chris Bonnington on top of Everest. The view from the top of Monte Irago was most impressive with the undulating countryside below and the tree-clad hills still covered somewhat in the low cloud that hung over the forests.

As we were beginning to descend the mountain, we came across a refugio to the right. It had a sign indicating that it was one of the only surviving remnants of the Knights Templars' dwellings. I could see that there were all sorts of pilgrim bric-à-brac on display in the distance, but rather than stop a second time so soon after the Cruz de Ferro, I was more anxious to continue along

Cyclist takes a rest along the pilgrim route.

the route. Those who did stop told me later that it had been fascinating to visit the place and to meet the local hospitalero, who dressed like a Knights Templar and resided for the entire summer period in the refugio. Apparently, he claims to have proof of direct lineage with the Knights Templars.

The descent from Monte Irago was very pleasant as the road wound its way in a zigzag fashion down towards El Acebo, a small town in the distance. We stopped along the roadside for a rest and as I lay there, I became aware of the strong desire in me to be alone. Carmen and I had said everything that we had to say to each other and I longed for solitude. Carmen herself was not to blame, though I was finding her regular complaining about the difficulty of the route rather hard to handle. As I lay there at the side of the road, I tried to understand how frightened she must be about going it alone, and it was this realisation of her real fears that helped me stay with her.

'Cruz de Ferro', meaning the iron cross, where pilgrims place a stone on the 'mounts of Mercury'.

The decent into El Acebo was quite steep but rather spectacular. I viewed the village from above and saw the interplay of light on the slanting roofs of the various dwellings and buildings. We called into the family-owned bar in the centre of the town and found it almost full with pilgrims, all sampling the home-made tortillas. We joined them and enjoyed the next 30 minutes or so assuaging our hunger and thirst. Many of the pilgrims I did not recognise, but it was good to be among them and feel a sort of communion with them all.

The road to Santiago is made special by the fact that so many different people are walking the route at the same time. The pilgrim feels in union with these fellow pilgrims and though it is only possible to meet a mere handful of them along the route, the knowledge that there are many more walking creates a sense of fraternity. However, I knew how easy it was to be in communion with everyone when what often counts more is communicating with the person with whom one walks. Could I be in communion with Carmen? That was the test. I was not sure how much longer I could stick with her.

We left El Acebo and passed through the village along the road, making our way to the small but picturesque hamlet of Riego de Ambrós. From there, we descended into the valley of the Arroyo Prado Mangas, named after the eponymous river. The scenery was spectacular. And it was at moments like this that I wished I had studied the flora of Spain. There was a variety of vegetation that warranted a better description than I could give.

We walked along the Prado Mangas river, and in the heat of the afternoon, the shelter from the trees was simply heavenly. Sitting on an old fallen tree, we stopped to allow our eyes to feast on the surrounding scene. The meandering stream as it wound its way through the valley created an idyllic picture of Spain at its best. No words of mine could describe the peace and contentment that filled my being at that moment. It was sheer bliss.

After what appeared to be a long time but was probably not more than 30 minutes of resting, we continued along the way and reached the road once more before descending again into another valley, that of the Rio de la Pretadura. We then had to climb up to a promontory towards the right and skirt around it as we made our way back to the road leading to Molinaseca. The going was rather tough, and we were beginning to feel the heat of the day and the effects of the early morning climb.

When we reached the road, we were just outside Molinaseca. As usual before any significant town, I stopped to get a photo of myself at the sign indicating the name of the place. This was just beside the Capilla de la Virgen, an eighteenth-century baroque chapel built against the hillside. Carmen was completely exhausted, as I was, and it didn't take much argument to decide to conclude our walk for the day at Molinaseca instead of continuing to Ponferrada, our planned stop.

We crossed over the impressive Romanesque bridge that spanned the River Boeza and entered the town along the Calle Real, which, until recently, had been called the Calle Peregrinos to indicate that it was the pilgrims' route. Noticeable as we walked through the town were some of the houses with the coats of arms of the original families who resided in them.

Much to our dismay, the refugio at Molinaseca was situated a kilometre outside the town in the recently restored Hermitage of San Roque. We had hoped that our walking for the day was over but there was still some 30 minutes to go before we arrived at the refugio.

The refugio was unusual, in that as well as having bunks inside, there were also bunk beds outside in the open air and situated on one side of the refugio under the eaves that acted as a shelter from the elements. Pilgrims could choose which sleeping arrangements they preferred. Carmen and I opted for the bunks inside, for there I felt more secure especially with regard to my rucksack and belongings.

We returned to the town later to buy some provisions for the next day and to find a place to have our supper. Eventually we came across a very typical Spanish restaurant just below the Boeza bridge and found that a Belgian pilgrim couple had already discovered the place before us. We joined them at their table for supper, but they were difficult to understand; indeed Carmen struggled to engage them in any meaningful conversation. They seemed shy or inhibited in some way, and the meal passed rather slowly and awkwardly.

Back in the refugio later on, I began to mingle with the younger pilgrims who had either cooked their own meal or simply eaten from their supplies. At the centre of the group sitting outside the refugio on the steps were a couple of American students who seemed to be the life and soul of the party. Roger, the Scottish walker and Emmanuelle, his companion, were also there.

On approaching the group, I listened to their goings on and found myself feeling very uncomfortable. The Americans seemed to be cynical of everything and everyone on the camino, laughing at people and their beliefs, scorning the idea that this was a religious event. No matter what aspect of the experience they discussed, it seemed that all they wanted to do was to scoff. Feelings of discomfort and sadness came upon me, and I found myself unable to stay in their company for long.

When I entered the refugio, I came across a young couple, Alberto and Carmen. They had arrived the day before in Astorga by bus from Madrid. It was not clear when they had started the camino, but it appeared that they may have only begun a day or so previously. Their feet were causing them problems; the dreaded tendonitis seemed to be lurking around. It was good to be able to offer them Feldene, for which they were most grateful. And although I was not able to communicate with them to any great extent, I felt so much better for having met them. In contrast to the cynicism of the Americans was the open simplicity of this young Spanish couple.

Before calling it a day, Carmen and Alberto began talking about the route via Ponferrada to Villafranca. They told me they had heard that the route through Ponferrada was most uninteresting and not worth following; that it was preferable to take a short cut that by-passed the centre of the city. This gave me food for thought but I decided to wait until the morning before making up my mind. And I was wondering what Carmen, my companion, would think. Part of me wished she would take off on her own. Then the example of Julia came to mind once more, and I felt guilty for the unkind feelings I was harbouring towards her. All I hoped was that the morning would bring wisdom and more charitable thoughts!

Day Twenty-Four
Ponferrada to Villafranca del Bierzo
Wednesday 15 July 1998

Ponferrada was supposed to have been the starting point for the walk on Day 24. However, having stopped at Molinaseca the previous day, it meant that there were some seven kilometres to be added to this day's stage, making a total of 31km. We hoped that we could reach Villafranca del Bierzo before the heat of the afternoon would become too oppressive.

We were on the road at 5.30am, and because we took the track that skirted the road and then the River Boeza, it was difficult in the dark to see exactly where we were going. Passing through the village of Campo, everything was silent except for the crowing of the cocks. From there, we crossed over the river and entered Ponferrada on the Puente Mascarón and continued along the Calle Hospital, where the Hospital de la Reina was built by Isabel la Catolica in 1498. By then, it was seven o'clock, and the day was growing brighter.

Ponferrada means 'iron bridge', referring to the one built over the Sil river that runs though the town and meets the River Boeza to the south. The bridge had been built on the orders of Osmundo, Bishop of Astorga, in order to make the town an obligatory passing place for pilgrims along the camino.

As we entered the town, the huge Templar Castle towered above us. It is supposed to be one of the oldest and best-preserved examples of Spanish military architecture. In the early morning light, it cast its shadows over us as we made our way into the centre of the town. Because we had decided to avoid the circuitous route on the advice of Alberto, we simply followed the main road as it curved around the castle.

We stopped for a coffee. As we sat in the café, I found myself thinking how I would make the break with Carmen. Increasingly I was finding her constant worry about making it to Santiago rather grating on the nerves and the further I continued with her the angrier I was beginning to feel. The moments of prayer and reflection that had been part of each day were being dissipated in superficial conversations and inane observations. The only solution I felt possible was to increase my walking pace and simply let Carmen realise that we should go our separate paths.

As we walked along the main thoroughfare, a local woman approached us to tell us that we had taken the wrong street for the camino. Thanking her, we continued along the same path; but the further we walked along the NVI, the more convinced I became that we should have stuck to the official route. Nothing could have been more uninteresting than the road through the city. Meeting some pilgrims later on confirmed my suspicion that the very route we had been advised to avoid was, in fact, the one described in Lozano's book and far preferable to the so-called short cut that we had taken.

Just outside the village of Camponaraya, which was situated along the main road, we cut into a path on the opposite side of the road and began walking along the borders of a wine-growing area. By this time, I had begun to quicken my steps and it was not long before I heard protests from Carmen that I was going too fast. At this stage I explained that we had to arrive at Villafranca without delay and simply continued walking at the increased pace.

Being alone again as I walked was sheer heaven. It allowed me to enjoy once again the surrounding countryside, and as I walked, I admired the local workers as they were cultivating their vines. The path dipped into the Arrohyo Magaz valley, and as it crossed the river, it lead though wooded land. I crossed the road and entered the town of Cacabelos, having passed through a farmyard and vineyards, then over a small hill that led down to the town.

Carmen was far behind me at this stage, but on entering the town, she eventually caught up with me, still complaining of the heat and the speed at which I was travelling. This confirmed the necessity to make the final break from her. It was obvious now that she would not be able to keep up to our schedule of stages, though I felt confident that she would arrive in Santiago at her own pace. This realisation eased my conscience. No longer would I feel guilty at deciding to leave her behind. The hope was too that she herself would make the decision and settle for a more relaxed pace over the subsequent few days.

The main street of Cacabelos is called Calle de los Peregrinos (Pilgrims' Road), as are many of the streets in towns along the camino. Having such a name on the streets reinforces the whole concept of pilgrimage and creates a real atmosphere of the pilgrim journey.

The town itself has a real touch of antiquity. Even though it had been destroyed in the eleventh century, the rebuilt town dates back as far as the twelfth century, with additions made throughout the Middle Ages. Above the entrance to the Church of Santa Maria de la Plaza stands the small stone statue of the Virgin, dating back to the thirteenth century. As I stood before this ancient image, I prayed for Rolf, Bernard and Liam.

The main street of Cacabelos was appropriately populated with pilgrims of all shapes and sizes. Some of the cyclist groups had congregated near the Plaza San Lazaro, simply soaking up the sun and taking a rest from the exertions of the early morning.

A young couple were making their way down the Calle de los Peregrinos. The girl was on crutches with her right knee heavily bandaged. Apparently, she had a severe case of tendonitis and had been ordered to give up the pilgrimage. However, the spirit of the pilgrim is stronger than the advice of any physician. So she was hoping to rest for a few days, then take a bus for a stage or two and take up the pilgrim way again.

Coat of Arms at Cacabelos, a town where many noble families resided in the thirteenth century.

Near one of the corner shops, a group of pilgrims had congregated. Some were eating ice cream, while others simply replenished their water supply. I joined the ice-cream brigade and relaxed as I listened and chatted to the pilgrims from different countries and to those who had started the pilgrim journey from different parts of Spain or France.

Carmen seemed very subdued and annoyed that I had left her on her own while I had walked ahead. However, she said nothing about it and joined me for the refreshments. Later, we went looking for some medication that she wanted; and soon after, we left to continue the route to Villafranca del Bierzo, which was some eight kilometres away.

We walked along the NVI for the next five kilometres. The road rose unrelentingly towards our destination. The going was very tough, and the gap between Carmen and myself grew once again. After Pieros, the yellow arrows pointed along a path, which crossed a narrow stream and continued through dense vegetation. The path was rising more steeply now along a wider track until, finally, we came to Villafranca del Bierzo. Carmen was doing well and following me towards the town.

The wide track known as the Camino de la Virgen passed the Romanesque Church of Santiago, famous for its 'Puerta del Perdón', the Door of Pardon. This is the door through which pilgrims who were unable to continue the camino to Santiago could pass through and receive a plenary indulgence equivalent to that given to those who completed the pilgrimage. The concession dates back to the Spanish Pope Calixto III, who was Pope from 1455 to 1458.

By the time I reached the refugio my feet were burning. The thought ran through my mind that I may have been walking too quickly and may have caused my feet to blister. It struck me as ironic that this would happen; and were it not that I do not believe in a vengeful God, I could have thought that such suffering was in retribution for my attempts to lose Carmen. A more likely explanation was that we had walked 30km, much of which was on asphalt roads. My feet had had very little respite from hard surfaces all day and were protesting loudly.

The refugio at Villafranca was big and modern, having been recently erected by the town council. Getting rid of the heavy rucksack and taking off the walking boots brought instant relief. And after our showers, both Carmen and myself were very civil, if not exactly friendly, to each other.

My main desire for the remainder of the day was to rest in preparation for the challenging walk that would face me the next day. So I wandered down to a local bar and found refreshments. As I sat in the cool of the early afternoon, I enjoyed the exercise of writing some of my journal.

The time given each day to journal writing had become something very important to me. There were times when tiredness, and sometimes laziness, led to skimpy notes and rather superficial comments. But generally, I took the time to reflect on the various events of the day and to dwell on their significance. Knowing how one

Albergue at Villafranca. This modern hostel provided the pilgrim with all the necessary services that go to make the pilgrimage more human.

day can so easily drift into the next and events become a haze of unremembered details, I was most anxious to devote what the Americans call 'quality time' to filling in each day's entry, recording my experiences and the impact that they had on my thoughts and feelings. And as I sat in the bar with the journal and my thoughts, I simply allowed myself to run through the happenings of the day from the early morning to the present.

Later on in the afternoon, I visited the town square and the other places of historical interest. However, that day I had had a surfeit of churches and monuments and found myself just wandering around without any desire to enter any particular building. Villafranca is built on various levels and when walking around the town, it was easy to tire as one climbed up the steep steps to the collegiate church or back down to the Church of San Nicolas.

Sixteenth-century castle of the Marquises of Villafranca del Bierzo, now owned by the Toledo family.

Towards late afternoon, I returned to the refugio to check my laundry and to see who had arrived. It gave me great joy to see that Javier and Nuria were there. They had just settled in, though Nuria was suffering from suspected tendonitis. Javier was tired but without any real difficulties. But they too were glad to meet; and we made arrangements for Carmen and I to join them for our evening meal.

There is a second refugio in Villafranca, which I had not noticed when I first arrived in the town. The refugio is owned by the Arias family and consists of a shanty-type construction made from a collection of buildings and what appeared to be wooden frames with plastic covering. Apparently, this refugio attracts many young people and indeed as I entered it, through the bar, there were many of them gathered there. Roger and Emmanuel greeted me. They had just arrived and were settling in. Roger was looking forward to some singing and chat with the young group that were arriving in a steady stream.

Part of me would have liked to have stayed in this more rustic setting, but I realised too that the cost of bedding down there would be that I would not sleep. I had no doubt that the singing, drinking and conversation would continue long into the night. The old conservative streak in me preferred the regularity of an early night and an early morning. I remember Roger saying that he would often leave the refugio after eleven in the morning and then walk during the hottest part of the day to the next stage of the camino, something I could never do.

That evening, Nuria, Javier, Carmen and I met outside the municipal refugio and we sauntered through the streets of Villafranca, enjoying the cooler air of the dying day. Nuria was limping a bit, but seemed unwilling to make anything of the disability. Eventually we found a small local restaurant off the main plaza and down a steeply slanting street. The evening meal was a great success. And although I had hardly any Spanish that would permit me to enter into the conversation, I found myself thoroughly enjoying their company.

What struck me forcibly was their willingness to meet with a total stranger who could hardly put two words of Spanish together. As we chatted about the journey from Ponferrada, with each of us telling our stories, I reflected how much I would enjoy walking with them the following day. This was something I kept to myself: I was conscious of Carmen and of her needs as well.

Towards 9.30pm, we began making our way back to the refugio. As I approached the Arias' family refugio, I could hear the strains of music and singing. No doubt the young people were having a wonderful time. But I knew that I was more at home with the company of the older pilgrims who had, over a meal, shared the story of their journey with me.

As I lay on my bed that night, I began to feel sorry for Carmen who still seemed so lost. As a fellow pilgrim, I found myself incapable of abandoning her. So many people had helped me along the route that I felt duty bound to support her on the journey. Certainly, I did feel the need for time to myself; yet, a greater need was to assist a fellow pilgrim on the way. So, before the peace of sleep overcame me, I made the decision to stay with Carmen as long as she needed. And with that decision, tranquillity soothed me and lulled me into a deep sleep.

Day Twenty-Five
Villafranca del Bierzo to O Cebreiro
Thursday 16 July 1998

There are two options for the beginning of the route to O Cebreiro. One way follows the NVI through the Valcarce valley. Apparently, this is the authentic pilgrims' route; unfortunately, it means the pilgrim has to follow the road along which very heavy traffic passes. The alternative route involves a steep three-kilometre climb up Monte del Real and offers a marvellous view over the Valcarce valley.

Still very aware of my own lack of fitness and despite having walked almost 600km, I decided to follow the original pilgrim's route and risk the perils of heavy morning Spanish traffic. Being very aware of Carmen as well, the only option was the route through the Valcarce valley.

Prior to leaving the refugio, Nuria and Javier invited us to share their breakfast with them. All they had was milk and doughnuts; yet the gesture was all the more touching for that. I am always moved by the generosity of so many pilgrims along the way. It challenges me on so many occasions to act in the same fashion, though often I found myself being selfish. It will take me many a pilgrimage to open my heart to the needs of others and the generosity that I was daily witnessing from other pilgrims.

Nuria and Javier had decided to take the mountain climb despite the fact that Nuria had been suffering from quite painful legs. She still seemed determined to face into the challenge, and all I could do was salute her courage.

Carmen and I departed the refugio at 6.00am in the dark and made our way alongside the imposing Monte del Real in a southerly direction towards the motorway. Even at that hour, the traffic was positively dangerous with gigantic juggernauts hurtling along the road at break-neck speeds. The space for pedestrians was almost non-existent, so we had to hug the crash barrier that bordered on the dense vegetation to the left of the road.

After about a mile, a yellow arrow on the other side of the road pointed to a route that led to a path clinging to the side of the mountain and overlooking the road. Walking along this path was infinitely preferable to battling with the traffic along the road verge; it also offered a pleasant walk through a tree-lined path. This led to the hamlet called Pereje, which contained a most beautifully appointed refugio alongside the main route through the sleeping village. Eventually this path led to Trabadelo whose main attraction for us was that it possessed a roadside café!

After about an hour's walk out of Villafranca, there developed quite an intense burning sensation in my feet. On occasions prior to this, my feet had been quite hot and to some extent burned. This time, however, the sensation of sharp pins and needles began to make walking rather uncomfortable. There was no real worry at the time, but walking had become somewhat less enjoyable and I looked forward to taking off my boots and socks to allow the cool morning air refresh my aching feet.

Trabadelo was the ideal place to rest. Once a cold drink was bought, I emerged from the café and sat down on a bench overlooking the roadway to examine my feet. The only sign of possible difficulty was the thickness of the skin that had formed on the soles. Whether this was causing the trouble was not certain, but I decided that a filing of the hardened skin might improve matters. The pain had been quite considerable, making it rather difficult to walk. What would happen if this condition deteriorated?

I was about six days walk from Santiago, and my confidence had been growing daily about my ability to make the 800km pilgrimage. Now difficulties were surfacing; a feeling of anxiety crept into me. Images of many pilgrims on crutches, or limping, or with bandages on various parts of their legs, flooded into my mind. Maybe I was to become part of the limping brigade. But for the moment, I intended continuing as long as I could possibly withstand the pain.

After Trabadelo, we continued along the motorway, and before long, we began to be overtaken by pilgrims who had taken the mountain track. James, the young English man, caught up with us. He had stayed in the Arias' family refugio in Villafranca, which was why I had not met him. He seemed in great shape and oblivious of the difficulties that lesser mortals like myself were beginning to experience. With a salute, he left us as he strode quickly away along the footpath leading to Ambasmestas.

Ambasmestas lies just at the confluence of the Rio Valboa and the Rio Valcarcel rivers in an area of rustic beauty. The view to the left of us, along the Rio Valcarcel, reminded me of the Dargal valley around Enniskerry and of my scouting days when we would walk along the river and under the trees that lined it. The memory made me think how good it was to be alive. The pain in my feet had eased considerably, and this allowed me concentrate on the beauty of the surrounding countryside.

Ahead we could see the imposing mountain that was to be our destination for the day. Its height of 1,293 metres reached to the unclouded blue sky inviting pilgrims to embark on what looked like a daunting climb for people not used to mountain climbing. And yet for others, this would only be considered a mere hillock in comparison to the Alps of France and Italy. For me, who had not even climbed Carrantuohill, the highest mountain in Ireland at 1040 metres, I knew that it would present a definite challenge, something, however, that I was anticipating with enthusiasm.

We walked along the path through some very beautifully named villages, such as Vega de Calcarce, Ruitelán and Herrerias. Each village lay along the banks of the River Valcarcel in idyllic surroundings. The river, the mountain and the abundance of trees along grass covered stretches of flat ground, created scenes almost similar to the Swiss views one sometimes sees on chocolate boxes.

Carmen seemed to have improved her mood and was walking quite well. I was glad not to have abandoned her completely. Even though I longed for some time with myself, I felt sure that this would eventually come about. From the struggle she had endured yesterday, I predicted that after the strenuous climb that lay ahead, she would eventually decide to take a rest-day. In this way, I felt happier that she would be the one making the decision and would not feel hurt by being left behind. But even today, I found myself walking somewhat ahead of her at times, and these moments of solitude created the necessary space for me to reflect on things personal. I found it ironic that prior to meeting her, I had been struggling with the challenges of chastity. Now these had ceased!

Just before I began the big climb, the path led to the small stone bridge that spans the River Valcarcel. There I met Nuria and Javier in the company of other pilgrims whom I did not know. They were taking a rest before the challenge of the climb. The entire group had 'conquered' Monte del Real that morning and seemed enthusiastic about the next challenge. I certainly could not have faced both mountains. At it was, I knew how difficult I would find this one. However, despite a certain tiredness, I looked forward to the challenge.

This was an ideal moment for a rest and a mouthful of truly refreshing cold water from the fountain near the bridge. And as we slaked our thirst, the group grew somewhat silent before the beauty that surrounded them. The sound of the river could be heard as it rushed by the small stone bridge, and a breeze blew gently through the trees.

In the silence of this sylvan scene, I thanked the Creator of this beauty; and as I thought of the Divine presence in all of creation, I felt a sense of well-being that filled me with peace and joy. Indeed, it was good for me to be there. It was at moments like these that I felt so privileged at having had the opportunity to undertake the camino and to have survived so far. Even had I to finish then, there was much for which I would be eternally grateful.

The climb was very steep, going along a winding path and amidst the tall heather on either side. Initially the path was paved with huge flagstones, which later gave way to a beaten path. Just beyond Laguna de Castilla there was a stone marking the boundary between Castile and Galicia and indicating that Santiago de Compostela lay 152km away. This raised my spirits even more as I thought of the arrival at Santiago that would, I hope, take place in five days time; that is, if nothing untoward happened in the meantime.

As I climbed the ever-ascending path, the view began to unfold beneath in all its splendour. It is at times like this that one begins to understand the motivation that drives mountain climbers to endure the challenges of scaling the heights. For all around me I could see sheer beauty in the distant hills and the tree-covered slopes beneath. I stopped now and again to recover some of my strength but also to savour the panoramic beauty.

Rounding a bend and near a farmyard, I came across Javier and Nuria who had sat down to rest and take a snack. They invited me to join them and encouraged me to eat. I had brought nothing in the rucksack by way of food, but they willingly thrust cheese, tomatoes and bread on me, saying that it would be necessary to feed the body for the remainder of the trek. It was a relief to pause for a while, for I had found the climb to that point quite difficult and there was further to go.

Carmen was still far behind. In the distance, I could hear her complaining aloud about the difficulty of the climb. But I kept going, knowing that to wait for her would have been a bad idea. But as we were finishing our snack, she joined us looking very tired and feeling rather depressed. We stayed with her until she settled down for a rest and then took off for the next stage.

The sun was at its strongest in the early afternoon. It was about three o'clock and there was no sign of the ascent coming to an end. Climbing is a humbling experience. As I walked slowly upward, I was overtaken by both young and old who saluted as they passed and continued on upwards. I had no inclination to increase my pace to keep up with them. I would not have been able to anyway. But I simply kept a steady slow pace and each bend in the path brought me closer to the summit.

Further on, I came across two pilgrims on horseback. This was a first for me. I had heard that people travel the camino on horseback but I had never seen any up to that point. That deserved a photograph. Indeed, most of the pilgrims who had recently passed me stopped to admire the mounted pilgrims and to photograph them. The horses seemed to enjoy the public interest and stood there calmly while the owners discussed the problems of being a pilgrim on horseback. The main problem apparently for them was to find suitable shelter for the horses each night. On the other hand, the riders did not have the problem of carrying their luggage. So there were some advantages, though personally I was pleased to be a pilgrim on foot, however sore they may have been.

Towards four o'clock, I came to a gap in a wall that led to the town of O Cebreiro. We had been walking since six that morning, and we were now feeling the effects of ten hours walking. The relief, however, was greater than the fatigue and I looked forward to a warm shower and a rest.

O Cebreiro is one of the ancient pilgrim stops along the camino. It dates back as far as the early eleventh century, when Alfonso VI entrusted the monastery to a group of French monks from Aurillac. Inside the beautiful Romanesque Church is the statue of Santa María la Real, venerated by many Spanish people. According to my guidebook, up to 30,000 pilgrims visit the shrine of Santa Maria la Real on her feast day on 8 September.

But O Cebreiro is most famous for the story of the 'Miracle of O Cebreiro'. This took place in the early part of the fourteenth century, when a peasant from the nearby village of Barxamaior struggled through the snow to attend Mass and receive Holy Communion. The priest celebrating the Mass saw the peasant arrive and thought to himself how simple and stupid the man had been to come to Mass on such a day. The priest's faith obviously was not that strong. As these condescending thoughts ran through his head, the bread and wine in the paten and chalice that he was holding turned literally into the blood and flesh of Christ. The reliquary that the Catholic kings donated is displayed together with the paten and chalice in a reinforced glass-fronted safe.

When I arrived at the refugio, I was horrified to see a queue of up to 70 people all waiting for the scheduled opening. They were seated in a neat and orderly line waiting patiently and in good spirits. This was the last straw for me. I had walked for ten hours in the heat of the day, and I could not bear waiting any longer for a shower. I immediately went hunting for

O Cebreiro, situated over 1100 metres above sea level, was one of the more important stops on the camino.

alternative lodging and inquired at a nearby pensión. The owner was looking for €30, which I told him was too expensive. He did not seem pleased with my remarks and simply shrugged his shoulders.

Just as I was about to go in another direction, I met Javier who suggested that we look for alternative accommodation. I went along with him; and to my embarrassment he went to the same pensión I had tried earlier. The man cited the same price he had quoted to me and Javier was willing to pay. When I agreed also to stay, the owner said that he had no space for me and told Javier why. I felt really stupid, and I'm sure Javier was wondering what I had been up to in trying to find my own lodging without reference to him and Nuria.

Soon after, however, I found a room in a pensión near the road that leads out of O Cebreiro and quickly accepted the price of €30 for a single room with shower facilities. Before washing, I left to see if Carmen had arrived. She jumped at the idea of getting a room and was lucky to obtain the last one in the same pensión. The Good Samaritan had not died completely in me!

Towards six o'clock, while in the Church of Santa María la Real, I came across a group of French pilgrims beginning to assist at a Mass. It was always very pleasant for me to get to a Mass during the camino, and I enjoyed hearing it celebrated in French. When it came to the homily, I found the priest going on interminably and after about 15 minutes of that, I decided to leave. It was good that I did because on my return to the church an hour later, the group was still listening to the extended homily. It seems that they were members of some religious movement and had a particular interest in sharing their ideas in the Scriptures.

O Cebreiro is also famous for its 'pallozas', round thatched houses that date back to prehistoric times. There was one fine example of these that had been transformed into a

O Cebreiro is famous for 'pallozas', round thatched dwellings for the local community.

museum, which I visited. It was very worthwhile and despite the fact that I could not fully understand the guide who explained the various aspects of peasant life in the past, I found the experience most enlightening. The struggles of a modern pilgrim fade dramatically in comparison with the hardship of the age-old peasant way of life.

That evening, Javier, Nuria, Carmen and myself came together for our dinner. Another Spanish pilgrim called Esteban joined us. He was a teacher and was using his long summer holidays to walk the camino. I had not met him to date along the pilgrim road, and although this may appear strange, it often happens that people can be walking the same route and hardly ever meet.

The restaurant was filled with pilgrims but again they were strangers to me. James was nowhere to be seen. Roger and Emmanuelle were more than likely in the refugio. I wondered where the young Emmanuel was. But that was the way things turned out. As I travelled along the route, I met some people for a day and then they disappeared. Even Francesco and Dominique had faded from the scene, and Frieda had vanished.

Towards nine in the evening, the restaurant began to empty, as pilgrims made their way to their beds. As our meal concluded, I thought to myself that the five of us could easily become separated during the next few days. I hoped, however, that Nuria and Javier would be around for the rest of the camino. I had become very fond of them.

Day Twenty-Six
O Cebreiro to Samos
Friday 17 July 1998

Carmen and I left O Cebreiro at 5.30am to be sure of a place at the Samos refugio. With the approach of the feast day of St James, it was getting increasingly difficult to be certain of a bed with all the groups from differing parishes organising shorter walks to Santiago to be there for the feast day. We decided, therefore, to set out in the belief that first come would be first served. It was not something I was very convinced of, and even though I agreed to see how the early start would work, I did not want to spend the time rushing to the end of the stage and thereby missing out on the experience of the journey. However, there we were in the dark, making our way out of the village.

The only light to guide us came from the stars that shone brightly in the dark morning sky but they were insufficient to indicate the route to take. As it turned out, the route simply followed the road down the side of Monte Pozo de Aréa.

As we went along, we passed an impressive statue of St Roque, the saint from Montpellier who travelled on pilgrimage to Rome in the fourteenth century and en route contracted the plague. He is usually seen pointing to his bared leg, which bears the scars of that terrible affliction. It was too dark to get a proper photograph of the statue even with the flash, but just standing beside this mighty Saint offered a fine vista of the valley below. It felt as if the Saint was bestowing his blessing on the pilgrims as they descended the valley.

I was beginning to experience great soreness in my right foot, and was glad to stop near the Hospital da Condesa, where I peeled an orange and allowed myself to savour the refreshing flavour of the ripe fruit. Oranges had become my favourite food for the journey. Having tried taking some bread and cheese on occasions, I had found it difficult to eat anything substantial in the heat of the day. But the fruit offered sustenance and quenched my thirst. Sitting down on the low wall alongside the road, I enjoyed the break and as I ate, I wondered how I would fare during the stage to Samos, a distance of 30km.

We climbed up to Alto de Poio at the junction of the NVI and found a small café that was luckily open. We were the first to arrive, but soon a crowd began to gather and pilgrims sat outside enjoying the strong coffee. Carmen was still fretful, making me suspect that she was near the point of resting for a day. I was determined not to push this. I would leave it up to her to make the decision, though I hoped more than ever that I could have some time to myself without offending her unnecessarily.

As we continued, I began to feel pain in my feet again and found it necessary to periodically stop and take off my boots to give my feet some respite. The stops were becoming more frequent as we began to descend towards Triacastela, appearing then in the distance. I was finding that the effects of the Feldene lasted only an hour or so. The situation was causing me increasing anxiety, but there did not appear to be any solution other than taking a day to rest, something I was avoiding at all costs.

The route went through some lovely countryside, with the valley of the Rio Ouribia stretching below as far as Triacastela. By now, I was descending through a shady track with trees almost forming a tunnel along the path. Eventually I came upon Ramil, a small hamlet nestling in the wooded area approaching Triacastela. Finally, I arrived at the town having used up all my Feldene and beginning to sense the pain increasing.

On the way into Triacastela I had passed by the refugio, which seemed quite inviting and while I had no intention of stopping there, I hoped Carmen would. She as much as intimated that she was ready for a rest day. Indeed, she was in no fit state to continue. She looked exhausted.

The main street leading through the town had quite a few cafés; at each of them there was quite a gathering of pilgrims. I spied Nuria and Javier, and they waved to invite me to join them. They were all tucking into an *impanada*, a savoury tart that I had not tasted up to that point and which may have been a speciality of the area. It appeared very tempting and soon I joined them as we munched away and drank plenty of liquids. Carmen came into view, looking under the weather. It seemed as if she had had enough. She appeared angry and crestfallen that things had come to the stage when she was going to have to give up. Most of the pilgrims by this time had experienced some of her complaining and were rather reluctant to pay her too much attention. Eventually, she went looking for a place to stay; we continued chatting and eating under the shade of the sun-umbrellas on the pavements outside the cafés.

The statue of St James at Triacastela with the traditional garb of the medieval pilgrim.

One of the pilgrims I was delighted to see and whom I had not set eyes on since Navarette was the friendly Miriam, as she introduced herself. She was the lady who had organised the group of four; the two young boys and the other woman, all of whom had arrived in Navarette drenched that afternoon.

Miriam turned out to be as friendly as I had supposed her to be. Her sunny outlook and caring approach to life was refreshing after the self-preoccupation of Carmen over the last week or so. Talking with her, I complimented her on her almost flawless English. She explained that she was married to an American who worked for a big corporation in Madrid.

Most of the pilgrims at our table were heading for Samos, about nine kilometres away; others were going straight to Sarria, a distance of 17km. I had intended going to Samos to visit one of the most ancient monasteries in Spain and was pleased that many of the more familiar faces would also be taking that route.

Before setting off, however, I scouted around for a pharmacy where I could replenish my supply of Feldene. It seemed likely that this would be essential for the remainder of the day at least, and should the pain continue, it could be necessary for the rest of the camino. So, once I had purchased the necessary supply, I was ready for the road.

We had to walk along the route towards Samos for the next six kilometres or so. As usual, I always resented having to walk along a motorway. Thankfully, the route of the camino offers the pilgrim a considerable portion of the way along earthen paths and through open countryside. I never worked out the exact distance but hazarding a guess, I would venture that seventy-five percent of the way is along pleasant country paths.

My guidebook informed me that I would have to walk for 10km along the motorway until Samos was reached. However, after about five or six kilometres, a yellow arrow pointed to the right and into a wooded section of the countryside. With relief, I turned off the horrible motorway and entered into an enchanting section of the route, leading through thickly populated landscapes, with trees and vegetation of all varieties. The sun was high in the sky, but the shade from the trees provided a welcome shelter from its unrelenting heat. Running through the woodland was the River Ouribio, gurgling as it flowed vigorously over the rocks and through gullies along its meandering way.

Miriam passed with her companion from Navarette, and as they saluted, I wondered what had happened to the two young men that had formed the quartet at Navarette. Miriam and her friend both seemed in great physical shape as they almost bounded along the woodland path.

The picturesque scene continued through farmyards and along other beautiful pathways. At one stage I stopped in sheer wonderment at a scene before me. The river had become a small cascade, which I could view through the remains of an ancient barn. It had once, it seemed, harnessed the water for what probably was a mill to grind the corn of the local district. This demanded a photograph, though none could capture the sheer beauty that filled me with such joy.

I arrived at the motorway to discover that I had still some distance to walk to reach Samos. The pain in my feet had become almost unbearable; and I was forced to stop walking and rest a while. It was difficult to understand what was causing the pain. A close examination revealed nothing strange. There were no blisters and although the soles of both feet had become very hard, it was difficult to imagine that this was causing the problem. There was no solution but to rest. By this time, I wanted to arrive at Samos without delay. The route I had taken was indescribably beautiful, but there comes a time at each stage of the camino when the focus shifts again to the destination rather than the journey. I had arrived at one such stage.

Eventually I came across the town of Samos; at that point, I was literally hobbling. Only with difficulty could I put my foot down on the ground and take a step. It was as if I were walking on red hot coals in my bare feet; people watching me must have wondered what had happened to this pilgrim.

The refugio in Samos consisted of a large dormitory-like room at the side of the monastic complex. Although it appeared basic, I was very relieved to have arrived and to find that there was room for me. Collapsing onto a bed, I found myself for the first time reluctant to get moving to do the laundry and have a shower. I simply wanted to sleep and rest. The sense of relief was indescribable, and I allowed sleep to overcome me. And there, for the best part of an hour, I forgot the pain that seemed to disappear once I had no pressure on the affected areas.

Reality must be faced eventually, however. On awakening, I realised that the situation was serious. There was no way I could continue the camino in my condition. Panic began to grow as I envisaged at best, a forced sojourn in Samos for some time and at worst, abandonment of the camino after 27 days walking. This beggared belief. How could I have arrived almost unscathed to this point only to find myself up against a pain barrier that appeared insuperable? I refused to even contemplate giving up, deciding that I would not even allow myself to imagine such a scenario. Instead, I gathered myself together and began preparing for the next day's walk by having a refreshing shower and doing the laundry.

Across from the refugio were two cafés and as I entered one, I greeted a group of people playing cards. There was no-one at the bar and when I asked to order something, one of the card players reluctantly rose to serve. As she was pouring the cider, I inquired if she could prepare a *bocadilo* (a sandwich). With little apology, the young woman informed me that they had ceased serving food and would not commence providing snacks until seven that evening. Nothing was going to interfere with the cards, I could see.

Having finished my pint of cider, I moved to the next bar to search for some food and was fortunate to find the staff there totally available to serve pilgrims. I sat at a table beside a group of four pilgrims, all of whom would have been in their sixties. They were probably two married couples and were speaking German. As I sat down, they smiled and appeared to want to talk. It turned out that they were from the German-speaking region of Switzerland and had walked some of the stages of the camino while their friends drove a back-up vehicle. In the course of the conversation, I told them of my difficulties with my feet. One of the women recommended that I buy a product called Volteren, recommended for the symptoms I described.

On leaving this very pleasant company of pilgrims, I made without haste for the local *farmacia* (pharmacy), which was quite a distance towards the outskirts of Samos. It was painful making my way there and frustrating to find the farmacia closed. No sooner, however, had I arrived than a woman rushed across from the bar opposite the chemist, introducing herself as the proprietor. She entered her chemist shop and without delay fetched the Volteren that I needed. She was most gracious and wished me good fortune for the remainder of the camino. What a difference from the card players!

The guidebook pointed out that Samos monastery is one of the most ancient monastic sites in Spain. Dating back to the seventh century, this Benedictine establishment would have offered hospitality to pilgrims down the centuries. Interestingly enough, the guidebook pointed out the following: 'Samos was never comparable to the other Benedictine monasteries at Sahagún, Nájera, Leyre, Carrión or Villafranca, whose principal mission was to offer aid to pilgrims.' I would later discover how true this statement was. But already I had compared the size and magnificence of the monastery with the very basic and rather primitive facilities made available to pilgrims in the refugio.

The monastery at Samos is one of the oldest in Spain, dating back to the seventh century.

As I could almost have predicted, when I approached the monastery for the guided tour, the sign indicated that they had all finished for the day. I had to make do with admiring the Renaissance and Baroque features of the façade displaying the figure of St Benedict, one of the founders of monasticism in Europe. However, a notice informed me that pilgrims were invited to join the community in reciting Vespers at six o'clock that evening in the community chapel. At least I would gain entry into the inner sanctum.

At exactly six, the Angelus bell began ringing, and a door leading into the monastery opened to allow pilgrims to follow a rather severe-looking monk inside. We climbed the stone steps into this formidable building and arrived on the first floor of the cloister. All along the walls were the most bizarre frescoes, which appeared to be of recent origin. None had the beauty of Fra Angelico in Sancta Croce. Rather, they were images of strange creatures that appeared to be characters in a nightmare.

We were shown into an uninspiring chapel with little decoration. There must have been about 80 pilgrims occupying the pews of this modest place of prayer. At the end of the chapel were a few elderly monks, dressed in their habits and kneeling in prayer.

The office began, and as it unfolded, I found myself both disappointed and angry at the lack of any effort on the part of the monks to offer pilgrims an opportunity to join in the prayers. They seemed to be simply going through the motions as they recited in choir the psalms of the day. The pilgrims were provided with books to follow the service but no effort was made to involve any of them. Nor was there any aspect of the ritual that would move the most devotional of pilgrims, never mind the more cynical or secular.

At the conclusion of Vespers, the pilgrims almost stampeded to exit from the chapel as if collectively recognising the emptiness of the ritual. Everyone began talking loudly in the chapel, to the consternation of the monks. An excited and annoyed monk clapped his hands and sternly admonished us for our lack of reverence, and as we emerged from the chapel, the same monk informed us that all pilgrims were invited to attend the Mass that followed Vespers.

At that stage, I happened to be beside Javier; I commented to him that I had had enough religion for the day. He seemed very amused, considering I had told him that I was a religious Brother. And as we walked towards the exit, in more subdued tones, I explained how disappointed I had been with the entire charade. Javier had not come across as particularly religious but I think he understood that something had been missing from the proceedings.

Javier and Nuria joined me for dinner. I was touched by their concern for my health. In comparison to the distant religiosity of the Benedictine monks, here was a couple who really cared and were willing to assist in any way they could. However, I knew that this was something that only I could deal with.

Eventually, pilgrims have to face that moment when they are on their own. I recalled the poor limping girl at the Hospital de Orbigo and the struggle she had with the group that were divided as to what to do with her. And the picture of the pilgrim on crutches in Cacabelos on the way to Villafranca came immediately to mind too. So I was very careful not to make Nuria or Javier feel any duty to assist me at this moment of difficulty. They had their own pilgrimage to complete, which I would never have permitted them to delay for any reason. This determination to underplay the difficulty facing me meant that the evening became a most enjoyable sharing of our pilgrim stories.

That night I found it difficult to sleep. A woman, one of the Swiss party I had met in the bar, was sleeping near me. I could not believe the sound that was coming from her. At first, I was convinced that it must be a man: never had I heard such snoring since the time of the Brazilian at Fromista. Here was a worthy competitor. The sound simply bored into my mind and made it impossible for me to sleep. I looked over to confirm that it was a woman as I had never heard a female snore so loudly: it was.

Eventually, I took my mattress, escaping reluctantly to the large bathroom that housed the toilets and showers. There I set the mattress on the ground. I hoped that away from the snoring Swiss lady I could get some rest. As I lay down in my new setting, I began thinking of the difficulty I was going to have to face the next day with my feet causing real concern. I did slip into sleep in the end, but only after much tossing and turning.

Day Twenty-Seven
Samos to Portomarín
Saturday 18 July 1998

From Samos to Sarria there are two options. One route follows the motorway and is about 12km in distance. The other route is far more circuitous, wending its way through the countryside. It was the second option that appealed to me that morning.

I awoke feeling hopeful that I could continue the camino despite the physical warnings of the previous day. I could feel that the soles of my feet had become somewhat numb, though the night's rest had at least mitigated some of the pain that I had felt the day before. Somehow, I felt that if I could avoid the unyielding asphalt roads, my feet would fare better and would have some respite from one of the camino's few negative effects.

It was a foggy misty morning as I set out on a new adventure. I had asked some locals about the alternative route and had been warned that it was very badly sign-posted and was much longer. Nevertheless, for health and survival reasons, I was prepared to take my chances among the pathways that followed the Rio Ouribio.

Soon after leaving the town, I saw the first yellow arrow pointing to a rise that brought me away from the main road. The trees quickly shielded me from the view of the road. Before long I was in the midst of country paths that wended their way through magnificent countryside shrouded in the early morning mist. It looked as if it could rain at any moment, but the cool morning air invigorated me and filled me with confidence that the difficulties of the previous day could be overcome.

Having the morning to myself away from Carmen was indeed a relief. How had we stayed together for so long, I wondered? For the best part of two weeks I had been with her and although the first few days were fine, what had followed was quite awkward. Initially I had enjoyed sharing our stories and our faith journey. But then, after three or four days, the interest began to wane; I found her becoming a burden.

I began questioning myself about whether it was charity that made me stay with her or the incapacity within myself to confront the issue and make the break. As I was mulling over the question, I simply decided to let the whole matter drop for then and enjoy the feeling of having space to myself. And as I walked near the river my spirits began to lift, as I repeated the morning offering and my pilgrim prayer.

There was not a pilgrim in sight. Nor indeed was there a soul from the locality to be seen. The quiet of the morning, with the sound of the river nearby filled my spirits with a peace and contentment that was powerfully felt. The blessing of the camino was indeed palpable as I strolled along the route, stopping periodically to examine a particular tree or plant. Just pausing along the route created a sense of peace and tranquillity that I had not felt for quite some time.

Soon, however, the pain returned and forced me to stop and apply Feldene. The previous night I had taken some Volteren in the hope that any swelling or inflammation could be checked. But it was Feldene that seemed to have the most immediate effect, and after about ten minutes, I was able once again to resume walking.

Many hours passed, and I began to feel somewhat uncertain about the way ahead. Since my guidebook did not describe this route, I was at the mercy of the yellow arrows. These had proved to be very regular and clear, contrary to what I had been told. However, I knew that the distance was 12km, which, under normal circumstances, could be completed in about three hours. Now it was nearly ten o'clock and I had been walking for more than four hours. Doubts filled my mind; and as I thought of what was before me after Sarria, I became seriously concerned. The journey from Sarria to Portomarín is 21km and I would be walking in the hottest period of the day.

Making my way along a minor road, I heard the bell of a bicycle and a shout of greeting. It was Georgie, whom I had first met at Rabanal and who had given me and many pilgrims such a welcome. She explained how she had spent only a few days in Rabanal before deciding to embark on the camino once again. She had continued on the route by bicycle but had no desire to rush things. Each day she only travelled the distance that a pilgrim would walk because, as she had previously explained, she had been a pilgrim on foot prior to hurting her leg and wanted to keep in contact with the walking fraternity.

It was great to see her, and when she expressed concern at my obvious limp, I explained the symptoms to her. She wondered from the description I gave her whether I could have a touch of gout! I could hardly believe my ears. It was true that each night at supper I had sampled quite an amount of the local wine. With each menu, an entire bottle of wine is included in the bill. And often, even if I did not finish the bottle completely (and sometimes I did), I would definitely take three glassfuls. But I had never even imagined that this could be the cause of the problem.

Georgie laughed at my surprised expression and playfully warned me of living the high life. With that, she left me with a sympathetic pat on the back and cycled away towards Sarria. She was a fine person, full of spirit and the courage to have faced her own problems and continued on the camino, albeit on a bicycle.

As I approached Sarria, I could see a distant figure ahead of me that seemed familiar. Not having good long-distance sight, I could not have been sure. Yet as I neared the town, my pace was obviously faster than the figure ahead and within some 200 metres of the town I realised that it was Carmen. She had obviously walked from Triacastela that morning and was continuing on the camino. My immediate reaction was to slow down and avoid meeting her. This I did, planning how to avoid to walk with her.

Entering Sarria at a much reduced pace, I approached the old part of the town, which had been built on the side of a hill, and made directly to leave Sarria without delay. I would like to have spent some time visiting the remains of the castle that crowned the town and to have visited the Monastery of La Magdalena. But I was more concerned not to meet Carmen and to have to explain that I wanted to walk alone.

As luck would have it, I bumped into her just as I emerged from a local grocer's shop, having purchased my supplies for the day. She appeared still concerned and anxious but seemed to brighten when she saw me. I was not looking forward to the encounter and wondered what way things would develop.

Castle ruins at Sarria where there was a pre-Roman settlement before the town was built in the sixth century.

"Are you going as far as Barbadelo, David?" She did not obviously want to go further. Barbadelo was just 3.5km away.

"No, I'm for Portomarín, Carmen."

"Oh, but that's miles away. I couldn't walk that distance today. It's too far." She gave all the appearances of someone who was tired. I said nothing to give her false hope. There was silence for a second or two. "Best of luck, David. Maybe we'll meet in Santiago!" There was disappointment in her voice.

"OK, Carmen, Take care!" There was nothing more to say, so we shook hands and I departed. I did hope that we could meet eventually in Santiago, but not before that. I needed more time to myself.

I passed the monastery of La Magdalena, noticing the fine stonework and the Romanesque portals, and made my way downhill, past the cemetery and along the road, until I crossed the bridge over the Celeiro river. Having crossed a railway line, I continued alongside it for some minutes before crossing a stream. Before heading uphill into an oak grove, I decided to rest and take some lunch in a nearby field.

The sun was high in the sky, but its intense heat did not reach me under the shade of some trees where a gentle breeze was blowing. At first, I simply lay down and felt my whole body relaxing. Eventually, I prepared lunch, and while enjoying the snack, I surveyed the scene around. It seemed as if the countryside had displaced any trace of suburbia though I had walked hardly more than a kilometre out of Sarria.

I heard the sound of boots on the stony path nearby and saw James passing. With a shout, I called to him to join me. He was in good form and obviously ready to make it for Portomarín without delay. But he seemed pleased to have the opportunity to rest a while and we shared the food we had.

James talked about himself and of his plans. He was obviously a highly intelligent young man but one who did not flaunt his gifts. He had spent the last few years in research into computers and was now moving to a new job in telecommunications. He talked about his studies and his life in a way that showed great humility and simplicity. But he was able nevertheless to pursue his own interests and dreams, despite being slightly modest. He was thoroughly enjoying his pilgrim walk and exploring the monasteries along the way.

As I listened, I found myself growing in admiration of him. We parted, and I made my way much more slowly than him up the hill and into an area of fields interspersed with farmhouses dotted in random fashion along the camino. The heat of the sun in a cloudless sky was very strong in the early afternoon.

The walk took me through a number of small villages with lovely-sounding names like Domiz, Leiman and Peruscallo and alongside clumps of chestnut and oak. The surrounding countryside lay before me like a patterned tablecloth laid out for some special occasion or important visitor. I was being treated to a real feast.

I spotted a type of farm guesthouse with tables and sun umbrellas in the garden and some pilgrims sitting having a drink. It was Miriam, from Navarette, who had joined the company of three other young women. So I joined the foursome, who were enjoying the shade from the sun. Miriam introduced Georgina, Inowa and Franca, three beautiful-looking young people who were walking the camino together. I have forgotten the details of each person, but I remember that they were nurses and that one, probably Inowa, was Finnish but doing her nursing practice in Madrid, where she met her two companions.

They were delightful company and obviously had found in Miriam the sort of person that was a pleasure to know. My own regret was that I myself had not come to know Miriam more during the camino. She seemed so balanced a person with a good sense of humour. The four girls were going to stay at a refugio in Ferreiros, some five or six kilometres away. They were, therefore, in no hurry to move on towards their destination. I would loved to have stayed with them, but I knew the road ahead was still challenging. Reluctantly, I bade my farewell and hoped that we would meet again.

As I walked along a narrow track that climbed gradually uphill, I came across the 100km stone to Santiago. It was covered with pilgrims' graffiti, celebrating the important event of having only 100km to walk before embracing the statue of St James in Santiago.

A moment of prayer seemed appropriate at this significant juncture. Gratitude for the Lord's protection was uppermost in my mind. I thanked God for his presence in me all along the route. The difficulty I was having with my feet further highlighted the fragility of the entire venture, and I prayed that I would accept whatever would happen over the next few days. I was even coming to accept that there was the vague possibility I might

Portomarín's reservoir was built in 1962 when the new town replaced the submerged one.

have to abandon the pilgrimage. But I still felt determined to continue if my feet would stand the pressure.

On through other villages I passed, until I began climbing towards Ferreiros. There on the top of the ascent was a rather ugly building, now used as a refugio. The place was packed and among the pilgrims struggling to settle in, I came across Caroline and Michael, whom I had first met outside León.

Caroline, in her enthusiastic manner, ran and embraced me, expressing her joy at meeting after such a long time. Michael, true to character, smiled in a quieter manner indicating his own pleasure at the reunion. I was delighted to meet them again and to see that they were still on the camino and in good shape. They had lived the experience to the full and had many stories to share about the journey.

When I expressed disappointment that they were stopping at Ferreiros, they decided to change plans and make for Portomarín as well. This would allow us to meet that night and chat over a beer. It would also mean that we could be together for the rest of the camino.

The remainder of the journey was quite tiring. The initial descent led to the villages of Mirallos and Pena and then on to Couto and Rozas. Then there was the climb to Pena do Cervo, before descending again towards Moimentos and the pleasant valley of the River Bocelo, where Moutras is situated.

One village led to the next but as the walk continued, I found myself thinking more of the arrival at Portomarín. It was approaching 6.00pm and I had been walking for almost 12 hours. As fortune would have it, the stretches on the pathways through the countryside had cushioned my feet from continuous pain. And as I approached Portomarín, I noticed a sign that indicated the distance to the town in kilometres and the time required to reach the destination. That was a real relief; I hoped that there would be room in the refugio for someone arriving so late. This was the latest I would ever arrive at a refugio. Normally, I tried to arrive towards two o'clock so that I would have time to wash clothes, eat and visit the sites. That night I would only have time to wash and eat. The laundry would have to wait for the next day.

Crossing the impressive bridge over the River Mino, I could see the town towering above me, with the road curving around as it rose to lead into the centre of the town.

Portomarín was originally situated on the banks of the River Mino, but in 1956 it was decided to construct a reservoir in the valley where the town stood. The village was submerged, and only the remains of the medieval bridge and the Church of San Nicolas were preserved. The church, also known as the Church of San Juan because it was the headquarters of the Order of St John of Jerusalem, one of the religious military orders, was deconstructed on-site and moved up to the town where it was reconstructed stone by stone on its present site.

At the refugio I was lucky enough to be given the last bed and had begun to settle in when Roger and Emmanuelle arrived. I felt for them, as they too seemed exhausted after their long walk. They had to go looking for lodging where they could be together.

Caroline and Michael had arrived earlier at Portomarín. Caroline kindly offered to buy me fruit before the shops closed. This extra time saved gave me the opportunity to wash the clothes that I had taken off and put in the drying-room in another part of the refugio.

The Church of San Juan at Portomarín was transported brick by brick from the flooded valley to its present position.

When she returned, we went for a drink, walking along the arcaded street of Portomarín. Nuria, Javier and Esteban joined us. Roger and Emmanuelle came later; and together we shared our stories of the walk that day. They all expressed great sympathy when I told them of my problems with my feet, but all were unanimous that I could not give up, now that I was within reach of Santiago! This encouragement and support was what I needed to banish my fears and apprehensions about the next few days.

My memory of that evening was of the group of us relaxing in a town I had not had the opportunity to visit but which had welcomed me as the last pilgrim searching for accommodation. The refugio was completely full that night; and I felt I had earned my place by the 12-hour walk from Molinaseca to Portomarín.

Day Twenty-Eight
Portomarín to Palas de Rei
Sunday 19 July 1998

It was 6.45am when I left Portomarín, the latest I had ever left a refugio. The long Saturday walk had caused me to sleep more soundly than usual, so I found myself almost the last pilgrim to pack their rucksack and set off down the main street. As I passed the Church of San Nicolas, I again admired the feat of relocating it from the river to where it now stood.

I found myself praising the Lord on the day that celebrates for all Christians the triumph of the cross. This resurrection day filled me with hope and courage as I crossed the narrow iron footbridge that spanned the River Mino. I made my way up a gradual slope through the trees on the north side of Monte San Antonio. The path led to the C135 and arrows indicated that the way forward was along the main road.

Before long, I found myself forced to stop for a Feldene treatment. As I sat at the side of the road, I acknowledged the sympathetic smiles and greetings of pilgrims who were passing by. Obviously, I had not been the last to leave Portomarín! Sitting on the side of the road afforded me the chance to thank the Lord for bringing me safely so far and to ask Him to be with me on this approach to the camino's end. I wondered how I would feel if, at the very final hurdle, I couldn't complete the journey. Part of me wished for the acceptance of poor Bernard and the resignation of my friend Rolf. But I wondered if I could be so accepting. I doubted it.

After Gonzar, a path led off the road down a track leading to the village of Castromaior and continuing through a country path amidst fields and trees. Easier on the feet, this comfort was short-lived as the harder-surfaced road came into view again, leading to Ventas de Narón.

It was time for breakfast. The sight of a small local café where a group of pilgrims had already gathered was too tempting to miss. It was a pleasant surprise to meet the Spanish family gathered there, the family I had first met at Nájera. This was the first time I had had the opportunity to chat with them.

Martín and his wife (whose name I have forgotten) were from Santiago; they had often thought of walking the camino, witnessing as they did the many foreign pilgrims arriving in the Plaza del Obradoiro at the cathedral. Eventually undertaking the walk with their two children Luis and Raquel, they had found the whole experience wonderful. They admitted that the children found the walking rather boring. But for themselves as a family, it had been a tremendous opportunity to be together for an extended period. Martín's wife was particularly fascinated with nature and found great joy in observing the flora and fauna in each region. Martín was rather taciturn, but during this chat with the family, I could see that his heart was in the right place.

The road from Ventas de Narón led through quiet countryside. I found myself alone and filled with the spirit of the Lord. I had forgotten to devote time for prayer because of my preoccupation with my hurting feet, but now I was finding walking much easier, so in the beauty of the countryside, I began the morning offering: 'Loving Father, thank you for the gift of this new day', followed by the pilgrim prayer and the Hail Mary, said in several languages.

The experience of reciting words of prayers has a soothing effect on me. Personally, I do not often say the Rosary. But alone and walking along the road, I found the rhythmical repetition of the prayers very calming. As I prayed, I surveyed the surrounding countryside and became aware of the glory of creation and of the Creator of all things.

Near the village of Lameiros I was joined by Barry, an American in his early fifties who had taken some time out from his accountancy business to embark on the camino. He was an exceptionally pleasant man who talked very freely about his family and his home in the States. The walk had been quite difficult for him. He initially suffered from blisters and these became septic. The situation became critical for him, and by the time he reached Burgos he could go no further and had to be hospitalised for a number of days. Yet here he was, fully recovered and approaching the end of the walk.

I was thoroughly enjoying the walk and the conversation, but I became aware of the strain of keeping up with him, and for fear of causing blisters to my own feet, I allowed him to go ahead at his own pace. It would have been very pleasant to have had such congenial company, but it was not worth the risk. As things were, I already felt a slight twinge at the side of my left foot, which was

Cross at Lameiros where there is a chapel dedicated to St Lazarus.

enough to call a halt to my quickening pace. So we saluted each other, and as Barry walked ahead, I looked forward to meeting him later on in the day.

After passing the village of Eirexe, I noted a sign that pointed to Vilar de Donas. The guidebook described the place as possessing one of the most outstanding small twelfth-century Romanesque churches of the area. Reading Lozano's account of the monument whetted my appetite to make a detour but considering that it was three kilometres there and another three kilometres to return to the camino route, put me off.

I was beginning to find the walk rather tiring and knew that I had another seven kilometres to reach Palas de Rei. Just as I was about to rest for a while, I came across a sign in Spanish and French that said, 'Courage! You're almost there!' Obviously, the owners of the house who had posted the notice had either walked themselves to Santiago or must have known the difficulty pilgrims sometimes experience as they near their destination.

Eventually, the municipal sports ground came into view, the last landmark before Palas de Rei, and as I passed it, I promised myself that I would take a private room for the night and refresh myself after the struggle of the last few days. Generally, I was anxious to sleep in the refugio so as to mingle with the other pilgrims. But now I was feeling the need to have some space to myself and to sleep undisturbed.

I found a room in 'Guntine', a bar-pensión that had been recently built. The facilities were second to none, with the en suite rooms beautifully finished and of ample size. As I lay on the

161

bed, I simply allowed myself to relax even before showering or washing my clothes. The peace and quiet filled me with a sense of well-being that I was reluctant to disturb. And so I remained for some time, until the need to have fresh clothes for the next day galvanised me into action.

Lunch consisted of a tortilla and a beer in the bar attached to the pensión. I was joined by a poor Spanish 'down-and-out', who wanted to talk. Although I could not understand much of what he said, I gathered that he had been a seminarian as a youth and had been expelled from the seminary. The people behind the bar looked on sympathetically. It seems that the unfortunate chap was a regular visitor here. With no desire to move to another bar, I was content to listen to the non-stop ramblings of this poor unbalanced man.

As I came to the end of my snack, the former seminarian insisted on paying. Initially, I protested, but then saw that it was a losing battle and graciously accepted his kind gesture. With that he departed, having found someone else to listen to him. I was touched by the incident, wondering what the whole story was of this disappointed clerical student who had found his life unmanageable.

I later met Nuria and Javier at the very modern refugio of Palas de Rei. We went for a walk through the town. The only monuments that interested me were the modern statue of St James as a pilgrim, just below where I was staying and the Church of San Tirso, with its Romanesque portal.

Being Sunday, I wanted to attend Mass and wondered if my two companions were that way inclined. Although hesitant at mentioning it, I decided it was better to tell them my intentions early on. To my delight, Nuria indicated that she would also like to attend. Javier showed no such interest. I had suspected that he was not overtly religious even though, like my Scottish friend Roger, I was sure that he had spiritual values.

A Spanish priest, who was leading a parish group of young people from Madrid to Santiago, celebrated the Mass. The group had spent most of the afternoon sitting outside the church singing both religious and popular songs for the entertainment

A modern statue of St James in the centre of the town of Palas de Rei.

of the local people. And now, during the Mass, they added great life and energy to the celebration. The priest presided at the Eucharist with great sincerity and although I could only understand about a quarter of what he said, the clear, simple tone of his sermon was most inspiring. Sitting with Nuria, a pilgrim with whom I had walked for some of the camino and dined with on several occasions, I found myself once more united to the spirit of pilgrimage and to the thousands of pilgrims on the route to Santiago.

That evening Nuria, Javier and Esteban came together for the evening meal. Barry was also there on his own at a table beside us, quite happy with this seating arrangement because he could not understand any Spanish. So I alternated between speaking pidgin Spanish to my companions and chatting with him in English. The evening passed most pleasantly and for a while, I had almost forgotten my sore feet. As we parted that evening, I looked forward to meeting these dinner companions along the route. I also hoped that Caroline and Michael, who must have been staying in the municipal refugio, would surface the next day.

Returning to the pensión, I entered the bar seeking to pay for the lodging before retiring so that I could leave early the next morning with no delay. The proprietor was behind the bar and willingly accepted the payment. When I requested a coke, he insisted that I accept it on the house. That in the commercial centre of Palas de Rei there were still people who valued the spirit of Santiago was indeed a pleasant surprise. I left the bar feeling really grateful for this small kindness. It had been a good end to a challenging but good day. I went to bed with a grateful and joyful heart.

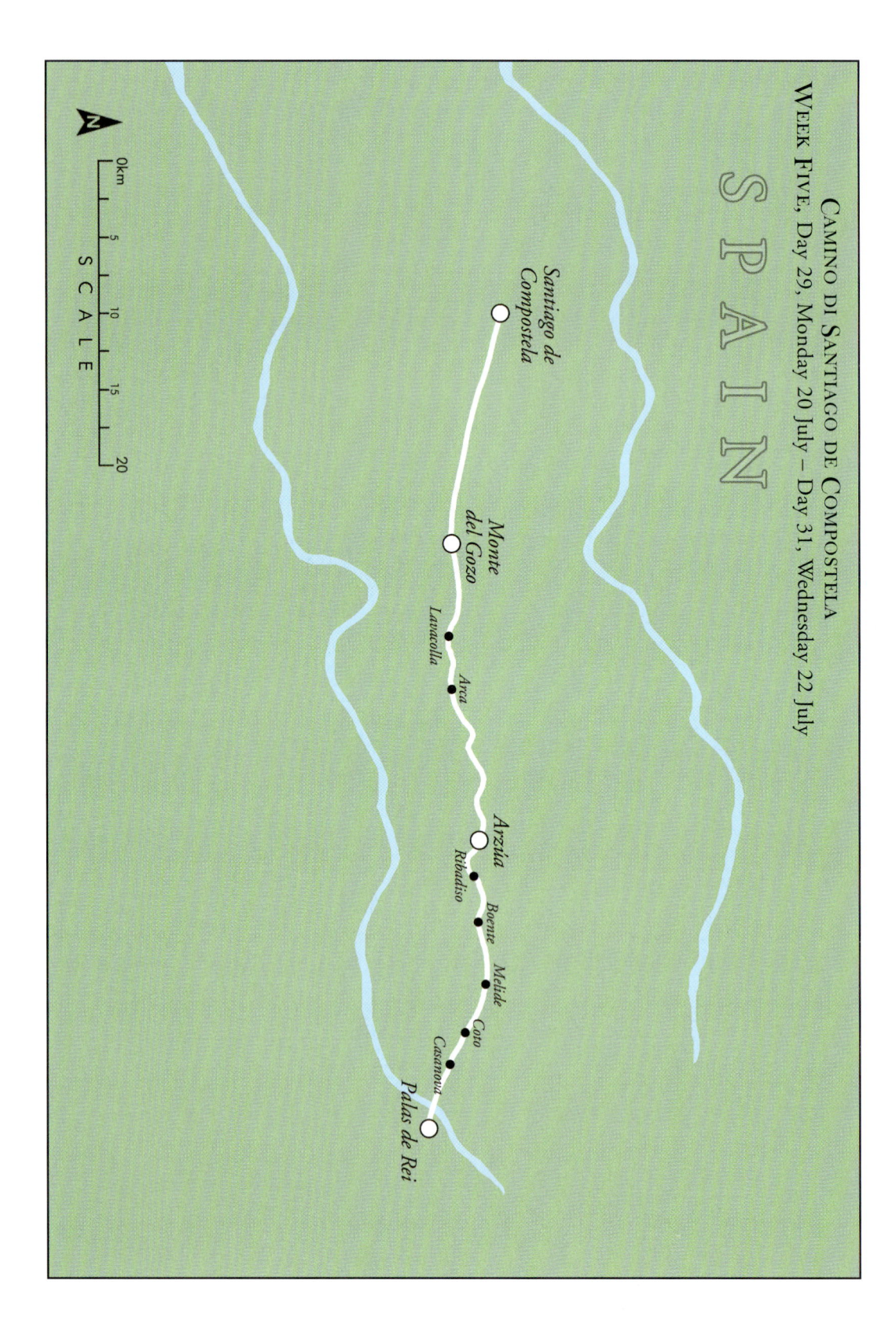

CAMINO DI SANTIAGO DE COMPOSTELA
Week Five, Day 29, Monday 20 July – Day 31, Wednesday 22 July

SPAIN

- Santiago de Compostela
- Monte del Gozo
- Lavacolla
- Arca
- Arzúa
- Ribadiso
- Boente
- Melide
- Coto
- Casanova
- Palas de Rei

Week Five

Day Twenty-Nine
Palas de Rei to Arzúa
Monday 20 July 1998

As I awoke that morning, I lay on the bed contemplating the fact that within two to three days I would be in Santiago. It seemed amazing that I had been walking for four weeks; that now the destination so hoped for was just within reach in a matter of days. Despite the fact that I had been having trouble with my feet, there could have been greater problems. And although there was still some 70km to go, I was feeling confident by now that I would arrive at Santiago. It was still dark outside; as I looked at my watch I wondered whether I should rise at 5.00am or wait for another hour until the sun made its appearance. Unable to rest, I got up and left the refugio at 5.30am, in almost total darkness.

Initially I descended along a paved walkway towards the village of San Xulián, and as I walked along a track, I found myself like someone with a blindfold over their eyes. I could hardly see a metre before me. Having posted home my torch with some other personal items at Burgos, a big mistake, I simply could not make out any yellow arrows or any indicators. I should have known that leaving so early was not such a good idea. This had already happened at Nájera, but then that was so long ago now.

As I stood in the dark, I heard voices. There behind me was a group of scouts walking quite confidently and carrying torches. With them were Nuria and Javier, who also had torches. These 'trailblazers' permitted me to follow, their pace being much faster than my morning dawdle. It would have been pleasant to accompany Javier and Nuria to Arzúa; instead, I looked forward to meeting them at the end of the day.

The track led up a gentle climb through pines and oaks, until I came to a sign indicating a refugio at Casanova. Beside the sign was a telephone, a very unusual sight in the middle of the countryside but for me, very opportune. Johnny, my brother, was leaving for Japan on holidays that morning, and I had planned to ring and wish him 'bon voyage'. This was the first time I had contacted the family since I embarked on the camino. I had purposely decided to avoid calling home, so that I could concentrate on the reality of Spain instead of living in two worlds. This, however, was different; I knew that a phone call would brighten his day.

Without delay, I was through. It seemed somewhat eerie to be talking to the family after what seemed like a long time; actually a month. Johnny was as delighted to hear me as I was to speak to him; yet I found myself struggling to describe the experience of the camino. It would have to wait until I returned and had meditated further on its significance before I could communicate the essential mystery of the camino to others.

Having rung Johnny, I then rang my sister Darina. The contact with family had caused a desire to touch base. Maybe I was feeling somewhat lonely. I probably was. Talking to her for a brief moment and assuring her that all was well provided me with sufficient human contact to alleviate whatever sense of isolation that had begun to surface at that early morning hour. When I finished talking, I found myself ready to set off with a lighter heart.

As I dropped down towards the Villar valley, I came across those strange constructions so typical in the Galician countryside called 'horreos'. They are stone or wooden structures that

These unusual constructions, called 'horreos', are used to store farm produce out of reach of rodents.

look like narrow miniature single-naved churches on a platform, the sidewalls consisting of what would appear like hundreds of narrow windows in three neat rows taking up the entire north and south walls. And on the roofs at the gable-ends, there is a cross on one end and at the other, some sort of orb-like motif. These unusual buildings, I learned, were for storing maize or other cereals. The idea of having the platform is to protect the farm produce from rodents.

Walking through this countryside, which so reminded me of a typical Irish scene, I found myself praying for my family. They had supported me in preparing for the camino, and having just made the phone calls home, each of my four brothers and my only sister came to mind. It was an ideal opportunity to pray for each of their intentions and for those of their families and friends. At that early morning hour, it was as if they walked with me along the camino. I would have plenty of stories to share with them when we met for our annual get-together in September. We had decided on the death of our parents to meet as an immediate family once a year so that the family spirit would continue. This had happened now for the last three years, and I looked forward to the imminent gathering. I would have plenty of photographs to bore them with!

Another group of scouts joined me as I was making my way along the track that went through some fields and led to a river. Two of them, José Maria and his companion Cristina, seemed happy to pull back from the group and walk with me for some of the journey. How refreshing it was to talk to such open and friendly young people. They chatted away, talking about their experiences of the camino, of their friends and families; and as I listened to them, I found myself thoroughly enjoying their company along the glorious trail.

No sooner had they said their goodbyes and moved on to catch up with their troop than two young Spanish girls came alongside and chatted away. They encouraged me to share the nuts and fruit that they felt were giving them energy for the journey. Not since Puente la Reina had I eaten nuts and raisins and as I walked with them, the memories of that early stage with Liam flooded to mind.

We were approaching the main road that forms the boundary between the provinces of Lugo and La Coruna, the last I would journey through as I approached Santiago. Already I had travelled through Navarra, La Rioja, Burgos, Palencia, León, Lugo and now La Coruna. Looking at the map inside the front cover of my trusted guidebook, I found myself marvelling at the journey that was coming to an end. The provinces stretched the entire breadth of Spain, and I had walked through each of them.

At Coto, I stopped at a bar while the girls continued on. Already there was a pilgrim taking his coffee and I joined him with an early morning salutation in Spanish. As it turned out, he was an Italian from Trieste. Antonio had two walking sticks, like young Emmanuel from Denmark whom I had not seen for some time now. What a joy it was to be speaking Italian again on the camino. Not since San Nicolas on the way to Fromista had I had the opportunity to connect once more with the beautifully musical language of Italy. I had no desire to hurry the coffee and was pleased when Antonio agreed to walk together for some of the journey into the busy town of Melide.

Antonio was an insurance risks calculator in his hometown of Trieste and had undertaken the camino to provide him with some space to reflect about his future. He was most unhappy with his lot, finding the job both stressful and life-draining. He hoped that the journey to Santiago would bring some sort of enlightenment as to what he might do instead. I could see that he was stressed and nervy. Obviously, the experience of somewhat dull work had affected him quite badly. He needed some form of help in this time of crisis. But for the moment, he was happy to have a listening ear as we walked together.

As we turned once more on to the road through the San Pedro district, I began to suffer with pains in my foot and had to bid farewell to Antonio to stop and apply Feldene for the first time that day. By this time, the procedure had become a routine. Initially there had been panic, especially on the journey through Triacastela and Samos; now I simply accepted that pain would be part of the journey and that I had been more fortunate than most in being able to continue walking.

At the supermarket in Melide, I bought some food for the next day's breakfast. The shop assistant could not have been more helpful; no order was too small. She sliced three thin slices of cheese and even offered to slice the bread roll I ordered, knowing I wanted to make a sandwich. Obviously, she was used to dealing with pilgrims and went about her work with efficiency and pleasantness. She was one of the angels of the camino, an ambassador for Spain.

I also bought a good bottle of wine. For some time now, Nuria and Javier had been commenting on the poor quality of the wine served on the pilgrim menu; so I thought it would be fun to celebrate with them the near approach of our destination before we lost each other along the route. I wanted also to express my gratitude to them for their company and support along the camino over the last few days. They had become good companions on the journey.

I was glad, however, to be leaving the town atmosphere. The camino crossed the River Lázaro, winding along earthen paths through oak woods, beautiful countryside and taking in small hamlets, eventually turning into asphalt minor roads. Antonio by this time was nowhere to be seen but I wished him well as he tried to work out his future.

The sun was high in the sky and hunger began to gnaw away at me, demanding attention and immediate action. I wondered when I would find a place to stop and eat. The road continued through the village of Peroxa, but the only sign of food there was in the local baker's van that sounded its horn as it travelled through the village.

Boente was the next village; it was almost attached to Peroxa. That this small village is mentioned in Picaud's *Pilgrim's Guide* and has a church dedicated to St James, did not interest me as much as the bar that I noticed at the entry to the village! I needed to eat.

The omelette sandwich that I was served in this small bar tasted like heaven! I had been really hungry and had even felt weak as I approached the village. So, sitting on the bar stool in the deserted hamlet, I allowed all the tiredness and hunger to drain away gradually. The beer was too tempting to resist. I ordered a glass and then another one. Life took on a different hue, as I relaxed and allowed my feet some respite from the heavy boots. I even took off my socks to allow the cool tiles of the bar to relieve the burning sensation.

As I made my way through a tunnel under the N547, and went downhill and across the River Boente, I began to feel

One of the few examples of a seated statue of St James in the local church at Boente.

drowsy and dizzy. My head felt light and I noticed myself walking all over the road. I felt as if I was slightly drunk! I could not believe it, but the combined effects of sun and drinking two beers made me feel unable to continue walking. I had to sit down in the shade for a while. What would people have thought had they known that I – a Christian Brother – was walking like a drunk along the roads of Spain!

When the effects of the beer began to wear off, I got up. As I was putting on the rucksack, the precious bottle of wine became dislodged from its moorings and went crashing to the ground. It smashed against a small rock, its contents pouring out onto the sandy soil. In a matter of seconds, the bull's blood had disappeared into the earth leaving me rooted to the spot. So much for the celebration with Nuria and Javier. My surprise party had ended in a shambles. A valuable lesson had been learned about taking beer during a hot day and when out walking.

I had to negotiate a partially built motorway bridge over a gorge. Then I continued downhill towards the River Iso and on to Ribadiso, where the fifteenth-century Hospital de San Anton de Ponte de Ribadiso had been converted into a fine refugio. The place was crowded with pilgrims, most of whom seemed to be scouts. The refugio was closed until four in the afternoon, and a queue had formed to ensure that the first arrived would gain entry.

I walked around looking for familiar faces. Antonio was there and seemed more relaxed. José Maria and Cristina ran over to shake hands and showed me their group, who were in the process of cooking a meal. But I could not see any sign of Nuria or Javier and supposed that they had continued on to Arzúa. There must have been close to 60 pilgrims forming the queue that circled the refugio. Knowing from the guidebook that the refugio only held 60, I saw that Arzúa was the only option. So I bade farewell to the young people and set off again.

It was beginning to rain lightly, though not heavily enough to stop and extract the raingear that I had not used since San Domingo de la Calzada. I was walking along the side of the N547 when I heard someone shouting out my name from behind me. It was Nuria and Javier, approaching fast.

They had been at Ribadiso but had not seen me. A chance remark of one of the pilgrims about the 'Irishman' caused them to leave Ribadiso and follow on to Arzúa. I was delighted to see them, and as we walked, I felt happy that we would have a chance to meet again and share stories.

We walked in the rain into Arzúa. As we made our way towards the refugio, we met a Frenchman wheeling a pram, in which his four-year-old baby was sitting contentedly. He had pushed the pram all the way from St Jean-Pied-de-Port. With great conviction, he told us that the refugio was horrible, badly organised and with unhygienic facilities. *"C'est déguelas!"* (It's stinking!), he spat out. This description was enough for us to turn about and look for alternative arrangements.

Monument at Arzúa, where there was an Augustinian refugio in the fourteenth century.

Casa Frade proved to be the ideal refugio. There was a warm, simple welcome, and as we climbed the stairs to our rooms, I noticed that the walls were covered with religious pictures and emblems. The house was old-fashioned but immaculately kept, and as we were shown to our bedrooms, I admired the old iron bed and the wooden dresser that would have dated back to the nineteenth century at least. Each room led on to a common veranda overlooking a side road. The veranda was crowded with pilgrims' washing hanging out to dry.

While Nuria and Javier were resting, I made for the church to get the pilgrim passport stamped. It was surprising to find the large parish church packed to the door. There was a funeral service taking place and had there been room, I would loved to have made my way in to see the altarpiece and statue of St James. But it was impossible. The congregation was spilling onto the pavement, almost preventing the traffic from passing. Instead, I made my way to the back of the church, hoping to find the sacristan who would stamp the passport. He informed me that the parish priest's housekeeper would do the job and pointed to a house diagonally across the square from the church. I knocked at the door but no-one answered. There was no hurry, so I simply sat down and began filling in my journal.

After some time, Nuria saw me and said that I should go to the Ayuntamiento (county council) offices where she herself had gone to obtain a stamp. Fearing it would be closed, she accompanied me and we found everything locked up. Undaunted, she rang the bell and convinced the cleaner who answered to allow us in to see if the official would oblige us and stamp my passport. I was amazed at Nuria's persistence: she made her way through all the bureaucracy and into the inner sanctum of the county council offices. She seemed to have done this before. The official was rather gruff and reluctant. But in the face of Nuria's winning smile, he relented, and I emerged triumphant with the precious stamp!

That evening, we made for the dining room, which had a few guests, including Marius from The Netherlands, whom I had met at Rabanal and along the road towards Triacastela. He was eating on his own and seemed to need the quiet time alone.

Nuria, Javier and myself enjoyed being together; they found it most amusing when I told them of the misadventure with the wine. As it turned out, the house wine was quite good, and we shared a bottle between us. Halfway through the meal, Marius interrupted us saying that he did not like the wine and offered us his almost untouched bottle, which we drank. He seemed in rather low spirits, complaining of the state of the refugios in Spain, which were, he contended, much inferior to those in France. I felt sorry for him, knowing that he had travelled so far from his home and was now in a rather negative mood, just as he was nearing the final destination.

Our evening, however, was very enjoyable, as I relaxed in the company of such fine people. We were near the end of the journey and feeling a sense of inner peace and a satisfaction that the camino had brought to each of us real blessings.

We decided that we would shorten slightly the final stage to Santiago – the longest section of the entire camino at 40km – and stay at Monte del Gozo, which overlooks Santiago. Apparently, this is an old custom for pilgrims. It means that Santiago is approached in the early morning of the following day, when pilgrims can arrive relaxed in the ancient city and pray quietly and privately at the shrine of St James before the tourist throng invade and take over the cathedral.

This would prolong the camino by a day; yet I felt something within myself that wanted to delay the pleasure of finally arriving at the tomb of the Saint in the Field of the Star – Compostela.

Day Thirty
Arzúa to Monte del Gozo
Tuesday 21 July 1998

Nuria, Javier and myself began the day with a large hot coffee and some croissants at the corner bar in Arzúa. We were all sleepy, finding ourselves almost reluctant to begin the day's journey. The previous night had been most enjoyable and had lulled us into such a relaxed state that we could easily have stayed an extra day in Arzúa.

Javier got us moving, and as he and Nuria set out, I encouraged them to walk ahead, giving me time to warm up the muscles and to get in touch with the Lord of the journey. I always found it important to raise my thoughts to the Lord in these early hours of the day.

The route led through vegetable patches and fields, passing an oak grove on the left. The N547 made its appearance for a short while before heading onto a earthen track that gradually climbed up to Raído and continued along minor roads and dirt tracks through a series of 14 hamlets, each within a kilometre of the other and hidden among the eucalyptus trees.

The scenery was spectacular but I was finding the going quite difficult. My feet were very sore and the stops for applying Feldene were becoming increasingly frequent. The now persistent pain prevented me from fully appreciating the surrounding countryside and admiring the typical small hamlets that dotted the way. All I could do was attempt to focus on Santiago and pray that things would not deteriorate. Although I had no real fears that the pain would prevent me finishing the camino, this last stage was proving to be more difficult than I had expected.

When I came onto the C547, the yellow arrow pointed to the right on the other side of the road; but by this time I needed a rest and decided to stop at a bar at Arca, another small hamlet further on along the road.

The waitress must have been having a bad day. When I asked her to explain what a *tortilla variada* meant she simply said that it was the same as the ordinary one. Being stubborn by nature, I kept at her, trying to get her to identify why the tortillas were 'varied', but she was having none of it. Just as I was about to give up, another girl behind the counter came over and explained the varieties available, much to the disgust of the other waitress. The smiling one took no notice of the mood of the first and tried her best to make me feel welcome. The contrast was remarkable. And the tortilla with ham that I ordered was served beautifully and perfectly cooked.

Having finished the meal and paid the bill, I went outside the restaurant and sat down to rest. I had been there about five minutes when the pleasant waitress came rushing out with a plastic bag that I had left behind. She obviously thought I had taken off on the camino and showed relief that I was still nearby. The kindness of this young girl was a real elixir for a tired pilgrim – another angel along the pilgrim road.

Leaving Arca, I came to a leafy pathway, where I met Marius resting in the shade of the trees. Sitting down beside him, I gratefully accepted his offer of fruit and we chatted for a while.

Marius talked of his life as a business consultant and how he had come to the stage where he felt that a change in direction was needed. The idea of the walk was to provide him with space to think clearly about his future. He shared very personal details about the journey from The Netherlands and through France; as I listened to him, I found myself admiring his honesty and openness. He was not only telling me the story of his camino to Santiago but also his journey through life, and I felt privileged to be privy to such revelations.

At one stage of the journey, we came to the distance marker that indicated there were just 13km to Santiago. Marius asked me to stop with him at this special place. He explained that he had marked the 45th to remember his own age. Then at the 35th marker, he paused to think of his partner. Now, at the 13km marker, he paused to remember his daughter. Attached to his rucksack, he had a key ring hanging down containing a photograph of his partner and his daughter. He showed it to me and asked me to remember them during the moment of silence, when we stood at the kilometre marking and placed a stone on it.

As we talked, he asked me how I could live a celibate life when such a choice seemed impossible to him. I explained how I had found the choice sometimes very difficult, but that it was a calling to which I had found myself attracted as a young person. I went on to explain that it only made sense in the context of loving service to those in need. The challenge, moreover, was to live a life of love in community and to share that love with a wider group than a family. At the heart of the call, I explained, is the conviction that I was being called to dedicate myself totally to the love and service of God. The vow of chastity was a direct sign of the seriousness of that intention. I admitted that there had been many times when I had found the vow of chastity very challenging; then I pointed out to him how difficult *any* committed life was, especially marriage.

In such a vein, we continued along the path, until I was forced to stop with the pain in my feet. Marius left me at that stage, with us wishing each other well for the remainder of the journey.

I found the rest of the walk that day very difficult. Arriving at Labacolla, I realised that my water supply had run out, and I continued along the road feeling parched and fearing dehydration. As luck would have it, I came across a bar at the end of the town. When I requested from the young girl behind the bar a bottle of water, she offered to fill my flask with tap water to save me some money. The angels were coming to my help this day.

As I sat outside the bar I read in the guidebook that Labacolla is so named because it was the tradition that pilgrims on their way to Santiago would take off their clothes and, thus naked, wash (laba) themselves completely including their nether regions – or colla! This tradition I decided to ignore, though I was looking forward to the shower at the end of the day's walk.

The last stretch of the walk climbed steeply out of Labacolla, and as I trod slowly uphill, a Spanish cyclist, who had ridden from Bilbao, joined me. He seemed anxious to talk and dismounted from his bicycle to walk alongside me up the steep climb. Soon after, a young Swiss man came along and he seemed to be very hyperactive. He talked non-stop, wanting us to know that he had walked 50km a day from his home town in Switzerland. On and on he continued, barely drawing a breath, and only when the two of us slowed down to almost a crawl did he decide to move ahead to keep up his schedule. We breathed a sigh of relief and with that, the Spaniard good-naturedly clapped me on the back and bade me, *"Ultreya!"*

Finally, I came to Monte del Gozo or 'the Mount of Joy', so named because it was there that pilgrims caught their first glimpse of Santiago. I was not sure from which vantage point I could view Santiago as all along the roadside where I walked, a huge hostel had been built. There must have been up to 20 individual units in the complex, each perhaps holding 50 pilgrims. It seemed to have been built for student games or something but it was now an eyesore. I wondered had I made a mistake in deciding to stay the night there.

Just as I arrived in the central concourse, Caroline came running to embrace and congratulate me on having reached the final destination, almost! It was a real joy to meet Michael and her and to share this last night of the camino with them. Nuria, Javier and

Esteban also appeared. We all agreed to meet in the self-service restaurant later that evening, and despite the very Americanised fast-food quality of the meal, we celebrated the fact that this would be the final night before reaching Santiago. And before retiring for the evening, we arranged to meet next morning for breakfast. Then we would walk together the final four or five kilometres into Santiago.

It was a fitting conclusion to a difficult day. As I lay on my bed, I found myself thinking of Rolf, Bernard and Liam and praying for their welfare. I wondered how Carmen had fared after I had left her at Sarria. I hoped that she had pulled herself together. Tomorrow and the following day would reveal who finally had managed to complete the camino.

And to the Lord I once again raised a prayer of thanksgiving for the protection afforded me along the Santiago trail. I had been truly blessed.

Day Thirty-One
Monte del Gozo to Santiago
Wednesday 22 July 1998

That Wednesday morning it was raining. But there was sunshine in my heart. I was about to arrive in Santiago de Compostela after 31 days of walking across the north of Spain. Our small group met at the arranged time of 8.00am and quietly celebrated our imminent arrival with a breakfast that was very subdued in spirit. It was as if the moment was too sacred for words. Each one was with their own thoughts and apart from knowing smiles to each other, we were happy to eat quietly and wait for the moment to make our move – to walk the final four or five kilometres to the shrine of St James. Nuria and Javier, Michael and Caroline, Esteban and Barry, together with myself, were all at the one table. It seemed more like a Eucharist than a breakfast as we sat in quiet reverence prior to our departure.

We descended in the light drizzle towards the N544 and the San Lázaro district, which in the twelfth century was a leprosarium. As we walked, I began to feel the pain returning to the soles of my feet, shifting from a dull pain to an almost unbearable agony. Nuria was also complaining of severe pains, but neither of us wanted to delay the arrival of our small group as we moved gradually towards the city walls.

The Puerta del Camino was ahead of us, the gate through which for over a thousand years pilgrims have made their way to this most sacred of shrines. All that remained of the gate was the junction of two roads, yet my imagination conjured up the original gate as we entered the old part of the town. I noticed that Nuria and Javier had joined hands as they walked, the first time I had seen this happen since I met them. So I slowed down and allowed them to go ahead together to enjoy their moment of special intimacy.

As I walked on my own past where the Puerta del Camino had once stood, I suddenly became aware that my feet no longer felt sore. It was the strangest sensation, and I stopped to check that this was really happening and not just my imagination. But all I could feel was the comfort of my boots that had carried me safely for almost 800km. The pain had vanished. I could not believe it, finding it difficult to accept that such an immediate healing could happen. But it had happened, and all I could do was express a prayer of gratitude to St James who had accompanied me since first leaving St Jean-Pied-de-Port. I continued alone across the Plaza de Cervantes and up the Calle de la Azabachería, through the eponymous plaza and into Plaza del Obradoiro.

Pilgrims there were all crowding together, as if disorientated after the long journey. We stood silent in the huge square. The cathedral was on the east side of the Plaza del Obradoiro; the Hostel de los Reyes Catolicos on the north side; the Ayuntamiento Palacio de Rajoy (Town Hall) on the west side, and the Colegio de San Jéromino completing the rectangle. For a second we simply greeted each other with embraces and remained in silent wonder at the moment we had all waited for.

Barry approached me with a clap on my shoulder and simply said, "Well done!" And somehow, this released the gates that held back my tears. Standing before the flamboyant façade of the cathedral, completed in 1750 by Fernando de Cassas y Novoa, with its twin towers sheltering the famous Romanesque Portico della Gloria, I unashamedly allowed the tears of gratitude to flow down my cheeks. I uttered a prayer of thanks to the Lord for His kindness to me and for His protection along the camino. It was a real miracle that I had made it when many of my companions had unfortunately fallen away.

The twin spires of Santiago Cathedral overlooking the Plaza del Obradoiro.

Eventually, we mounted the double-ramp staircase that led up to the Portico della Gloria. This ancient Romanesque portal would require someone more versed in the history of architecture to describe its beauty and significance. All I could do was to marvel at the sheer magnificence of the detail in each panel in the door and place my hand on the stone where millions of pilgrims down through the centuries had placed their hands, forming an indentation on the now polished stone.

Pilgrims were also touching with their heads the small sculpture of the head of architect Master Mateo situated just behind the stone with the imprinted hand. I followed their example to express my humble admiration for this man who, together with Bernardo and Esteban, was the main architect of this thirteenth-century cathedral. Then I entered into that unique interior, shaped in the form of a Latin cross measuring 98 metres long and 67 metres across at the transept.

We all made for the shrine of St James over the main altar. Unfortunately, the entire altar was under restoration, which made it difficult to appreciate the beauty and majesty of this

Baroque work of art. We were, however, able to mount the stairs leading up to the seated statue of the saint, dressed as a pilgrim but gilded in sparkling and precious stones. Each pilgrim then embraced the saint from behind, following the ancient custom, and, after a silent prayer, we descended the steps on the other side.

Below the high altar is the crypt housing the relics of St James. The guidebook informed me that excavations in 1956 brought to light that the apostle's tomb – first discovered between AD 820 and AD 830 – was a stone mausoleum situated in a necropolis that had been in use from 100 BC to AD 500.

Pilgrims stood or knelt in silent reverence before the remains of what, in the light of the above archaeological research, is likely to be the remains of the apostle James the Elder. When my turn came, I simply stood before this casket, praying that I would continue to be a pilgrim on my journey towards the fullness of life. I prayed that I would be of help to fellow pilgrims along that continuing journey.

Nuria and Javier led the way to the Oficina de Acogida del Peregrino in Rúa del Villar No.1, where pilgrims go to get the 'Compostela', the certificate which, since the fourteenth century, has been awarded to those who have completed the camino, irrespective of where they started out from. Once a pilgrim has walked over 150km, they are entitled to get their certificate.

At the entrance to the pilgrim office, the atrium was filled with bordóns, the staffs that pilgrims had used to help them negotiate the uneven terrain of the camino and had now abandoned at the end of the walk. As I mounted the stairs to the office and looked down on the assortment of abandoned walking staffs, I now fully grasped the magnitude of the walk that I had undertaken. I hadn't originally appreciated the difficulties involved.

Obtaining the final stamp in my passport and supplying my name for the Compostela brought to an end a magnificent adventure that had brought with it immense blessings and had touched my life in ways I still did not fully appreciate.

Nuria, Javier and I went walking along the streets of Santiago, taking in the spirit of excitement that was building up in preparation for the 25 July, the feast of St James. There were pilgrims everywhere, as well as visitors who had come to Santiago for this special time.

We entered a rather up-market café to taste the hot chocolate and *churrios*, special finger donut-like cakes that are typical of the area. And as we sat together, we examined each other's Compostela and chatted about our plans for the next few days. Javier was determined to continue walking to Finesterre, a distance of 100km. Originally, I had hoped to walk to Finesterre also but the nearer I approached Santiago, the more convinced I was that this was the destination I desired, and I therefore would not continue further. Nuria had no interest either and would have loved to have convinced Javier to stay with her. But he was adamant that he wanted to walk the extra stages.

Instead of staying at the pilgrim refugio, I decided to book myself into a hotel in the centre of the town in order to be near the hub of activity. The Barbantes Hotel proved to be ideal, and though it cost €30 a night, I considered it worthwhile, especially for its prime location beside the cathedral.

Nuria and Javier found another hotel, and for the rest of the day we went our own ways. It was important for me not to interfere too much in the short time that remained for them together.

I spent most of the afternoon in the Plaza Obradoiro enjoying the sun, writing cards and watching out for pilgrims with whom I had travelled along the camino. I met Miriam (returning to Barcelona the next day) and Georgina, and enjoyed listening to how they had been overcome with tears of joy on their arrival into Santiago. It was lovely to hear of people talking about such emotional reactions, especially for one who is inclined to avoid showing tears!

That evening I found myself alone and feeling rather sorry for myself. I would love to have dined with Nuria and Javier; but naturally they were taking advantage of the last moments of this time together. Michael and Caroline had vanished. I presumed they were in the refugio at the other side of the town. Barry was nowhere to be seen. As I sat eating my evening meal, I felt lonelier than I had ever felt along the pilgrim path; it took me a while to remember the philosophy of attempting to move from loneliness to solitude. It was a lesson that was taking time to learn.

The following day, I decided to take the bus to Finisterre to see the 'Finis Terrae', the end of the earth. I found the bus journey very disappointing. As I travelled and admired the countryside, I could make out pilgrims amidst the trees. For the entire trip I found myself thinking that I should either have walked to Finisterre or else remained in Santiago. Taking the bus-ride felt like cheating, and the day had an air of unreality and discontent about it. Walking in Finisterre was a lonely affair. There were no pilgrims to be seen. Instead, the place was sparsely populated, with only the occasional tourist wandering around. I could not wait for the evening bus to bring me back to Santiago.

That evening I met for dinner with some of the pilgrims I knew. Nick and Naomi had arrived and announced their plans to marry. James, Barry and Esteban joined us, as did Adrian, the budding broadcaster who had interviewed pilgrims along the camino. There were still many others I hoped to meet the next day.

On the eve of St James, I attended Mass in the cathedral. I had been looking forward to the ceremony of the 'botafumeiro'. A huge thurable, some 1.25 metres in size, is hoisted high above the centre of the transept by a group of burly robed attendants and swung across until it almost touches the ceiling. The spectacle was as magical as I had expected: gasps of wonder and excitement burst forth from the congregation as the incense-filled thurable began to swing like a giant pendulum across the transept of the crowded cathedral. It is said that in the Middle Ages, the thurable broke loose from its rope and flew straight through the rose window, landing in the middle of the wooden houses and setting the town of Santiago alight. But on the eve of the feast day, the event passed without a hitch.

In the afternoon, I saw Emmanuel from Denmark. He was beaming, having at last completed the camino. I took a photograph of him before the temporary hoarding that were being erected in front of the cathedral in preparation for the son et lumière on the eve of the feast day. He told me that he had heard that Bernard was expected to arrive that day or in the next few days. Apparently, Bernard had recovered from his troubles and had continued walking after some days rest in Burgos. This was great news, and I hurried off to write a note of welcome and congratulations to him, which I posted on the notice board in the office for pilgrims.

Later, I saw Liam sauntering down Rua del Villar as if he owned the place. With a shout, I awoke him out of his reverie and we embraced like long lost friends. He had arrived that morning, having spent two days in Belorado thanks to the kindness of the hospitalero. He had then proceeded along the camino without further mishap. We sat on the terrace of a bar while he shared some details of his walk and I, in turn, told him of my adventures. I was so delighted that at least half of the original quartet had made it to Santiago.

I was completely taken aback when I met Julia and Georgie in one of the side streets of the city. Julia explained that she left Rabanal the following day after a serious disagreement with

Statue of St James the 'Moor-slayer' in the cathedral in Santiago.

Roger, the hospitalero, whom she had kindly offered to help. She discovered, in fact, that the reason his assistant had left in a hurry was the same reason she refused to remain with him. It was a real pleasure to meet Julia and Georgie, who had been so kind to me and to many pilgrims in that wonderful refugio of Rabanal.

I was half-expecting to meet Carmen in Santiago. We had made an arrangement when we separated at Triacastela that we would meet outside the cathedral at noon on 24 July. She did not make it. I heard from others that she had arrived, but I never saw her again. All I hoped was that the remainder of her journey had been more enjoyable than the earlier part.

That evening, many pilgrims gathered at the corner of the Plaza del Obradoiro to book their place for the fireworks display due to take place around midnight. It seemed that all those who had travelled with me had miraculously appeared. Nick and Naomi sat together. Phil the American cartoonist was there with his pencil and pad. Marius joined us, seemingly in much better form. Dominique and Francesco, always inseparable, joined in. And despite the fact that most of us were speaking English, Francesco kept on talking Spanish and French with gay abandon and much to the amusement of all.

Sitting beside me was Rooker, the American artist whom I had seen for the first and only time at El Burgo Raneros. She spoke with a wisdom and maturity far beyond her years, discussing the impact that the camino had had on her. It was a privilege to have finally spoken to her. Liam was smiling and chatted away in his own relaxed way, while Emmanuel was discussing with great intensity his opinions of agriculture in Europe.

I missed the presence of Bernard and Rolf. But I felt somehow that they were there in spirit. I hoped that the cards I had sent them from Santiago would, in some way, make them part of the group of pilgrims they had come to know.

As the evening approached, I saw Kristen arrive, much to the delight of many of those who had walked with her. Once again, she had shown her wonderful spirit in remaining for a few days in León with a fellow pilgrim who fell ill and had to be hospitalised. I was delighted to meet once more my first companion on the camino, with whom I had travelled along the road, albeit by taxi.

Almost at midnight, the fireworks began, creating a spectacle that transformed the Plaza into a surreal arena of music and light. Everyone went wild, with dancing and festivities of all sorts taking place. Together with a small group of pilgrims at the side of the Plaza, I joined in with joy and enthusiasm to celebrate the completion of a wonderful walk along the camino to Santiago de Compostela.

Epilogue

When I returned home to Ireland there was a card in the shape of a scallop shell awaiting me. It was from Bernard. He had stayed in Burgos for four days while his leg had a chance to mend, then setting out again to complete the camino. After a day's walking, he suffered from serious dehydration and could go no further. His son drove from Saintes to meet him and take him home. But the undaunted Bernard insisted that he be driven to within a few kilometres of Santiago, where, with his faithful bordón, he walked into the city and claimed his Compostela. In fact, he had arrived some two weeks ahead of me, and I was in no doubt that his prayers had been with me along the route.

Rolf also wrote. I was delighted to hear that his wife had improved and was fully back to health. I was glad also that he was still determined to complete the walk and hoped that I might have the opportunity to accompany him on that future journey, God willing.

Bernard and Rolf remain faithful friends, and we keep in touch promising each other that we will one day set out together on another pilgrim walk.

Caroline has written on many occasions, telling me about her life. She and Michael have gone their separate ways but are still good friends, Michael having completed his course as a master carpenter.

I have been in contact with Julia and look forward to meeting her some day in London. Until then, we continue to be in contact by email.

Marius still sends the occasional email. He has moved from business consultancy and now works at assisting people to plan their future careers. We exchange cards at Christmas; and were it not for my laziness in writing letters, we could still have been in contact.

Emmanuel sent a Christmas card designed by himself, with various symbols of the pilgrimage to Santiago on it. He is becoming an eco-farmer.

Nuria and Javier were in touch initially, and their present of a linocut executed by Javier of St James sits on my desk to remind me of their support during the walk. At the time of writing, I do not know where they are living but someday they may get in touch again. They had been very good to me along the camino; I hope that I had offered them something in return.

Liam and I have lost contact with each other, and Carmen has faded from the scene.

Obviously not all contacts made during the walk could possibly continue afterwards.

For me, I often remember those days along the pilgrim trail and pray for everyone I met during that summer of 1998. In many ways, and in ways I may not fully appreciate, the people with whom I walked have touched my life and have become part of my ongoing journey. I pray for them; that the experience of pilgrimage has transformed their lives in ways still mysterious yet enriching. I know that the camino has changed me and made me better aware of the great gift that God's presence is during my journey through life. That old Spanish word and its poignant sentiment still rings in my ears as I continue along the pilgrim road of life – *"Ultreya!"*

Bibliography

Most of the books listed below are on my library shelf. I have also included ones that have assisted me in my research and writing. The list is by no means exhaustive or even comprehensive.

ENGLISH:

Coelho, Paulo *The Pilgrimage, A Contemporary Quest for Ancient Wisdom*, Harper, 1995. Fiction.

Hogarth, James (Translator) *The Pilgrim's Guide, A 12th Century Guide for the Pilgrim to St James of Compostela,* Confraternity of St James, 1992. Stimulating.

Hopkins, Adam *Spanish Journeys, A Portrait of Spain,* Penguin, 1993. Background reading.

Lodge, David, *Therapy,* Penguin, 1995. Fiction.

Laffi, Domenico (translated by J. Hall) *A Journey to the West: The Diary of a Seventeenth Century Pilgrim from Bologna to Santiago de Compostela,* Leiden, The Netherlands: Primavera Pers. 1997. Detailed period account.

Lozano, Millán Bravo *A Practical Guide for Pilgrims, The Road to Santiago,* Editorial Everest, 1996. The best guidebook available on the camino, packed with historical and practical information.

Luard, Nicholas *The Field of the Star, A Pilgrim's Journey to Santiago de Compostela,* 1999, Penguin Books. A very personal account of the author's walk during the illness of his daughter.

Morris, Jan, *Spain,* Penguin, 1982. Background reading.

Nootsboom, Cees *Roads to Santiago,* The Harvill Press, 1997. Background reading.

Raju, Alison *The Way of St James, Le Puy to Santiago, A Walker's Guide,* Cicerone Press, 1999. Succinct and very practical.

Selby, Bettina *Pilgrim's Road, A Journey to Santiago de Compostela,* Abacus, 1994. Very enjoyable account of the camino on bicycle.

Valiña, Elías Sampedro *The Pilgrim's Guide to the Camino de Santiago,* Galaxia, 1992.

FRENCH:

Aavv *Les Chemins de Saint-Jacques de Compostelle*, MSM, 1999. Pictorial guide.

Clouteau, Jacques *Il est un beau chemin semé d'épines et d'étoiles.* 3rd Edition, Editions du Vieux. Crayon, 1997. Amusing travelogue.

Grégoire, Jean-Ives *Le Chemin des Etoiles, en marche vers Saint-Jacques-de-compostelle,* Rando Editions, 1999, Pictorial travelogue

Grégoire, Jean-Ives *Sur le chemin du Puy du Puy-en-Velay a Roncevaux,* Rando Editions, 1999, Pictorial travelogue.

Huchet, Patrick et Ynon Boëlle *Sur les chemins de Compostelle.* Editions Ouest-France, 1999. Pictorial guide.

ITALIAN:

Gandini, Davide *Il Portico della Gloria, Lourdes-Santiago de Compostela-Finisterre a piedi 1luglio-18 agosto 1992*, EDB, 1996. A very personal and religious testimony.

Lamberti-Bocconi, Anna *Sola sul cammino, il pellegrimaggio a Santiago de Compostela*, Xenia, 1999. A very poetic account.

SPANISH:

Bango Torviso, Isidro G. *El Camino de Santiago,* Espasa Calpe, 1994. Excellent pictorial and historical account. A magnificent treasure of information and images.